THE SHAPE OF
SOLA SCRIPTURA

KEITH A. MATHISON

canonpress
Moscow, Idaho

Published by Canon Press
P.O. Box 8729, Moscow, ID 83843
800–488–2034 | www.canonpress.com

Keith A. Mathison, *The Shape of Sola Scriptura*
Copyright © 2001 by Keith A. Mathison

Cover design by David Dalbey.
Printed in the United States of America.

Library of Congress Cataloging-in-Publication Data
Mathison, Keith A.
      The shape of sola scriptura / Keith A. Mathison.
    p. cm.
    Includes bibliographical references and index.
    ISBN-10: 1-885767-74-9 (pbk.)
    ISBN-13: 978-1-88576-774-5 (pbk.)
    1. Bible—Evidences, authority, etc. 2. Protestant churches—Doctrines.
    I. Title.
    BS480 .M36 2001
    220.1–dc21   2001000512

09 10 11 12 13 14 15   12 11 10 9 8 7

To my father and mother.

Parents are the pride of their children
Proverbs 17:6

Contents

Acknowledgments

As I reflect upon the completion of this book, I cannot help but smile in wonder at the amazing providence of God. When I began to study this topic almost five years ago, I did not think that I wanted to write a book on the subject. After several years of study my thoughts on the matter changed somewhat. I became absolutely certain that I did not want to write a book on the subject. It is not that I do not like the topic. One cannot study something in depth for five years unless he has at least some interest in it. The problem was the sometimes overwhelming complexity involved. It seemed at times as if every question raised ten further questions, and each of those ten questions raised ten more and so on.

This book only exists because Doug Jones at Canon Press asked me to write it. I want to thank him for asking me to do this because I may have never attempted it otherwise. I would also like to thank my beautiful wife Tricia for putting up once again with almost daily trips to and from the library. I want to thank my daughter Sarah for being such a joy and for reminding me to take frequent breaks for "play time." I also want to thank my mom and my dad for their constant encouragement.

There are several others who contributed to this project in different ways. I would like to thank Roy Bennett, David Temples, Darren Edgington and Tom Forest for numerous conversations and discussions during the years when I was beginning to study this issue and wrestle with the many implications involved. I would also like to thank Ethan Harris for once again bearing the heavy burden of reading the first draft.

Foreword

As Christians continue to struggle against modernity and post-modernity, the term "medieval" is slowly and wonderfully becoming more of a crown than a term of abuse, especially in thoughtful Protestant circles. C.S. Lewis once quipped that the more medieval he became in his outlook, the farther from Roman Catholicism he seemed to grow. The history of the doctrine of *sola Scriptura* tends to produce the same effect in many of us. Once one gets beyond the superficial, individualistic, confused accounts of the doctrine presented in contemporary Evangelicalism, this teaching becomes very natural, organic, medieval, and apostolic.

In contrast, Roman Catholic and Eastern Orthodox accounts fall out of rather perfectionistic and rationalistic commitments that are alien to the earthiness of biblical reality. Submitting to an infallible magisterium requires relatively little faith; everything is, in principle, neat and clean, like a doctor's office or a robot husband. A perfect husband would make for a very easy marriage; faith wouldn't be hard at all. He could never go wrong. But most wives require great faith. Submission takes on much more fascinating dimensions when marriage involves sinners.

Biblical history reveals that God's ways are often more ragged around the edges than we might wish. In the Old Covenant, we see the Spirit working through broken institutions, illegitimate priesthoods, and lonely Elijahs. The Sanhedrin of Christ's time presented delicious institutional unity and pomp, but the Spirit happened to be working through a locust-eating prophet and a band of unordained fishermen.

In this light, the various, widely publicized departures of many Evangelicals to Roman Catholicism and Eastern Orthodoxy have the distinct aroma of youthful haste and short-term zeal. The Sanhedrin was far better organized than the fishermen, and it had a grand liturgy, an authoritative line of oral tradition, and a succession of leaders. In a healthy church, those forms are good and holy. But to have turned to the Sanhedrin at *that* time would have been to embrace apostasy. Truth, beauty, and goodness were with the fishermen.

God's ways are not our ways. Such disheveled times ought not to be the norm: an established Temple and the unified Church are the norm. Christendom is currently scattered east, west, and Evangelical, but it won't always be that way. We should have Elijah's hope in the midst of disarray. And a mature and ancient understanding of *sola Scriptura* will be at the heart of recovery.

The practice of the ancient and medieval understanding of *sola Scriptura* can often be messy in history, and it requires a maturity that can wisely balance creedal authority and the rare need for Josiahs, a trinitarian one and many. But that is our life on earth. We are to walk by maturity, not by sight. Keith Mathison's work is a grand step in this direction, and, over the past few years, I have been privileged to share in his thinking about these questions. I am even more grateful that he agreed to write this book. He carefully peels away the thick misconceptions concerning *sola Scriptura,* many of which have been key to those claiming to abandon the doctrine. While many Roman and Eastern apologists have been able to ignore such corrections over the past decade, I hope Keith's book will significantly shift the debate and provoke more genuine dialogue.

Douglas M. Jones III
New St. Andrews College
Moscow, Idaho

Introduction

The doctrine of *sola scriptura*, "by Scripture alone," has been the focal point of intense disagreement between Roman Catholics and Protestants since the Reformation of the sixteenth century. In recent years the subject has gained renewed attention due to the growing number of converts from Protestantism to both Roman Catholicism and Eastern Orthodoxy who claim that their conversion was due in large part to their "discovery" that the doctrine of *sola scriptura* was indefensible.[1] In addition, a new generation of Roman Catholic and Eastern Orthodox apologists has been publishing an ever increasing number of books critical of the doctrine of *sola scriptura*.[2]

Many of these men and women who have left Protestantism claim to have grown increasingly frustrated at the tendency within evangelical Protestantism to divide continually over numerous differences of interpretation and at its seeming inability to even begin resolving these differences. They cite the numerous theological fads that permeate Protestantism and the

---

[1] E.g., Patrick Madrid, ed., *Surprised by Truth*, (San Diego: Basilica Press, 1994); Scott and Kimberly Hahn, *Rome Sweet Home*, (San Francisco: Ignatius Press, 1993); David Currie, *Born Fundamentalist, Born Again Catholic*, (San Francisco: Ignatius Press, 1996); Peter Gillquist, ed., *Coming Home: Why Protestant Clergy are Becoming Orthodox*, (Ben Lomond, CA: Conciliar Press, 1992).

[2] E.g., Robert A. Sungenis, *Not by Scripture Alone: A Catholic Critique of the Protestant Doctrine of Sola Scriptura*, (Santa Barbara: Queenship Publishing Co., 1997); Mark Shea, *By What Authority?* (Huntington, IN: Our Sunday Visitor, 1996); Clark Carlton, *The Way: What Every Protestant Should Know About the Orthodox Church*, (Salisbury, MA: Regina Orthodox Press, 1997).

numerous heretics that are readily given a hearing in evangelical circles as long as these heretics claim to be preaching "what the Bible says." Seeking shelter from the theological chaos that is modern evangelicalism, these men and women fled to communions which claim to have the answer. Part of that answer is a rejection of *sola scriptura*.

Within evangelicalism, many professing Christians use *sola scriptura* as a battle cry to justify endless schism. Other professing evangelicals use the slogan *sola scriptura* to justify every manner of false doctrine imaginable. The numerous ways in which *sola scriptura* has been misused have provided its critics with further evidence of the practical "unworkability" of the doctrine. If *sola scriptura* is true, these critics ask, then why are Protestants unable to come to agreement on what that Scripture teaches? For these reasons and more, it is absolutely imperative that the heirs of the Reformation be able to define accurately their concept of authority and be able to defend it against its opponents.

This will require not only answering the relevant criticisms of Roman Catholic and Eastern Orthodox apologists but also doing away with a large number of faulty concepts which are often wrongly identified with *sola scriptura*. Roman Catholic and Orthodox apologists have been effective in their criticisms in large part because of the fact that most Protestants have adopted a subjective and individualistic version of *sola scriptura* that bears little resemblance to the doctrine of the Reformers. As long as Protestants attempt to maintain this defective version of *sola scriptura*, and as long as this version of the doctrine is allowed to be identified as *the* Protestant position, Roman Catholic and Orthodox apologists will continue to effectively demolish it and gain frustrated seekers.

What this means is that, like the Reformers, our battle must be on two fronts. Just as they had to combat the Roman Catholic position which effectively made the Church autonomous and the Radical Anabaptist position which effectively made the individual autonomous, so we too must combat both of these defective views. Roman Catholic apologists have regrouped, and Eastern

Orthodox apologists are making numerous inroads. We must continue to stand firm against their view which ultimately results in a Church which is a law unto itself. But we must also take a strong stand against those Protestants whose view ultimately results in each man being a law unto himself. Both positions are a deadly poison in the body of Christ, and both are condemned not only by Scripture itself, but also by the witness of the communion of saints throughout the history of the Church.

The purpose of this book is twofold. First, it is an attempt to clear away some of the often misleading historical and theological rhetoric surrounding this debate. Much of the apologetic output from proponents on all sides has either ignored or mishandled crucial historical evidence, presented confusing and often contradictory definitions of terms, and in many cases simply annihilated armies of straw men. The second purpose of this book is to outline a consistent doctrine of the authority of Scripture. Nothing novel will be said in this study, though much might be new to some ears in this debate. It is the conviction of this author that the view of the relationship between Scripture, tradition, and the Church that the Reformers attempted to restore to the Church is substantially correct. It is a doctrine for which they coined the term *sola scriptura*. It is a doctrine which has been vigorously attacked by its opponents and often misused by its supporters, but it is the Christian doctrine, and therefore it is the doctrine that will prevail.

PART ONE:

THE HISTORICAL CONTEXT

1

The Early Church

In order to understand the present nature of the debate over the authority of Scripture it is necessary to gain some historical perspective. Much of the confusion surrounding this discussion is due to the failure of Christians to honestly examine the historical teaching of those believers who have preceded us in the faith. More often than not, the historical records are used for the sole purpose of extracting proof-texts to support a currently entrenched viewpoint. The result is an anachronistic reading of modern ideas and theories back into the writings of the church fathers. This practice may be observed among both Roman Catholic and Protestant apologists, and diligent effort must be made to avoid it. While it is obviously impossible to present an exhaustive examination of the patristic understanding of scriptural authority in a single chapter, a summary overview of the writings of the fathers themselves and of the conclusions of patristic scholars does shed valuable light on the historical question of scriptural authority.

Much of the problem involved in the historical debate over the authority of Scripture concerns the ambiguity surrounding the meaning of the word "tradition." In present day usage, the term commonly denotes unwritten doctrines handed down orally in the Church. It is therefore often contrasted with Scripture. However, a remarkable scholarly consensus shows that in the early church, Scripture and Tradition were in no way mutually exclusive concepts because they coincided with each other completely.[1]

---

[1] See Ellen Flessemann van Leer, *Tradition and Scripture in the Early Church* (Assen,

What this means is that throughout the history of the Church, including the Protestant Reformation, what we find is a battle that cannot often be characterized accurately in terms of Scripture vs. tradition. Instead what we find are competing concepts of the relationship between Scripture and tradition.[2] This will become clearer as the study proceeds.

THE APOSTOLIC FATHERS

The term "apostolic fathers" is normally used in reference to the earliest Christian authors whose writings were not included in the New Testament. Because they were written in the century immediately following the death of Christ (ca. A.D. 70–135), they are considered to be extremely valuable primary sources. These documents offer invaluable insight into the life and thought of the Church during this crucial transitional period.[3] It was during this period of time that Rome sacked Jerusalem, leaving the Church to wrestle with the question of its identity *vis-a-vis* Judaism. It was also during this period of time that the rapid growth and geographical expansion of the Church forced it to confront pressing questions of administration and government. And it was during this period of time that the last of the Apostles died, forcing the Church to confront the question of authority.

Among the apostolic fathers, one will search in vain to discover a formally outlined doctrine of Scripture such as may be found in modern systematic theology textbooks. The doctrine of Scripture did not become an independent *locus* of theology until the sixteenth century. What we do find throughout the writing of

---

1953); J.N.D. Kelly, *Early Christian Doctrines*, Rev. Ed., (San Francisco: HarperCollins, 1978), 29–51; R.P.C. Hanson, *Tradition in the Early Church*, (London, 1962); Heiko Oberman, *Dawn of the Reformation*, (Edinburgh: T&T Clark Ltd., 1986), 269–296; *The Harvest of Medieval Theology*, (Cambridge: Harvard University Press, 1963); Jaroslav Pelikan, *Obedient Rebels*, (London: SCM Press Ltd., 1964); F.F. Bruce, *Tradition: Old and New*, (Grand Rapids: Zondervan, 1970).

[2] Cf. Oberman, *Dawn of the Reformation*, 270.

[3] See J.B. Lightfoot and J.R. Harmer, *The Apostolic Fathers*, second edition, Edited by Michael W. Holmes, (Grand Rapids: Baker Book House, 1989), 1–15.

the apostolic fathers is a continual and consistent appeal to the Old Testament and to the Apostles' teaching. During these first decades following Christ, however, we have no evidence demonstrating that the Church considered the Apostles' teaching to be entirely confined to written documents.[4] This first generation of the Church saw many laymen and elders (e.g., Polycarp) who had been personally acquainted with one or more of the Apostles and who had sat under their preaching. We have no reason to assume that the apostolic doctrine could not have been faithfully taught in those churches which had no access to all of the apostolic writings. Copies of the writings of the Apostles were in circulation among the churches and were quoted by the apostolic fathers, but not every local church had a complete collection of all of the twenty-seven books later referred to as the New Testament.

As already noted, we have broad scholarly agreement that Scripture and tradition were not mutually exclusive concepts in the mind of the early fathers. The concept of "tradition," when used by these fathers, is simply used to designate the body of doctrine which was committed to the Church by the Lord and His Apostles, whether through verbal or written communication.[5] The body of doctrine, however, was essentially identical regardless of how it was communicated. No evidence suggests that the apostolic fathers believed they had recourse to any type of secret oral traditions. At this point in the Church's history, Scripture and tradition were coinherent concepts; "there was simply no way of imagining possible conflict between the Christian Scripture and the Christian tradition—and, therefore, no necessity to choose between them."[6] In fact, at this early point in the history of the Church, the use of the term "tradition" to denote the apostolic deposit of faith would, strictly speaking, be anachronistic.

[4] J.N.D Kelly, *Early Christian Doctrines*, 33.

[5] The term *paradosis* (tradition) was only rarely used in the period of the apostolic fathers. Clement, for example, uses the phrase "the glorious and holy rule of our tradition" to describe the deposit of faith (7:2). The verb *paradidonai*, on the other hand, is much more common, but it had not yet, at this point in history, acquired any specific technical meaning.

[6] Albert C. Outler, cited in Jaroslav Pelikan, *Obedient Rebels*, 173.

The concept of an apostolic deposit of faith existed, but no specific term, including "tradition," was universally used at this point to denote it.[7]

The fact that the Lord committed his teaching to the Church is also significant in the thought of the apostolic fathers. We do not find in their writings a dichotomy between the apostolic teaching and the apostolic Church. The Church is distinguished from Scripture, but the two are not opposed.[8] The true apostolic doctrine could only be found in the true body of Christ—the Christian Church.

THE SECOND AND THIRD CENTURIES

In the second and third centuries, the Church's struggle with the Gnostic heresy resulted in further clarification of the relationship between Scripture, tradition, and the Church. Because the Gnostics utilized scriptural texts to prove their points and because they also appealed to alleged secret apostolic traditions, the fathers were forced to explain the true relationship between Scripture and tradition.

IRENAEUS (CA. 130–200)

Irenaeus, the Bishop of Lyons, was on the front lines in the early Church's battle against Gnosticism. He has left the Church an immensely valuable work entitled *Against Heresies*. The book is devoted to destroying the various forms of the Gnostic heresy while at the same time defending the truth of Christianity. According to the Gnostics, the revelation of redeeming knowledge was not generally available to all men. Instead it was contained in secret apostolic traditions that were available only to those inducted into the Gnostic mysteries.[9]

---

[7] Kelly, op. cit., 34–35.

[8] Geoffrey W. Bromiley, "The Church Fathers and Holy Scripture," in *Scripture and Truth*, ed. by D.A. Carson and John D. Woodbridge, (Grand Rapids: Zondervan Publishing House, 1983), 218–219.

[9] Jaroslav Pelikan, *The Christian Tradition, Vol. 1: The Emergence of the Catholic Tradition,*

In his defense of apostolic Christianity, Irenaeus developed the concept of the *regula fidei* or the "rule of faith."[10] The *regula fidei* was essentially the content of the profession of faith that every catechumen was asked to recite from memory before his or her baptism. It was a summary of the faith taught by the Apostles and committed to their disciples.[11] Whereas the Gnostics appealed to a secret unwritten tradition, Irenaeus appealed to the public tradition of the Church. Does this mean that Irenaeus subordinated Scripture to unwritten tradition? No. As Heiko Oberman points out,

> Irenaeus insists that the rule of faith or the rule of truth (*regula fidei* or *regula veritatis*) is faithfully preserved by the apostolic Church and has found multiform expression in the canonical books. There is an unbroken continuation of the preached kerygma into Holy Scripture. One may speak here of an "inscripturisation" of the apostolic proclamation which in this written form constitutes *the* foundation and cornerstone of faith.[12]

This "inscripturisation" means for Irenaeus that the apostolic faith had been safeguarded by being permanently written in the Holy Scripture.[13] The two were not somehow opposed, nor was Scripture "subordinate" to the other. Irenaeus simply appealed to this *regula fidei* as a necessary hermeneutical principle. The Orthodox scholar Georges Florovsky points out that in the early Church, exegesis was "the main, and probably the only, theological method, and the authority of the Scriptures was sovereign and supreme."[14] But the *regula fidei* was the necessary context for the correct interpretation of that authoritative Scripture.[15] F.F. Bruce summarizes this early understanding of the rule of faith:

(Chicago: The University of Chicago Press, 1971), 92. Cf. H.E.W. Turner, *The Pattern of Christian Truth*, (A.R. Mowbray & Co. Ltd., 1954), 310.

[10] It may be found, for example, in Book III, 4, 2 of *Against Heresies*.

[11] Bruce, op. cit., 115–116.

[12] Oberman, op. cit., 272. See also Kelly, *Early Christian Doctrines*, 38–39.

[13] *Against Heresies* III, 1, 1. Cf. Kelly, op. cit., 38.

[14] Georges Florovsky, *Bible, Church, Tradition: An Eastern Orthodox View*, (Bucherver-triebsanstalt, 1987), 75.

[15] Ibid.

When the summary of the apostolic tradition is called the rule of faith or the rule of truth, the implication is that this is the church's norm, the standard by which everything must be judged that presents itself for Christian faith or claims to be Christian doctrine, the criterion for the recognition of truth and exposure of error. If at times it is formally distinguished from Scripture in the sense that it is recognized as the interpretation of Scripture, at other times it is materially identical with Scripture in the sense that it sums up what Scripture says. Plainly what was written down by the apostles in their letters and what was delivered by them orally to their disciples and handed down in the church's tradition must be one and the same body of teaching.[16]

This concept of the *regula fidei* remained a crucial tool in the early Church's arsenal against Gnosticism and other heresies.

CLEMENT OF ALEXANDRIA (CA. 150–CA. 215)

One of the lengthiest explanations of the relationship between Scripture, tradition and the Church in early Christian literature is found in the *Stromata* of Clement of Alexandria. Written within the historical context of the battle with Gnosticism, chapter 16 of Book VII is devoted to an elucidation of Scripture as the criterion by which truth and heresy are to be distinguished. In the very first sentence of chapter 16, Clement declares the necessity of having all things proven from Scripture: "But those who are ready to toil in the most excellent pursuits, will not desist from the search after truth, till they get the demonstration from the Scriptures themselves."[17] Like Irenaeus, Clement recognizes the necessity of the *regula fidei* as the interpretive context of Scripture and the Church as the interpreter of Scripture, and he explains this relationship further in chapter 17; but throughout this chapter it is the Scripture itself that is considered the criterion of truth.[18]

---

[16] Bruce, op. cit., 117–118.

[17] Unless otherwise noted, all patristic citations are taken from the 38 volume English edition of the fathers co-published by Wm. B. Eerdmans and T&T Clark.

[18] It is interesting to note that the doctrine of the perpetual virginity of Mary, for which Rome claims a universal and continuous tradition, is explicitly declared by Clement to be false in this chapter.

TERTULLIAN (CA. 155–220)

Tertullian's explanation of the relationship between the Scripture, tradition, and the Church does not differ in any significant way from that of Irenaeus. Like Irenaeus, he does not contrast Scripture and tradition; instead he claims the oral preaching of the Apostles was written down in Scripture.[19] For Tertullian, as Kelly explains, "Scripture has absolute authority; whatever it teaches is necessarily true, and woe betide ["befall"] him who accepts doctrines not discoverable in it."[20] In refuting a particular tenet of Docetism, for example, Tertullian writes, "But there is no evidence of this, because Scripture says nothing."[21] When contending against the patripassianism of Praxeas, he writes, "Let us be content with saying that Christ died, the Son of the Father; and let this suffice, because the Scriptures have told us so much."[22] In contending against Hermogenes' teaching that matter is eternal, he says, "But whether all things were made out of any underlying Matter, I have as yet failed anywhere to find. Where such a statement is written, Hermogenes' shop must tell us. If it is nowhere written, then let it fear the woe which impends on all who add or take away from the written word."[23]

We also find in Tertullian "a marked insistence on the decisive difference between the tradition of God, preserved in the canon and the traditions of man (*consuetudines*)."[24] In chapter 13 of *On Prescription Against Heretics*, Tertullian condemns as madness the idea that the Apostles "did not reveal all to all men" but instead "proclaimed some openly and to all the world, whilst they disclosed others (only) in secret and to a few." This Gnostic idea of a secret apostolic tradition Tertullian heartily condemns.

Like Irenaeus, Tertullian outlines the *regula fidei* in a number of

---

[19] Kelly, op. cit., 39.

[20] Ibid.

[21] *On the Flesh of Christ*, ch. 6. Docetism (from the Greek *dokein*, meaning "to think or suppose") was an early heresy that denied the reality of the incarnation. According to the Docetists, Christ's human body only "appeared" to be real.

[22] *Against Praxeas*, ch. 29.

[23] *Against Hermogenes*, ch. 22.

[24] Oberman, op. cit., 274.

places throughout his writings.[25] In chapter 13 of his treatise *On the Prescription Against Heretics*, for example, he describes the rule of faith as

> the belief that there is only one God, and that He is none other than the Creator of the world, who produced all things out of nothing through His own Word, first of all sent forth; that this Word is called His Son, and, under the name of God, was seen "in diverse manners" by the patriarchs, heard at all times in the prophets, at last brought down by the Spirit and Power of the Father into the Virgin Mary, was made flesh in her womb, and, being born of her, went forth as Jesus Christ; thenceforth He preached the new law and the new promise of the kingdom of heaven, worked miracles; having been crucified, He rose again the third day (then) having ascended into the heavens, He sat at the right hand of the Father; sent instead of Himself the Power of the Holy Ghost to lead such as believe; will come with glory to take the saints to the enjoyment of everlasting life and of the heavenly promises, and to condemn the wicked to everlasting fire, after the resurrection of both these classes shall have happened, together with the restoration of their flesh.

One will immediately notice the similarity in overall form between this early outline of the rule of faith and what later became known as the Apostles' Creed. The rule of faith, like the Apostles' Creed, follows a Trinitarian outline, beginning with a confession of faith in the Father, followed by a confession of faith in the Son and the Holy Spirit. It must also be noted that as in the case of Irenaeus, for Tertullian, the Scriptures are in no way subordinated to this "rule of faith." It is the Scriptures, according to Tertullian, that "indeed furnish us with our Rule of faith."[26] But it is the rule of faith that is the hermeneutical context for a proper interpretation of Scripture. Because both the apostolic Scriptures and the apostolic rule of faith have as their source the Apostles, they are mutually reciprocal and indivisible for Tertullian.[27]

---

[25] Eg., *On Prescription Against Heretics*, ch. 13; *Against Praxeas*, ch. 2; *On the Veiling of Virgins*, ch. 1.

[26] *Against Praxeas*, ch. 11.

[27] *On Prescription Against Heretics*, ch. 19.

HIPPOLYTUS (CA. 170–236)

Further testimony demonstrating patristic belief in the one source understanding of God's self-revelation may be found in the writing of Hippolytus. In a work entitled *Against the Heresy of One Noetus*, Hippolytus explains the source of our knowledge of God.

> There is, brethren, one God, the knowledge of whom we gain from the Holy Scriptures, and from no other source. For just as a man, if he wishes to be skilled in the wisdom of this world, will find himself unable to get at it in any other way than by mastering the dogmas of philosophers, so all of us who wish to practice piety will be unable to learn its practice from any other quarter than the oracles of God. Whatever things, then, the Holy Scriptures declare, at these let us look; and whatsoever things they teach, these let us learn; and as the Father wills our belief to be, let us believe; and as He wills the Son to be glorified, let us glorify Him; and as He wills the Holy Spirit to be bestowed, let us receive Him. Not according to our own will, nor according to our own mind, nor yet as using violently those things which are given by God, but even as He has chosen to teach them by the Holy Scriptures, so let us discern them.[28]

Hippolytus does not divorce the Holy Scriptures from the Church or from the *regula fidei*. In fact, he includes a summary of how the Church used the *regula fidei* in their condemnation of Noetus,[29] but the Holy Scripture is held forth as the unique standard and only source for the knowledge of God.

CYPRIAN (CA. 200–258)

Further insight into the early Church's understanding of the relationship between Scripture, the Church, and tradition may be gained through an examination of the letters of Cyprian, the Bishop of Carthage. The question of lapsed Christians was a

[28] *Against Noetus*, ch. 9.
[29] Ibid., ch. 1.

contentious issue at this time, and Cyprian quarreled extensively with Pope Stephen over the question of baptism.[30] What is of interest at this point is not the subject of the debate so much as the manner of the debate and the principles expressed. In a letter written to explain Stephen's actions, Cyprian directly accuses the pope of error. He writes, "I have sent you a copy of his reply; on the reading of which, you will more and more observe his error in endeavoring to maintain the cause of heretics against Christians, and against the Church of God."[31] He continues,

> Let nothing be innovated, says he, nothing maintained, except what has been handed down. Whence is that tradition? Whether does it descend from the authority of the Lord and of the Gospel, or does it come from the commands and the epistles of the apostles? For that those things which are written must be done, God witnesses and admonishes, saying to Joshua the son of Nun: "The book of this law shall not depart out of thy mouth; but thou shalt meditate in it day and night, that thou mayest observe to do according to all that is written therein."[32]

Cyprian grieves over this error of Stephen: "What obstinacy is that, or what presumption, to prefer human tradition to divine ordinance, and not to observe that God is indignant and angry as often as human tradition relaxes and passes by the divine precepts."[33] He laments the fact that "that which is done without against the Church is defended within the very Church itself."[34] And arguing against the pope's own claim that he is merely defending the ancient tradition of the Church, Cyprian counters, "Nor ought custom, which had crept in among some, to prevent the truth from prevailing and conquering; for custom without truth is the antiquity of error."[35]

---

[30] William La Due, *The Chair of Saint Peter: A History of the Papacy*, (Maryknoll: Orbis Books, 1999), 33–39.
[31] *Epistle* 73:1.
[32] *Epistle* 73:2.
[33] *Epistle* 73:3.
[34] *Epistle* 73:8.
[35] *Epistle* 73:9.

In a letter from Firmilian, the Bishop of Caeserea, to Cyprian regarding Pope Stephen's actions, we gain another witness to the attitude of the early Church towards authority. Firmilian writes, "they who are at Rome do not observe those things in all cases which are handed down from the beginning, and vainly pretend the authority of the apostles."[36] He argues that by advocating heresy, Pope Stephen has broken the peace and unity of the Catholic Church.[37] There is no intimation here, or anywhere in the ante-Nicene fathers, of a *charism* or gift of infallibility given to the Roman bishop which automatically preserves him from doctrinal deviation from the apostolic faith. Not only is the possibility of grievous error assumed, it is expressly declared to have been embraced.

THE FOURTH AND FIFTH CENTURIES

The fourth and fifth centuries of the Church's history were a period of great theological controversy and great theological consolidation. It was during this period of time that the intense Trinitarian and Christological battles reached their climax. It was also during these two centuries that the standards of Trinitarian and Christological orthodoxy were clarified and explained at the ecumenical councils of Nicea (A.D. 325), Constantinople (A.D. 381), Ephesus (A.D. 431), and Chalcedon (A.D. 451) and officially set forth in the Nicene-Constantinopolitan Creed and the Definition of Chalcedon.

ATHANASIUS (CA. 296–373)

Considered to be the greatest theologian of his time, Athanasius, the Bishop of Alexandria, was a key player in the fourth-century battle with the Arian heresy. His tireless efforts were largely responsible for the great ecumenical council at Nicea in

---

[36] *Epistle* 74:6.
[37] Ibid.

A.D. 325, which officially condemned Arianism and vindicated the orthodox doctrine.[38]

Like earlier heretics the Arians appealed to Scripture and, in fact, insisted that all discussion be restricted to the text of Scripture. Athanasius's critique of these heretics, therefore, proves invaluable to a study of the early Church's concept of authority. Athanasius does not deny the sufficiency of Scripture for the defense of the truth. Instead he often explicitly affirms it. He states in one place that "the sacred and inspired Scriptures are sufficient to declare the truth."[39] Elsewhere he argues that "holy Scripture is of all things most sufficient for us" and urges "those who desire to know more of these matters to read the Divine word."[40] And again he says, "divine Scripture is sufficient above all things."[41]

The error of the heretics, according to Athanasius, is not in their appeal to Scripture but in their appeal to Scripture taken out of the context of the apostolic faith, that which Irenaeus referred to as the *regula fidei*. As Florovsky notes,

> This "rule," however, was in no sense an "extraneous" authority which could be "imposed" on the Holy Writ. It was the same "Apostolic preaching," which was written down in the books of the New Testament, but it was, as it were, this preaching *in epitome*.[42]

According to Athanasius, Holy Scripture *is* the apostolic *paradosis* or "tradition."[43] There is no second source concept of tradition. In his entire debate with the Arians, Athanasius never appeals to any plural "traditions."[44] He appeals to the sufficiency of the Holy Scripture as interpreted within the context of the apostolic *regula fidei*.

---

[38] For a history of the events and debates surrounding the Arian controversy and the Council of Nicea, see Leo Donald Davis, *The First Seven Ecumenical Councils (325–787): Their History and Theology*, (Collegeville, MN: The Liturgical Press, 1983), 33–80; cf. Kelly, op. cit., 280–309.

[39] *Against the Heathen*, I: 3.

[40] *To the Bishops of Egypt*, I:4.

[41] *De Synodis*, I, 1, 6.

[42] Florovsky, op. cit., 82–83.

[43] *Ad Adelphium*, 6.

[44] Florovsky, 83.

HILARY OF POITIERS (CA. 300–367)

The concern for interpreting the authoritative Scriptures within the context of the apostolic faith is repeated in the writings of Hilary, the Bishop of Poitiers. The apostolic rule of faith and the Holy Scripture are essentially one and the same for Hilary. In his treatise *On the Councils*, he provides a brief outline of the evangelical and apostolic tradition and then concludes, "For all those things which were written in the divine Scriptures by Prophets and by Apostles we believe and follow truly and with fear."[45] The same truths he refers to as the apostolic tradition he refers to as written in the Scriptures.

These Scriptures, however, cannot be interpreted apart from the context of the apostolic faith without destroying their meaning. He writes of heretics, "Such is their error, such their pestilent teaching; to support it they borrow the words of Scripture, perverting its meaning and using the ignorance of men as their opportunity of gaining credence for their lies."[46] Scripture is the final doctrinal authority, according to Hilary, but only when it is interpreted rightly. The mere use of Scripture does not guarantee the right use of Scripture.

CYRIL OF JERUSALEM (CA. 315–CA. 384)

One of the most fascinating statements made by any of the early Church fathers concerning the authority of Scripture is found in the *Catechetical Lectures* of Cyril, Bishop of Jerusalem. He writes,

> For concerning the divine and holy mysteries of the Faith, not even a casual statement must be delivered without the Holy Scriptures; nor must we be drawn aside by mere plausibility and artifices of speech. Even to me, who tell thee these things, give not absolute credence, unless thou receive the proof of the things which I announce from the Divine Scriptures. For this salvation which we believe depends not on ingenious reasoning, but on demonstration of the Holy Scriptures.[47]

45 *On the Councils*, 29–30.
46 *On the Trinity*, IV:14.
47 *Catechetical Lectures*, IV:17.

Here we find stated, about as clearly as possible, the necessity of firm scriptural proof for every article of faith. Cyril tells his catechumens not to rest their faith upon plausibility or ingenious arguments or even upon his own authority as a Bishop, but to rest it upon clear proof from the Holy Scripture.

THE TRANSITIONAL PERIOD

Thus far the testimony of the early Church fathers regarding the question of authority is consistent. Scripture is the authority, but it must be interpreted according to the apostolic *regula fidei*. As noted by G.L. Prestige, "The voice of the Bible could be plainly heard only if its text were interpreted broadly and rationally, in accordance with the apostolic creed and the evidence of the historical practice of Christendom."[48] In a number of historical studies, the church historian Heiko Oberman describes the characteristics of this early patristic position. As he explains, this one source concept of "tradition" has two primary qualities:

1. The immediate divine origin of tradition together with the insistence on a clearly circumscribed series of historical acts of God in the rule of faith or the rule of truth.
2. The rejection of extra-scriptural tradition.[49]

For the sake of clarity, Oberman terms this "single exegetical tradition of interpreted scripture 'Tradition I'."[50] It is this view which was universally held for the first three centuries of the Church. During the fourth century, however, a transitional period began as several prominent fathers started to hint at a two-source concept of tradition.

---

[48] Cited by Florovsky, 80.

[49] Heiko Oberman, *The Dawn of the Reformation*, (Edinburgh: T&T Clark Ltd., 1986), 276. Cf. also Oberman, *The Harvest of Medieval Theology*, (Cambridge: Harvard University Press, 1963), 361–393.

[50] Ibid., 280. Because of the value of Oberman's thesis and because it has been built upon by other historical scholars, this study will continue to use his terminology.

BASIL THE GREAT (CA. 330–379)

It is in the fourth-century writings of Basil the Great that we find for the first time the suggestion "that the Christian owes equal respect and obedience to written and to unwritten ecclesiastical traditions, whether contained in canonical writings or in secret oral tradition handed down by the Apostles through their successors."[51] The passage in question is found in Basil's treatise *On the Holy Spirit*. He writes,

> Of the beliefs and practices whether generally accepted or publicly enjoined which are preserved in the Church some we possess derived from written teaching; others we have received delivered to us "in a mystery" by the tradition of the apostles; and both of these in relation to true religion have the same force. And these no one will gainsay; no one, at all events, who is even moderately versed in the institutions of the Church. For were we to attempt to reject such customs as have no written authority, on the ground that the importance they possess is small, we should unintentionally injure the Gospel in its very vitals; or, rather, should make our public definition a mere phrase and nothing more.[52]

As we shall see, these comments by Basil were seized upon in the late Middle Ages by canon lawyers and theologians seeking to defend an authoritative second extra-Biblical source of revelation. And while it is very possible that Basil's teaching is the first explicit instance of what Oberman terms "Tradition II," the case has been made by the Orthodox theologian Georges Florovsky that Basil meant nothing of the sort. He notes,

> In any case, one should not be embarrassed by the contention of St. Basil that *dogmata* were delivered or handed down by the Apostles, *en musterio*. It would be a flagrant mistranslation if we render it as "in secret." The only accurate rendering is: "by the way of mysteries," that is—under the form of rites and

---

[51] Oberman, *Harvest of Medieval Theology*, 369.
[52] *On the Holy Spirit*, 66.

(liturgical) usages, or "habits." In fact, it is precisely what St. Basil says himself: *ta pleista ton mustikon agraphos hemin empoliteuetai.* [Most of the mysteries are communicated to us by an unwritten way]. The term *ta mustika* refers here, obviously to the rites of Baptism and Eucharist, which are, for St. Basil, of "Apostolic" origin. . . . Indeed, all instances quoted by St. Basil in this connection are of ritual or liturgical nature.[53]

All of these liturgical rites, according to Basil, come from a "silent" and "private" tradition. But, as Florovsky notes, "[t]his 'silent' and 'mystical' tradition, 'which has not been made public,' is not an esoteric doctrine, reserved for some particular elite." In fact, "the 'elite' was the Church."[54] The historical context sheds some light on this obscure concept:

> St. Basil is referring here to what is now denoted as *disciplina arcani.* [The discipline of secrecy]. In the fourth century this "discipline" was in wide use, was formally imposed and advocated in the Church. It was related to the institution of the Catechumenate and had primarily an educational and didactic purpose. On the other hand, as St. Basil says himself, certain "traditions" had to be kept "unwritten" in order to prevent profanation at the hands of the infidel. This remark obviously refers to rites and usages. It may be recalled at this point that, in the practice of the Fourth century, the Creed (and also the Dominical Prayer) were a part of this "discipline of secrecy" and could not be disclosed to the noninitiated. The Creed was reserved for the candidates for Baptism, at the last stage of their instruction, after they had been solemnly enrolled and approved. The Creed was communicated, or "traditioned," to them by the bishop *orally* and they had to recite it by memory before him. . . . The Catechumens were strongly urged not to divulge the Creed to outsiders and not to commit it to writing. It had to be inscribed in their hearts.[55]

It is against this historical context and background that Basil's comments must be interpreted and understood.

[53] Florovsky, op. cit., 86–87.
[54] Ibid., 87.
[55] Ibid., 87–88.

The only difference between *dogma* and *kerygma* was in the manner of their transmission: dogma is kept "in silence" and *kerygmata* are "publicized".... But their intent is identical: they convey the same faith, if in different manners.... Thus, the "unwritten tradition," in rites and symbols, does not actually add anything to the content of the scriptural faith: it only puts this faith in focus.... St. Basil's appeal to "unwritten tradition" was actually an appeal to the faith of the Church.... He pleaded that, apart from this "unwritten" rule of faith, it was impossible to grasp the true intention and teaching of the Scripture itself. St. Basil was strictly scriptural in his theology: Scripture was for him the supreme criterion of doctrine.[56]

Basil explicitly declares Scripture to be his supreme criterion in one of his many letters. Writing about his controversy with the heretics, he says,

> Their complaint is that their custom does not accept this, and that Scripture does not agree. What is my reply? I do not consider it fair that the custom which obtains among them should be regarded as a law and rule of orthodoxy. If custom is to be taken in proof of what is right, then it is certainly competent for me to put forward on my side the custom which obtains here. If they reject this, we are clearly not bound to follow them. Therefore let God-inspired Scripture decide between us; and on whichever side be found doctrines in harmony with the Word of God, in favor of that side will be cast the vote of truth.[57]

The evidence seems to indicate that, despite the inherent ambiguity of his infamous words, Basil did not intend to be understood as teaching a two-source concept of revelation.

GREGORY OF NYSSA (CA. 335–CA. 394)

Gregory, his brother Basil the Great, and their lifelong friend Gregory of Nazianzus, are known to historians as the Cappado-

---

[56] Ibid., 88–89.
[57] *Letters*, 189:3.

cian Fathers. These men are best known for their detailed defense of Nicene Trinitarianism against the attacks of the Arian heretics. Gregory, who was ordained Bishop of Nyssa, wrote a large number of philosophical, theological and apologetic treatises. One of these works, entitled *On the Soul and the Resurrection*, contains a summary statement of his view of the authority of Scripture. The book is set forth in the form of a dialogue between Gregory and Macrina, who is referred to as "the Teacher." Throughout the book, Gregory raises the objections of the philosophers to the Christian doctrine, and the Teacher answers. Near the beginning of the tract, Gregory summarizes the orthodox Christian answer to the speculations of philosophers. He writes,

> But while the latter proceeded, on the subject of the soul, as far in the direction of supposed consequences as the thinker pleased, we are not entitled to such license, I mean that of affirming what we please; we make the Holy Scriptures the rule and the measure of every tenet; we necessarily fix our eyes upon that, and approve that alone which may be made to harmonize with the intention of those writings.[58]

Although written in the context of a philosophical debate, the intent of Gregory's statement is clear. The Scripture is the doctrinal norm of the Christian faith.

J.N.D. Kelly suggests that Gregory differentiated between Scripture and an extra-scriptural tradition when, in his desire to prove the unique generation of the Son, he argued that it is sufficient that "we have the tradition descending to us from the fathers, like an inheritance transmitted from the apostles along the line of holy persons who succeeded them."[59] It is unclear, however, that Gregory meant anything different here than what the earlier fathers meant by their use of tradition. In fact, Gregory himself explains in another place:

---

[58] *On the Soul and the Resurrection.* There are no book or chapter divisions in the Eerdmans English edition of this text. See, Philip Schaff and Henry Wace, eds. *The Nicene and Post Nicene Fathers*, Second Series, Vol. V, 439.

[59] Cited in Kelly, op. cit., 45.

The Christian Faith, which in accordance with the command of our Lord, has been preached to all nations by His disciples, is neither of men, nor by men, but by our Lord Jesus Christ Himself. . . . He, I say, appeared on earth and "conversed with men," that men might no longer have opinions according to their own notions about the Self-existent, formulating into a doctrine the hints that come to them from vague conjectures, but that we might be convinced that God has truly been manifested in the flesh, and believe that to be the only true "mystery of godliness," which was delivered to us by the very Word and God, Who by Himself spake to His Apostles, and that we might receive the teaching concerning the transcendent nature of the Deity which is given to us, as it were, "through a glass darkly" from the older Scriptures—from the Law, and the Prophets, and the Sapiential [Wisdom] Books, as an evidence of the truth fully revealed to us, reverently accepting the meaning of the things which have been spoken, so as to accord in the faith set forth by the Lord of the whole Scriptures, which faith we guard as we received it, *word for word*, in purity, without falsification, judging even a slight divergence from the *words delivered to us* an extreme blasphemy and impiety. . . . In the Faith then which was delivered by God to the Apostles we admit neither subtraction, nor alteration, nor addition, knowing assuredly that he who presumes to pervert the Divine utterance by dishonest quibbling, the same "is of his father the devil," who *leaves the words of truth* and "speaks his own," becoming the father of a lie.[60]

The emphasis throughout this passage is that the faith—the tradition—that is handed down is clearly written "word for word." In other words it is the apostolic Scriptures, together with the older Scriptures, from which Gregory admits no subtraction, alteration or addition.

JOHN CHRYSOSTOM (CA. 347–407)

Considered one of the "doctors" of the Church, John spent a number of years as a deacon and elder in the church at Antioch.

---

[60] *Against Eunomius*, II: 1. Emphasis mine.

His gift of preaching was so admired that it later earned him the nickname *Chrysostomos* or "golden mouth." In A.D. 398, John became the Bishop of Constantinople, one of the great sees of the ancient Church, but it is his gifted preaching for which he is most remembered.

Unlike Basil and Gregory of Nyssa, whose support of Tradition II is ambiguous at best, John seems to clearly embrace a two-source concept of revelation. While he will without hesitation assert the authority of Scripture, he also seems to assert the existence of authoritative unwritten apostolic traditions. An explicit declaration of John's view of the authority of Scripture is found in his sermon on 2 Timothy 3:16–17. In his examination of this passage, John carefully comments on each phrase. He writes regarding the ways in which Scripture is profitable for doctrine:

> For thence we shall know, whether we ought to learn or to be ignorant of anything. And thence we may disprove what is false, thence we may be corrected and brought to a right mind, may be comforted and consoled, and if anything is deficient, we may have it added to us.
>
> "That the man of God may be perfect." For this is the exhortation of the Scripture given, that the man of God may be rendered perfect by it; without this therefore he cannot be perfect. Thou hast the Scriptures, he says, in place of me. If thou wouldst learn anything, thou mayest learn it from them. And if he thus wrote to Timothy who was filled with the Spirit, how much more to us![61]

One of the most interesting comments John makes here is his assertion that the Scriptures are what the man of God now has "in place of" an Apostle. The authority of the Apostles is now found in their writings—the Scripture. In another place John tells his hearers, "I exhort and entreat you all, disregard what this man and that man thinks about these things, and inquire from the Scriptures all these things."[62]

---

[61] *Homilies on II Timothy*, IX.
[62] *Homilies on II Corinthians*, XIII.

This, however, is not all that John has to say. In a homily on 2 Thessalonians 2:15, John says that,

> It is manifest that they [the Apostles] did not deliver all things by Epistle, but many things also unwritten, and in like manner both the one and the other are worthy of credit. Therefore let us think the tradition of the Church also worthy of credit. It is a tradition, seek no farther.[63]

While it is possible that John may have meant no more than Basil, the specific distinction between what is written and what is unwritten is clear.

AUGUSTINE (354–430)

Probably the greatest theologian in the first thousand years of the Church, Augustine, the Bishop of Hippo, is known popularly for his *Confessions*. Equally important, although less familiar to most, are his numerous theological works such as *On the Trinity*, the anti-Pelagian writings, and his massive and highly influential philosophy of history—*The City of God*.

According to Oberman, Augustine is clearly an early proponent of Tradition II—the concept of tradition that allows for an authoritative extra-biblical source of revelation. On the one hand he repeatedly asserts the primacy and authority of Scripture. For example, in his moral treatise *On the Good of Widowhood*, he writes,

> What more can I teach you, than what we read in the Apostle? For holy Scripture setteth a rule to our teaching, that we dare not "be wise more than it behoveth to be wise." [64]

Likewise in *The Unity of the Church*, he writes,

> Let us not hear: This I say, this you say; but, thus says the Lord. Surely it is the books of the Lord on whose authority we both

---

63 *Homilies on II Thessalonians*, IV.
64 *On the Good of Widowhood*, 2.

agree and which we both believe. There let us seek the church, there let us discuss our case. . . . Let those things be removed from our midst which we quote against each other not from divine canonical books but from elsewhere. Someone may perhaps ask: Why do you want to remove these things from the midst? Because I do not want the holy church proved by human documents but by divine oracles.[65]

Augustine also makes it clear that the *regula fidei* is essentially a summary of Holy Scripture. In a sermon to catechumens, he declares that the words of the Creed "which ye have heard are in the Divine Scriptures scattered up and down; but thence gathered and reduced into one."[66]

If this were all Augustine said, we could confidently conclude that he shared the same concept of tradition taught in the first three centuries. However, while Augustine clearly asserts the authority of scriptural revelation, he also suggests that there is an authoritative extra-scriptural oral tradition. This comes out most obviously in his writings on issues such as baptism. He writes, for example, in one treatise on the subject, "if any one seek for divine authority in this matter, though what is held by the whole Church, and that not as instituted by Councils, but as a matter of invariable custom, is rightly held to have been handed down by apostolic authority."[67] And in a comment on Cyprian's controversy with Pope Stephen, he adds,

"The Apostles," indeed, "gave no injunctions on the point;" but the custom, which is opposed to Cyprian, may be supposed to have had its origin in apostolic tradition, just as there are many things which are observed by the whole Church, and therefore are fairly held to have been enjoined by the apostles, which yet are not mentioned in their writings.[68]

---

[65] *The Unity of the Church*, 3. Cited in Martin Chemnitz, *An Examination of the Council of Trent*, Vol. I, (St. Louis: Concordia Publishing House, 1971), 157.

[66] *On the Creed: A Sermon to the Catechumens*, I.

[67] *On Baptism, Against the Donatists*, IV:24.

[68] Ibid., V:23.

On the face of it, this statement and the others like it appear to indicate that Augustine advocated a two-source concept of tradition. And it is very possible that he did embrace this view. It is certainly true that his statements were later interpreted in that way. But when we consider the fact that his suggestive comments (like those of Basil) almost all occur within the context of debates over liturgical and ritual issues, the possibility must remain open that Augustine meant nothing more than what Basil meant and that neither intended to advocate a new concept of tradition.

In addition to the comments Augustine made regarding Scripture and tradition, there are numerous statements in his writings regarding the authority of the Church. Perhaps the most infamous statement of Augustine that bears on the question of ecclesiastical authority is one he made in his anti-Manichaean writings. The statement itself reads as follows: "For my part, I should not believe the gospel except as moved by the authority of the Catholic Church."[69] This brief comment has become a foundational proof-text for modern Roman Catholicism's ecclesiastical claims, but it remains to be seen whether it can bear the weight placed upon it. As Oberman explains, Augustine's assertion of "practical priority" was later interpreted as an assertion of "metaphysical priority."[70] The actual language and context of Augustine's comment, however, will not allow for this interpretation. Oberman points out that "moved" is a translation of the Latin *commovit me* and that here "the Church must be understood to have an authority to direct (*commovere*) the believer to the door which leads to the fullness of the Word itself."[71] Florovsky explains the importance of a contextual reading of Augustine:

> The phrase must be read in its context. First of all, St. Augustine did not utter this sentence on his own behalf. He spoke of the attitude which a simple believer had to take, when confronted

[69] *Against the Epistle of Manichaeus*, ch. 5.

[70] Oberman, *The Dawn of the Reformation*, 278.

[71] Heiko Oberman, *Forerunners of the Reformation*, (London: Lutterworth Press, 1967), 56.

with the heretical claim for authority. In this situation it was proper for a simple believer to appeal to the authority of the Church, from which, and in which, he had received the Gospel itself: *ipsi Evangelio catholicis praedicantibus credidi.* [I believed the Gospel itself, being instructed by catholic preachers]. The Gospel and the preaching of the *Catholica* belong together. St. Augustine had no intention "to subordinate" the Gospel to the Church. He only wanted to emphasize that "Gospel" is actually received always in the context of Church's catholic preaching and simply cannot be separated from the Church. Only in this context it can be assessed and properly understood. Indeed, the witness of the Scripture is ultimately "self-evident," but only for the faithful, for those who have achieved a certain "spiritual" maturity,—and this is only possible within the Church. He opposed this teaching and preaching *auctoritas* of the Church Catholic to the pretentious vagaries of Manichean exegesis. The Gospel did not belong to the Manicheans. *Catholicae Ecclesiae auctoritas* [the authority of the Catholic Church] was not an independent source of faith. But it was the indispensible principle of sound interpretation. Actually, the sentence could be converted: one should not believe the Church, unless one was moved by the Gospel. The relationship is strictly reciprocal.[72]

In this Augustine is in agreement with the earlier fathers who insisted on the necessary role of the Church. The evidence simply does not support later medieval concepts of a Church that has metaphysical priority over Holy Scripture. This interpretation (which persists today) stems from taking one sentence out of context and reading far more into it than that context will allow.

The evidence does, however, lend possible support to Oberman's assertion that Augustine is one of the first, if not the first, Latin father to explicitly endorse a two-source concept of revelation. This is significant because, as Pelikan notes, "in a manner and to a degree unique for any Christian thinker outside the New Testament, Augustine has determined the form and the content of church doctrine for most of Western Christian history."[73]

[72] Florovsky, op. cit., 92.
[73] Pelikan, op. cit., 293.

THE VINCENTIAN CANON

As we have seen, the question of how to distinguish truth from heresy has always faced the Church. From the first century onward, heresies have arisen, and Christians have been forced to combat them. We've seen the manner in which the concept of the *regula fidei* developed and guided patristic apologetics. One of the fullest and most influential treatments of the question of discernment to be found in the early Christian fathers is Vincent of Lerins's *Comonitory*.

VINCENT OF LERINS (D. CA. 450)

Little is known of the author of the *Comonitory*. The book is written under an assumed name, but it is attributed to Vincent of Lerins by Gennadius in the late fourth century, and his judgment has been almost unanimously accepted. The object of the book is to provide a standard or rule by which apostolic Christian truth may be distinguished from heresy.[74] Because of its significance, the relevant parts of Vincent's comments are quoted in full.

> [W]hether I or any one else should wish to detect the frauds and avoid the snares of heretics as they rise, and to continue sound and complete in the Catholic faith, we must, the Lord helping, fortify our own belief in two ways; first by the authority of the Divine Law, and then, by the Tradition of the Catholic Church.
>
> But here some one perhaps will ask, Since the canon of Scripture is complete, and sufficient of itself for everything, and more than sufficient, what need is there to join with it the authority of the Church's interpretation? For this reason—because, owing to the depth of Holy Scripture, all do not accept it in one and the same sense, but one understands its words in one way, another in another; so that it seems to be capable of as many interpretations as there are interpreters. . . . Therefore, it is very necessary, on account of so great intricacies of such various error, that the rule for the right understanding of the prophets and apostles should be framed in accordance with the standard of Ecclesiastical and Catholic interpretation.

[74] *Comonitory*, I.

Moreover, in the Catholic Church itself, all possible care must be taken, that we hold that faith which has been believed everywhere, always, by all. For that is truly and in the strictest sense "Catholic," which, as the name itself and the reason of the thing declare, comprehends all universally. This rule we shall observe if we follow universality, antiquity, consent. We shall follow universality if we confess that one faith to be true, which the whole Church throughout the world confesses; antiquity, if we in no wise depart from those interpretations which it is manifest were notoriously held by our holy ancestors and fathers; consent, in like manner, if in antiquity itself we adhere to the consentient definitions and determinations of all, or at the least of almost all priests and doctors.[75]

For the purposes of this study it must be determined whether Vincent embraced a one-source or two-source concept of tradition. Did he embrace "Tradition I" or "Tradition II"?

Oberman notes that Vincent's view does not allow for an authoritative extra-scriptural tradition. Vincent does not reject the material sufficiency of Scripture, only the formal sufficiency.[76] He argues that Scripture must be interpreted by the Church because heretics have repeatedly promoted their own various false interpretations. However, "the sole purpose of interpretation is preservation: the faith once declared to the Apostles has to be protected against change, which represents for him perversion."[77] As Florovsky notes,

Tradition was not, according to Vincent, an independent instance, nor was it a complementary source of faith. Ecclesiastical understanding could not add anything to the Scripture. But it was the only means to ascertain and to disclose the true meaning of Scripture. Tradition was, in fact, the authentic interpretation of Scripture. And in this sense it was coextensive with Scripture. Tradition was actually Scripture rightly understood. And

[75] Ibid., II.
[76] Oberman, *The Dawn of the Reformation*, 279.
[77] Ibid., 279.

Scripture was for Vincent the only, primary and ultimate, canon of Christian truth.[78]

In this Vincent was completely consistent with the early fathers' concept of tradition. Vincent does not establish any secret oral tradition as the standard of proper interpretation; instead he finds this standard in the consensus of the fathers. And yet, it is important to note, as Oberman observes, that "Vincent does not want the interpretation of the Church, which one may call the exegetical tradition, to become a second tradition or source apart from Holy Scripture."[79] Even the most godly of the fathers "are in principle *magistri probabiles,* teachers whose utterances are probable but do not yet constitute proof."[80]

In Vincent, we find one of the fullest early examinations of the vexing problem of authority. The standard Vincent sets forth by which one may distinguish truth from error is consistent with the one-source concept of tradition (Tradition I) found universally throughout the early fathers. His view of an authoritative exegetical tradition is directly opposed to any kind of two-source concept of tradition.[81]

THE AUTHORITY OF COUNCILS, CREEDS, AND FATHERS

The patristic attitude toward the authority of the Councils, the creeds, and their predecessors also plays into this debate. The discussion of Irenaeus and Tertullian illustrated the importance of the *regula fidei* in the early decades of the Church's history. It is interesting to note the gradual way in which the earliest creeds built upon the rule of faith. As F.F. Bruce explains,

> In Irenaeus, Tertullian and Origen alike this summary of the content of the apostles' teaching is in three sections, relating respectively to God the Father, to the Son, and to the Holy Spirit. This

[78] Florovsky, op. cit., 74–75.
[79] Oberman, op. cit., 280.
[80] Ibid. Cf. *Comonitory,* III.
[81] Ibid.

is comparable to the primitive baptismal confession of the Gentile churches, which consisted of an affirmative answer to the threefold question, framed more or less like this: Do you believe in God the Father? And in his Son Jesus Christ? And in the Holy Spirit? The response to this threefold question forms the skeleton on which were built up the early creeds, best known of which is the Roman creed, the ancestor of what we call the Apostles' Creed. But even the old Roman creed, and to a much more marked degree the creeds of the eastern churches (culminating in the Creed of Nicea and what we traditionally call the Nicene Creed) amplify the original threefold response by means of such a summary of the faith as we find in Irenaeus, Tertullian and Origen. Thus, even if the baptismal confession and the "rule of faith" were independent in origin, they came in time to interpenetrate each other, until from the fourth century onward the ecumenical creed supersedes the appeal to the rule of faith.[82]

The Creed was essentially a continuation of the *regula fidei*, expressing the same truths in a fuller way.

In the first three centuries of the Church, councils were occasional meetings held to discuss and decide upon issues of concern to the many local churches. The earliest councils were regarded more as "charismatic events" than ecclesiastical institutions.[83] Councils were never accepted as valid in advance in spite of the appearance of formal regularity. That this is true is clearly observed when we realize that many councils were disavowed.[84] In the fourth and fifth century there were four councils which gained a place of special prominence in the Church and were termed "ecumenical councils."[85] These councils dealt with significant Trinitarian and Christological issues that were rending the Church apart.

Until the division between the Eastern and Western churches,

---

[82] Bruce, op. cit., 115–116.

[83] Florovsky, op. cit., 96.

[84] Ibid.

[85] Nicea in A.D. 325; Constantinople in A.D. 381; Ephesus in A.D. 431; and Chalcedon in A.D. 451. For a good summary of the history of the ecumenical councils see Leo Donald Davis, op. cit.

an ecumenical council was defined "as a synod the decrees of which have found acceptance by the Church in the whole world."[86] Their acceptance in the early Church is illustrated by the way in which some early Christians referred to the Church as "the Church of the four Gospels and the four councils."[87] Their purpose, however, was not to supplant Scripture. Their purpose was to defend the apostolic interpretation of Scripture against the attacks of the heretics. Athanasius, for example, wrote the following in response to Arians calling for another council after Nicea: "Vainly then do they run about with the pretext that they have demanded Councils for the faith's sake; for divine Scripture is sufficient above all things."[88]

Similarly, we find that a patristic appeal to earlier fathers is not an appeal to an authority equal to or above Scripture. As Florovsky reminds us, "It must be kept in mind that the main, if not also the only, manual of faith and doctrine was, in the ancient Church, precisely the Holy Writ."[89] Appeal to the fathers was made in order to guarantee faithfulness to the proper interpretation of that authoritative Holy Scripture. As J.N.D. Kelly observes, "the authority of the fathers consisted precisely in the fact that they had so faithfully and fully expounded the real intention of the Bible writers."[90] Scripture was the doctrinal norm of the fathers. The clearest evidence of this is the fact that

> almost the entire theological effort of the fathers, whether their aims were polemical or constructive, was expended upon what amounted to the exposition of the Bible. Further, it was everywhere taken for granted that, for any doctrine to win acceptance, it had first to establish its scriptural basis.[91]

[86] Henry R. Percival, *The Seven Ecumenical Councils of the Undivided Church*, Vol. XIV of *A Select Library of Nicene and Post-Nicene Fathers of the Christian Church*, Second Series, Philip Schaff and Henry Wace, eds. (Grand Rapids: Wm. B. Eerdmans Publishing Co., 1997), xi. Since the split, Rome has redefined the definition of an ecumenical council to emphasize the role of the Bishop of Rome. Cf. Leo Donald Davis, op. cit., 323.

[87] Pelikan, op. cit., 335.

[88] *De Synodis*, I, 1, 6.

[89] Florovsky, op. cit., 102.

[90] Kelly, op. cit., 49.

[91] Ibid., 46. Kelly illustrates this by pointing out the difficulty that faced those who championed novel theological terms like *homoousios*. The objection that was

This is why the fathers were cited in the early Church—because they were faithful interpreters of Scripture. They were not cited as a second source of revelation or a second authority on par with Scripture.

SUMMARY

For the first three centuries, we find a general consensus regarding authority. The New Testament which was the "inscripturisation" of the apostolic proclamation, together with the "older Scriptures," was the source of revelation and the authoritative doctrinal norm. The Scripture was to be interpreted by the Church and in the Church within the context of the *regula fidei*. If it was taken out of its apostolic context, it would inevitably be mishandled. Yet neither the Church nor the *regula fidei* were considered second sources of revelation or equal authorities on par with Scripture. The Church was the interpreter and guardian of the Word of God, and the *regula fidei* was a summary of the apostolic preaching and the hermeneutical context of the Word of God. But only the Scripture *was* the Word of God. In other words, for the first three centuries, the Church held to the concept of tradition defined by Oberman as "Tradition I."

In the fourth century the first hints of a two-source concept of tradition—one which allows for an extra-scriptural revelation as authoritative as Scripture itself—begin to appear. This two-source position, or "Tradition II," is possibly suggested in the writings of both Basil and Augustine. And while it is uncertain that either of these fathers actually intended to advocate "Tradition II," it is certain that this understanding of tradition would have been foreign to the earliest church fathers. Its suggestion in the writings of Augustine, however, ensured it a place in the thought of the Middle Ages.

---

vigorously raised in both orthodox and heretical circles was that these terms were not found in the Bible. The opposition was finally overcome only when they were able to demonstrate that, even if the terms were not found in the Bible, the meaning of those terms was the meaning of the Bible.

2

The Middle Ages

The period of Western History commonly referred to as the Middle Ages spans approximately a thousand years, yet for most Christians it is one of the least familiar eras of Church history. Its importance, however, for a proper understanding of our subject cannot be overstated. Spanning the period of time between the fifth century and the beginning of the Renaissance and Reformation, the medieval era was not the static age that it is often portrayed to be. This is the age that gave birth to such great thinkers as Anselm and Aquinas and to such great universities as Oxford and Cambridge. It is the age that witnessed the rise and gradual centralization of the papacy as popes battled emperors and the constant temptation of temporal power. It is the paradoxical age that gave us the bloody cruelty of the Inquisition and the Crusades and yet also gave us the awe-inspiring beauty of the great cathedrals.

Like the preceding summary of the early Church fathers, the overview of the medieval discussion of Scripture and tradition will obviously not be exhaustive.[1] Instead, by briefly explaining some of the main biblical, hermeneutical, and theological trends of the Middle Ages, a coherent picture will emerge. As noted, the doctrine of Scripture did not develop as an independent *locus* of

[1] For a good general introduction to the theology of the Middle Ages, see Jaroslav Pelikan, *The Christian Tradition*, Vol. 3, *The Growth of Medieval Theology*, (Chicago: The University of Chicago Press, 1978). For an overview of the history of the Church in the Middle Ages, see R.W. Southern, *Western Society and the Church in the Middle Ages*, (London: Penguin Books, 1970).

systematic theology until the later Middle Ages and the Reformation. Therefore, in order to gain an understanding of the medieval Christian view of Scripture and tradition, we must approach
the subject somewhat indirectly. It will be necessary to discern
first what was believed and taught about a number of related—
and often overlapping—issues including the text of Scripture, the
canon of Scripture, hermeneutics, authority, and the relevance of
non-Christian philosophical systems.

After briefly examining these important contextual issues, we
will be able to see the medieval Church's concept of the relationship between Scripture and tradition more directly. It will become clear that both Tradition I and Tradition II had their
medieval adherents, although Tradition II doesn't seriously begin
to emerge until the twelfth century.[2] As the Oxford historian and
theologian Alister McGrath observes, "it is becoming increasingly clear that the medieval period in general was characterized
by its conviction that Scripture was the sole material base of
Christian theology."[3] In order to demonstrate the truth of this
thesis, however, some context is important.

THE DEVELOPMENT OF THE PAPACY

Any discussion of the concept of authority in the medieval
Church must take into account the development of the Roman
papacy from its humble beginnings to the position of power it oc-
cupied throughout much of the Middle Ages.[4] The growth of the

---

[2] Heiko Oberman, *The Dawn of the Reformation*, (Edinburgh: T&T Clark Ltd., 1986),
280. Cf. Richard Muller, *Post-Reformation Reformed Dogmatics*, Vol. 2, *Holy Scripture: The
Cognitive Foundation of Theology*, (Grand Rapids: Baker Book House, 1993), 40–41; Brian
Tierney, *Origins of Papal Infallibility 1150–1350*, (Leiden, E.J. Brill, 1988), 16.

[3] Alister McGrath, *The Intellectual Origins of the European Reformation*, (Oxford: Blackwell Publishers, 1987), 140. Cf. Beryl Smalley, *The Study of the Bible in the Middle Ages*, second edition, (Oxford: Basil Blackwell, 1952); Yves Congar, *Tradition and Traditions*, (New
York: The Macmillan Company, 1966), 86–87; Jaroslav Pelikan, *Obedient Rebels*, (London: SCM Press, Ltd., 1964), 21.

[4] For a good history of the papacy from a critical perspective see William J. La Due,
The Chair of Saint Peter: A History of the Papacy, (Maryknoll: Orbis Books, 1999).

papacy as an institution and its emerging role in European politics throughout the Middle Ages has considerable implications for any study of the nature of authority in the Church. Some of the more significant of these medieval developments provide the necessary historical and ecclesiastical context for our study.

Although Rome traces the origins of the papacy to the Apostle Peter, the historical evidence indicates that there was no monarchical bishop in Rome until sometime between A.D. 140–150.[5] Instead of a single bishop, it appears that the Roman church was organized under a college of presbyters or presbyter-bishops. No evidence exists for any claims to jurisdictional supremacy by Rome in the first century. The first historical instances of Roman bishops claiming any type of jurisdictional priority outside of Rome itself occurred in the late second century and early third century. Sometime between A.D. 190 and 195 Pope Victor attempted to sever communion with sister churches over the dating of Easter observance, but his actions had virtually no effect. In the middle of the third century, Pope Stephen was at odds with Cyprian of Carthage over the rebaptism of heretics. Cyprian's response to Stephen, however, rather clearly indicates that he did not believe that Stephen had any jurisdictional authority over Carthage.[6]

In these early centuries up to the time of Constantine, as Geoffrey Barraclough points out, "the bishop of Rome . . . was in no sense a pope and laid no claim to the position of pope."[7] But in the period of time between the death of Stephen (A.D. 257) and the accession of Pope Gregory the Great in A.D. 590, the papacy underwent enormous development. Much of this early development was due to the work of Pope Leo I, who reigned from A.D. 440–461. Leo's influence is most obvious in his famous *Tome to Flavian*, a letter that was very influential at the Council of

[5] Raymond E. Brown and John P. Meier, *Antioch and Rome*, (New York: Paulist Press, 1983), 204.

[6] See Chapter 1.

[7] Geoffrey Barraclough, *The Medieval Papacy*, (New York: Harcourt, Brace & World, Inc., 1968), 10.

Chalcedon in 451.[8] His reign greatly expanded the respect and prestige of the papacy in the Western Church.

The fifth century witnessed dramatic events in the western half of the Roman Empire. In A.D. 410 Rome fell to the invasion of Alaric the Visigoth, and in 455 the city was ruthlessly sacked by the Vandals. The end of the Roman Empire in the West in A.D. 476 is marked by the deposition of the boy emperor Romulus and the enthronement of Odovacer as king. After the fall of the Roman Empire in the West to the barbarian invaders, a centuries-long period of warfare and violence settled on Western Europe that was later termed the "Dark Ages."[9]

Despite the fall of Rome, the Roman Empire itself continued for another thousand years in the East. The capital of the Empire had been moved to Constantinople in A.D. 330, and the Empire would continue in the East until the city's fall in 1453. The changes wrought by the collapse of the western half of the Empire, however, dramatically impacted the ecclesiology of the Christian Church in the East and in the West. As C.W. Previte-Orton observes,

> In the Eastern Empire the relation of Church and State was more and more settling down . . . to a common, if sometimes mutinous dependence on the Emperor. In the dissolving Empire of the West the weakening Emperors were glad to fortify unity by encouraging the growing prerogatives of the Pope of Rome . . . . To Pope Gelasius I (492–6), when the Western Empire was no more, belongs the celebrated and long-lasting definition of the spheres and rank of the rulers of Church and State. In a letter to the Emperor Anastasius he declared that there were two powers which ruled this world, "the sacred authority of pontiffs and the royal power," and that of the priests was the weightier because they had to render account to God even for kings. Among the priesthood stood impregnable the primacy of the Roman Church. Thus the foundations of the medieval conception of the

---

[8] Davis, *The First Seven Ecumenical Councils*, 170–206.
[9] Previte-Orton, op. cit., I:77–102.

government of Christendom were laid in high-sounding phrases, that were to be developed and enlarged and diversely interpreted. Roman unity in the West was finding its refuge, as yet a matter of claim and influence, in the papacy.[10]

These fifth-century political and ecclesiastical events had long-lasting effects which are felt even today. Summing up the effects of these events, Previte-Orton continues,

> In the East they fostered provincial particularism, vastly enlarged the alienation of non-Hellenized lands from the Byzantines, and eventually contributed to their estrangement from Christianity altogether and their loss to the Empire. On the other hand they provided a national faith, identical with patriotism, for the Balkans and Asia Minor, which was not least among the forces which preserved the Eastern Empire. In the West they furnished the unifying culture and organization which gave its character to all subsequent history. Civilization, damaged and degraded as it might be, was preserved in the Dark Ages by the Latin Church, and the medieval civilization that was to arise was inspired and directed by that community and that inheritance.[11]

The survival of the papacy during the Dark Ages is a complicated story of political and ecclesiastical intrigue. The bishops of Rome often "played off one party against another, and occasionally the support of a barbarian ruler enabled them to assert a more independent position in their dealings with Constantinople."[12]

In the centuries between A.D. 590 and 1000, the independence of the papacy was developed even further under the guidance of such able popes as Gregory I who reigned from A.D. 590–604. Gregory was a gifted administrator, and with the weakening of the secular rulers of state, much of the responsibility for civil government in Italy fell upon him and upon the other Italian bishops. His numerous letters give us insight into how the bishop of

[10] Ibid., 124–127.
[11] Ibid., 127.
[12] Barraclough, op. cit., 28.

Rome viewed his own ecclesiastical office at this time. His letters to the patriarchs of the Eastern churches (Alexandria, Constantinople, Antioch, and Jerusalem), for example, indicate his belief that the five were on an equal footing as regional heads of the Church, with none exercising universal jurisdiction.[13]

The political developments over the next several centuries played a major role in the shaping of the papacy. William La Due explains,

> As the Byzantine emperors became less concerned about the West during the seventh and eighth centuries, due to pressing problems of their own, they offered the pope no security against his political rivals in Italy. It was in the eighth century that the popes began to move toward the Frankish kings in order to seek out military assistance against the Lombards. Under Popes Gregory II (715–31) and Gregory III (731–41), the duchies of Rome, Perugia, and in some respects Ravenna, were beginning to converge as a distinct political entity which eventually came to be called the Papal States. This arrangement was acknowledged by Charlemagne, who offered protection to the popes and their land. . . . In the ninth century, as the descendants of Charlemagne became more and more ineffective as rulers—allowing the original Carolingian Empire to disintegrate—popes such as Nicholas I and John VIII claimed ever expanding spiritual and temporal powers over all the churches. These claims, however, were never really taken seriously in the East. As a matter of fact, by the end of the first millennium the papacy and the eastern churches were drifting unalterably apart.[14]

The first three hundred years of the second millennium witnessed further developments in the papacy—some positive, some very negative. Much of the change that occurred during these years can be traced to the reign of Pope Leo IX (1049–54). R.W. Southern observes that "nearly everything that we associate with the papacy in its most expansive period can be traced back

[13] La Due, op. cit., 66–67.
[14] Ibid., 90–91.

to his initiative: the political alliance with the Normans; the exacerbation of relations with the Greeks; the reform of papal administrative machinery; the beginnings of a consistent plan of government through legates, councils, and a vastly increased correspondence."[15]

One event of major significance that occurred during the reign of Leo was the dispute with the Eastern churches in 1052–1054 regarding the different rites used in the worship of Latin churches in the East and Greek churches in the West. On July 16, 1054, after a disastrous meeting between the strong-willed Patriarch Cerularius and the hot-tempered papal legate Humbert, a bull of excommunication against Cerularius was laid down by the papal legates. Cerularius then called a synod which returned the favor and excommunicated the papal legates. Although it would be the Crusades which would eventually mark the definitive break between East and West, the events of 1054 were a major turning point.[16] Much of this dispute was initially caused by papal claims of universal jurisdiction. As one Catholic historian notes, "Rather than being a largely unifying influence, the papacy must be considered as one of the principal agents of this most tragic division among Christians."[17]

The twelfth century saw a dramatic increase in papal administrative and judicial power. This was followed naturally by a massive increase in litigation which bogged down the papal courts. The end of the twelfth century also saw the election of the most influential pope since Gregory I. Pope Innocent III reigned from A.D. 1198–1216 and was the first to emphasize the title "vicar of Christ," a term first used by Pope Eugene III in the middle of the twelfth century. Innocent III also claimed the prerogative of

[15] Southern, op. cit., 100.

[16] For a detailed history of how the Eastern and Western churches drifted apart and eventually split, see Timothy Ware, *The Orthodox Church*, New Ed., (London: Penguin Books, 1997), 43–72; Cf. Kenneth Scott Latourette, *A History of Christianity*, Vol. I., *Beginnings to 1500*, Rev. ed., (San Francisco: Harper Collins Publishers, 1975), 571–575; Southern, op. cit., 67–72.

[17] La Due, op. cit., 108.

plenitudo potestatis, or "fullness of power," which he would use as
the justification for placing entire nations under interdict,
thereby depriving the populations of the public celebrations of
the sacraments. Church historians commonly agree that the medieval papacy reached its highest level of influence under the
reign of Innocent III.[18]

Following the reign of Innocent, the prestige of the papacy
dropped rapidly. The College of Cardinals made numerous
efforts to expand their power and financial status, and the cen-
tralizing tendencies in the Church continued. As La Due notes,
"the smoldering resentment against the ceaseless expansion of
papal provisions and the ever increasing tax burdens imposed by
Rome broke into flames in the second half of the thirteenth century."[19]

The two hundred years prior to the Protestant Reformation
witnessed the degeneration of the papacy into an extreme form
of worldliness. Papal historian William La Due sums up these tu-
multuous centuries:

> With Pope Clement V, the papal sojourn at Avignon began in
> 1309 and lasted for nearly seventy years. The Avignon papacy,
> with its luxurious life style and exploding bureaucracy, multi-
> plied almost beyond counting the financial demands placed on
> the various dioceses, chapters, parishes, monasteries, and reli-
> gious houses all over Western Christendom. Papal reservations
> of benefices were expanded to the point where almost every ma-
> jor office and a great many minor offices throughout the entire
> western Church were now conferred by the pope, giving him
> hitherto unheard of opportunities for levying taxes and fees on
> the officeholders. This escalated the general unrest and notably
> increased the level of frustration everywhere. . . . Gregory XI
> ended the Avignon papacy, returning to Rome in 1377. How-
> ever, within six months after his death in 1378, there were two
> popes—one in Rome and the other in Avignon. This arrange-
> ment resulted in deep divisions in every nation, with some

---

[18] Barraclough, op. cit., 112–117.
[19] La Due, op. cit., 131.

dioceses and religious institutions pledging their allegiance to Rome, while others were sworn to Avignon. To solve this pathetic situation, cardinals from both camps met at Pisa in 1409, creating a third papal line which only further exacerbated the state of things. It was the Council of Constance (1414–18)—a masterpiece of moderate conciliarism—that finally brought the scandalous and extremely corrosive Great Western Schism to an end. Popes Martin V (1417–31) and Eugene IV (1431–47) managed to thwart the moderate conciliarists and returned the papacy to its monarchical moorings. The last half of the fifteenth century witnessed the rise of the Renaissance popes, who proceeded to shrink the office down to the size and shape of a regional Italian duchy, whose lord and ruler manifested less and less interest in the wider concerns of the Christian world.[20]

Under Pope Leo X, who reigned from 1513–1521, abuses reached a breaking point. Nepotism and simony reached scandalous levels under his reign. His need for money led to all kinds of strange deeds. For example, he created hundreds of unnecessary curial posts which he then sold to the highest bidder. He also allowed Albert of Brandenburg to hold three German bishoprics for a fee of 25,000 gold florins. In order for Albert to repay the money which he had borrowed from the German banking house of Fugger, Rome gave him the exclusive rights to sell Leo's new indulgence in the territories of Mainz and Brandenburg. The indulgence was to be sold for the purpose of raising money to rebuild St. Peter's in Rome. Approximately half of the proceeds were to go directly to the pope, and the other half would go to Albert in order to help him repay his debt. The man Albert called to spearhead the publishing of this new indulgence was the Dominican, John Tetzel. It was the shameless preaching of Tetzel that prompted a young Martin Luther to speak out publicly against the abuses of indulgences in 1517.

---

[20] Ibid., 181–182.

EXCURSIS: THE DOCTRINE OF PAPAL INFALLIBILITY

One theological development of profound importance for our study is the late medieval introduction and development of the doctrine of papal infallibility.[21] The origins of the doctrine of papal infallibility in the years around 1300 are a fascinating story, but the scope of this work focuses on the main points. Because some have traced the origins of the doctrine of papal infallibility to the canon lawyers, that will be the starting point.[22] In the century between 1150 and 1250, a study of the writings of the canon lawyers and theologians reveals that "they did not know of any magisterium conferred on Peter with the power of the keys; they believed that in matters of faith a general council was greater than a pope; they did not maintain that papal pronouncements were irreformable *ex sese*."[23] As Tierney points out, "Above all the canonists did not teach that the pope was infallible."[24] Instead the position that was generally held contrasted the indefectibility of the church's faith with the fallibility of individual popes. The theologians, who wrote much less on the subject, shared this general viewpoint.

In 1254 a dispute arose between mendicant friars and secular masters at the University of Paris.[25] Both Dominicans and Franciscans were involved, but it is the Franciscans who require our attention. Their order had received papal privileges beginning as early as 1230, and their dependence on these privileges would prove to be problematic. The problem stemmed from their assertion that their doctrine of "apostolic poverty" was not simply a good way of life or the best way of life but that it was an essential

---

[21] For an outstanding historical study of this issue, see Brian Tierney, *Origins of Papal Infallibility: 1150–1350*, (Leiden: E.J. Brill, 1988).

[22] Canon lawyers or canonists were those who studied and systematized canon law—those rules of the church established for the practical purposes of order and discipline. Quite often canons of order and discipline were set forth at councils (such as Nicea in A.D. 325). But the collection and standardization of canon law reached its high point with the work of Gratian, whose *Decretum* was the standard textbook throughout the later Middle Ages.

[23] Tierney, op. cit., 57.

[24] Ibid.

[25] A "mendicant" is one who depends upon alms for a living.

aspect of the perfect way of life Christ taught His apostles.[26] Many of them claimed that St. Francis was the first Christian to correctly understand the gospel since the time of the Apostles and that Franciscans were the only members of the Church leading truly Christian lives.[27] Of course these were highly controversial claims that raised no small opposition. Bonaventure, the head of the Franciscan order, responded to the arguments against the order by developing a theory of poverty he termed "condescension." Without going into all of the details, suffice it to say that in 1279, in the bull *Exiit qui seminat*, Pope Nicholas III gave papal sanction to the doctrine of Bonaventure and asserted that the "Franciscan way of life did indeed correspond to the way of perfection that Christ had taught to the apostles."[28]

The first major medieval Christian to assert a doctrine of papal infallibility was Peter Olivi, a highly influential Franciscan in the decades following the death of Bonaventure. He lived and wrote at a period of time when the Franciscans were splitting into two major camps: the larger and less strict "Community" and the rigorous "Spirituals." Olivi himself was a prominent spokesman for the Spirituals.[29] The reason that Olivi, unlike Bonaventure, developed a theory of papal infallibility was that he, unlike his predecessor, lived under the constant fear of the possibility that a future pseudo-pope would seek to overturn the true faith (i.e., the Franciscan way of life). It was necessary in the mind of Olivi that the decrees of true popes (such as Nicholas III) "should be regarded as, not only authoritative for the present, but immutable, irreformable for all time to come."[30] This, however, was impossible within the framework of the canonists' doctrine of papal sovereignty. They recognized that a doctrine of infallibility would limit the sovereignty of an individual pope. Olivi recognized this as well. His "new theory of papal infallibility was designed to

[26] Cf. Latourette, op. cit., I:429–436.
[27] Tierney, op. cit., 67–72.
[28] Ibid., 69–70.
[29] Ibid., 93–101.
[30] Ibid., 125.

limit the power of future popes, not to loose them from all re-
straints."[31]

Olivi's new doctrine was virtually ignored for forty years, but
in 1322 Pope John XXII revoked the pro-Franciscan provisions of
Exiit and issued a new statement on the doctrine of Christ's poverty.[32] The Franciscans were dismayed and reacted by issuing two
encyclical letters defending their doctrine. Pope John responded
in late 1322 in the Bull *Ad conditorem.* To John, "the idea that any
decisions of his predecessors might be irreformable presented
itself . . . simply as a threat to his own sovereign authority."[33] This
Bull evoked an impassioned response from the Franciscans who
appealed against the Bull to the pope himself. In November of
1323, Pope John issued his final judgment on the issue of Christ's
poverty in the Bull *Cum inter nonnulos.* The Bull refers to the view
that "Jesus Christ and his apostles did not have anything singly or
in common" as erroneous and heretical.[34] Because this Bull explicitly contradicted the earlier Bull *Exiit,* the Franciscans began
to assert the irreformability of the former to the degree that they
condemned John's view as heretical. As Tierney notes,

> The first overt condemnation of the pope's Bull came from . . . a
> group of dissident Franciscans who had taken refuge at the court
> of the excommunicated Emperor Lewis of Bavaria. Their pro-
> test, included as a sort of excursus in the emperor's Sachsen-
> hausen Appeal of May 24, 1324, not only defended the doctrine
> of evangelical poverty and denounced John XXII as a heretic for
> attacking that doctrine, but also presented a novel formulation
> of the theory of papal infallibility. In this work, for the first time,
> the ancient teaching that one of the keys conferred on Peter had
> been a "key of knowledge" was used to support a doctrine that
> the pope was personally infallible when he used this key to define
> truths of faith and morals. It was a major theological break-
> through.[35]

[31] Ibid., 130.
[32] La Due, op. cit., 146–47.
[33] Tierney, op. cit., 178–179.
[34] Cited in Tierney, op. cit., 181.
[35] Ibid., 182.

The Sachsenhausen Appeal drew the discussion into the main-stream of Catholic thought for the first time.

In November 1324, John responded in the Bull *Quia quorun-dam* that the "father of lies" had led his enemies to maintain the er-roneous thesis that "what the Roman pontiffs have once defined in faith and morals with the key of knowledge stands so immutably that it is not permitted to a successor to revoke it."[36] Tierney comments on the significance of this:

> The exchanges of 1324 are of fascinating interest for a historian of the doctrine of papal infallibility. Here, for the first time, a doctrine of infallibility based on the Petrine power of the keys was overtly propounded. But the doctrine was fathered by anti-papal rebels not by curial theologians. And, far from embracing the doctrine, the pope indignantly denounced it as a pernicious novelty.[37]

The striking thing about the doctrine of papal infallibility is that it "was invented almost fortuitously because an unusual concentra-tion of historical circumstances arose that made such a doctrine useful to a particular group of controversialists."[38]

> There is no convincing evidence that papal infallibility formed any part of the theological or canonical tradition of the church before the thirteenth century; the doctrine was invented in the first place by a few dissident Franciscans because it suited their convenience to invent it; eventually, but only after much initial reluctance, it was accepted by the papacy because it suited the convenience of the popes to accept it.[39]

The doctrine of papal infallibility was not declared official Ro-man Catholic dogma until Vatican I in 1870, but its origins can be traced to this obscure thirteenth-century battle between radical Franciscans and the papacy.

[36] Cited in Tierney, op. cit., 186.
[37] Ibid., 187–188.
[38] Ibid., 274.
[39] Ibid., 281.

THE TEXT AND CANON OF SCRIPTURE

In order to intelligently discuss the medieval concept of Scripture, we must first know what medieval Christians meant when they used the term "Scripture." In Western Christianity, a reference to "Scripture" is almost always a reference to the text of the Vulgate—Jerome's Latin translation of the Bible. It is often assumed that medieval Christians were naïve in their approach to textual issues, but the historical evidence does not support this stereotype. Because of the fact that the text of the Vulgate was passed down in numerous forms with significant variations, many Christian scholars were critical of the "received" text.[40] We find in the Middle Ages men such as Robert Grosseteste (d. 1253), the bishop of London, emphasizing the importance of the original Hebrew and Greek languages for a proper interpretation of Scripture and calling for a re-translation of the Old Testament from Hebrew into a more accurate Latin version. We also find criticisms of the text of the Vulgate coming in the twelfth century from men such as Stephen Harding, Nicholas Manjacoria and Hugh of St. Victor. In the thirteenth century, we find criticisms of the Vulgate text coming from Roger Bacon among others.[41]

Despite its problems, however, Jerome's Latin translation of the Hebrew and Greek manuscripts was the version of Scripture used throughout the Western Church in the Middle Ages. As it gradually replaced the old Latin version it became known as the "Vulgate" or "common edition."[42] Although he could not have foreseen it, the questions raised in Jerome's mind during his work of translation would become critical questions which would be the source of endless debate in the Church. Jerome's studies of the Hebrew Old Testament brought to the attention of the

---

[40] Alister E. McGrath, *Reformation Thought: An Introduction*, second edition, (Oxford: Blackwell Publishers, 1993), 136. McGrath notes the existence of several different versions of the Vulgate in the Middle Ages, a problem that eventually resulted in the adoption of a standard version in the thirteenth century.

[41] Muller, op. cit., 11, 16–17.

[42] F.F. Bruce, *The Canon of Scripture*, (Downers Grove: InterVarsity Press, 1988), 98.

Church the problem of the "apocryphal" books—books that were included as an addendum in the Greek translation of the Old Testament but were not found in the Hebrew Bible. The first Latin Bibles of the second century had been translated from the Greek Septuagint rather than from the Hebrew text and so had naturally included these books. Jerome, however, insisted on distinguishing these apocryphal books from the canonical books, and thus he relegated them to a secondary position. At the Council of Carthage in 397, however, it was decided that the apocryphal books were suitable for reading in the churches despite Jerome's reservations.[43]

In the Middle Ages, the apocryphal books were commonly regarded as "deuterocanonical." Hugh of St. Victor and John of Salisbury, for example, both noted that these books were not truly canonical although they could and should be read for the purposes of edification.[44] Hugh of St. Victor, however, also illustrates the relative confusion inherent in the medieval understanding of the canon by including in his concept of the "New Testament" not only the apostolic writings but also the canonical decrees of the Church and the writings of the "holy fathers" such as Jerome, Augustine, Ambrose and Gregory.[45] This confusion is also demonstrated by the inclusion of an "Epistle to the Laodiceans" after Galatians or Colossians in the text of numerous medieval Bibles.[46] Other medieval Bibles include books such as the Shepherd of Hermas, the Acts of Paul, Barnabas, and the Revelation of Peter.[47] Clearly the issue of the extent of the canon was not completely and universally settled in the Middle Ages.

[43] Ibid., 87–93.

[44] Muller, op. cit., 13.

[45] James Leo Garrett, Jr., *Systematic Theology: Biblical, Historical, and Evangelical*, Vol. 1, (Grand Rapids: Wm. B. Eerdmans Publishing Co., 1990), 172.

[46] Muller, op. cit., 12.

[47] Ibid.

THE SENTENCES AND THE GLOSSA ORDINARIA

In recent years many scholars have begun to realize that the study of Scripture was foundational to the theological work of the Middle Ages. The Bible, as Richard Muller notes, was "before the late twelfth century . . . the only 'set text' in the medieval schools."[48] In the late twelfth century, however, a transition began to occur. In the schools, the course on Holy Scripture began to be followed by a course on doctrine organized topically around a study of *sententia* or "statements." The most famous and influential example of this is the *Book of Sentences* by Peter Lombard (ca. 1100–1160)— a book that is, in the words of Alister McGrath, "perhaps one of the most boring books that has ever been written."[49] The book is a collection of statements by Church fathers and medieval writers arranged topically and organized into a systematic statement of Christian doctrine.[50] From the thirteenth century onward both the Bible and the *Sentences* were considered essential to proper theological education. Robert G. Clouse notes that "Lombard's work was introduced as the text-book in a theological course by Alexander of Hales (1222), and it gained in popularity to such an extent that for several centuries candidates in theology at European universities were required to comment on it as preparation for the doctoral degree."[51] From this time forward, the Bible was no longer the only set theological textbook in the schools.

Another important medieval development in biblical study was the tradition of the gloss. Muller explains its origins and development.

> Although certain elements of the *Gloss* were derived from commentaries written in the ninth and tenth centuries, the actual

---

[48] Ibid., 13. Cf. Smalley, op. cit.

[49] Alister McGrath, *Christian Theology: An Introduction*, (Oxford: Blackwell Publishers, 1994), 31.

[50] Previte-Orton, op. cit., I:629. Cf. Kenneth Scott Latourette, *A History of Christianity*, 2 vols. (San Francisco: Harper Collins, 1953), I: 505–6.

[51] Robert G. Clouse, "Peter Lombard," in *Evangelical Dictionary of Theology*, ed. Walter A. Elwell, (Grand Rapids: Baker Book House, 1984).

production of a running commentary on the whole text of Scripture belonged to the twelfth century and was the work of Anselm of Laon and his assistants. Between 1100 and 1130, the scholars of Laon gathered together all of Jerome's prologues, joined them to other prefatory material, and copied out the whole together with the text of Scripture and with a composite, running commentary consisting in marginal and interlinear discussion of the text. . . . Later in the twelfth century, Gilbert de la Porree and Peter Lombard expanded Anselm's *Gloss*. . . . The text of Scripture, as in the case of the great Paris Bibles of the second quarter of the thirteenth century, was frequently copied out together with the *Gloss*, for use as a text-book for theological study. In many cases, the text itself was accommodated to the *Gloss* on the assumption of the correctness of patristic interpretation. . . . The gloss developed in the first half of the twelfth century by Anselm of Laon and his school became, through the efforts of Anselm's pupil, Gilbert de la Porree, and of Peter Lombard, the standard or ordinary gloss (*Glossa ordinaria*) used in basic biblical instruction from the twelfth century onward.[52]

This mutual interdependence of text and commentary served to complicate the issue of the relationship between Scripture and tradition in the late Middle Ages.

THE INTERPRETATION OF SCRIPTURE AND THE QUADRIGA

An understanding of the medieval concept of scriptural authority must also take into account the development of scriptural interpretation or hermeneutics in the Middle Ages. The hermeneutical method known as "allegorization" gained a strong foothold in the early Church due to its extensive use by fathers such as Origen and Jerome. This nonliteral, and sometimes quite fanciful, methodology was commonly accepted throughout most of the Middle Ages. Its widespread use led to the development of what is technically termed the *quadriga,* or fourfold exegesis, which is

---

[52] Muller, op. cit., 14–15.

explicitly defined in the *glossa ordinaria*. In the gloss we learn that the four senses of a text are:

1. The Historical (*historia*)—The literal sense of the text that explains what happened.
2. The Allegorical (*allegoria*)—The spiritual sense of the text that is represented by the literal sense.
3. The Tropological (*tropologia*)—The moral declaration of the text.
4. The Anagogical (*anagoge*)—The sense of the text that draws the reader to heavenly contemplation.

The latter three senses of the text represented the Christian virtues of faith, love, and hope. As Muller explains, "allegory teaches 'things to be believed' (*credenda*), tropology 'things to be loved' or 'done' (*diligenda* or *agenda*), and *anagoge* 'things to be hoped for' (*speranda*)."[53]

The beginnings of a shift away from allegorization toward a more literal method of interpretation may be discerned at least as early as the twelfth century in the writings of Hugh of St. Victor. In the following century an even stronger push toward grammatical and literal hermeneutics may be observed in the work of Albert the Great and Thomas Aquinas. Because the influence of Platonism and Neo-Platonism was so strongly felt in the early middle ages, it has been suggested that one of the causes of this dramatic hermeneutical shift was the impact of Aristotle upon these scholastic theologians. Thomas F. Torrance observes that the rediscovery of Aristotelian philosophy

> challenged the sharp distinction between sense and thought. According to the Platonic philosophical orientation, there is a world of ordered forms above and apart from the world of sense experience; they are reflected in it, but knowledge of them is reached only by transcending sense experience. That belief made it

[53] Ibid., 17–18.

possible for the late patristic and early medieval ages to develop an entire world of elaborate allegory and spiritual meaning in detachment from history and event. Many think that such a perspective dominated the entire medieval view of the Scriptures. According to the Aristotelian view, however, the universal ideas exist only as expressed in the individual objects of the sensible world, and one has knowledge of them not apart from but only through sense experience. That belief had a sobering effect on exegesis. It disparaged the development of a world of meaning that could be correlated on its own without scientific reference to the historical sense of Scripture and careful examination of its words and concepts.[54]

This would mean, for those scholastic theologians who adopted an Aristotelian philosophical position, that one cannot interpret Scripture correctly by attempting to radically separate the "letter" and the "spirit." The "spirit" of the Scripture is not hidden behind the text; instead it is only expressed in and by the text.

This phenomenon is readily observable in the commentaries of Aquinas which are almost exclusively expositions of the literal sense of Scripture. Aquinas insists that each word of a text has one and only one meaning—the literal sense. All of the other senses are based upon this literal sense. Muller notes this fact:

> Aquinas concludes that the literal sense alone is ground for argument and insists that every truth necessary for salvation is offered somewhere in Scripture in the literal sense of the text. Thus the spiritual senses, although useful and highly enlightening, are not absolutely necessary.[55]

The gradual abandonment of the allegorical method of scriptural interpretation had enormous repercussions for the Church. As we shall see in examining the medieval concept of tradition, many

[54] Thomas F. Torrance, "Scientific Hermeneutics According to St. Thomas Aquinas," *Journal of Theological Studies* 13 (1962), 259, cited by John F. Johnson, "Biblical Authority and Scholastic Theology," *Inerrancy and the Church*, ed. John D. Hannah, (Chicago: Moody Press, 1984), 78.

[55] Muller, op. cit., 19.

doctrines and practices of the Church were validated by appeals to nonliteral interpretation of Scripture. Once this method of interpretation began to be questioned, it became necessary to discover another foundation for these doctrines and practices. Thus, at the same general time the allegorical method of interpretation begins to decline, the two-source concept of tradition begins its ascendancy.

REASON AND REVELATION IN THE MIDDLE AGES

In the Middle Ages the problem of the relationship between reason and revelation was central to the theological endeavor, and the question of scriptural authority was intimately tied to this issue. The position early medieval Christians adopted on this question was essentially that of Augustine. Unaided human reason, according to Augustine, is an insufficient means to reach truth. Instead one must begin with faith as the starting point of rational thinking. This does not mean that there are not valid rational reasons to believe that God exists and that He has revealed Himself but, as John F. Johnson explains,

> when all is said, perhaps the most forceful reasons to believe that God has spoken truly cannot take one further than that belief itself. To believe that God has spoken and that what God has said is absolutely true is something essentially different from a rational comprehension of the truth that one holds by faith. For Augustine, that is to say, one *believes* that it is true; but no Christian can hope to know, at least in this life, the truth that he believes. Yet among those truths that he believes, the Christian finds the divine promise that he will later contemplate the God of his faith and in that contemplation find eternal beatitude. Thus already in this life he attempts to investigate the mysteries of revelation by the natural light of reason. The result of such an effort is precisely what Augustine called *intellectus*—some rational insight into the contents of revelation. Such is the ultimate meaning of Augustine's famous formula "Understanding is the reward

of faith. Therefore seek not to understand that you may believe, but believe that you may understand."[56]

For Augustine, the truths of the Christian faith are true because they are revealed by God. Once one accepts the divine truth his reason will enable him to begin to understand those truths. Faith is higher than reason, yet cannot do without it; therefore when used properly, reason serves faith.[57] This early medieval attitude is expressed clearly in the writings of Anselm (1033–1109). Two phrases he used summarize his position: *fides quarens intellectum* ("Faith seeking understanding"), and *credo ut intellegam* ("I believe, in order that I may understand"). In other words, while faith precedes rational understanding, faith is itself rational.[58]

In the tenth and eleventh centuries the beginnings of a trend away from the Augustinian concept of reason and revelation may be detected. The rise of the nominalist and realist schools of thought brought the question to the forefront once again and other formulations began to emerge. As Johnson notes,

> The realist school of thought, with its belief in universals, did not challenge the authority of the Church. Realists treated logic and dialectic as useful but clearly subordinate tools. The nominalists, on the other hand, were inclined to give a very important place to human reason.[59]

The debate between realism and nominalism is at heart a debate over the existence of "universals." Realists asserted that universal concepts, such as "redness" *really* exist and are embodied in particular things.[60] Nominalists, on the other hand, deny the

---

[56] Johnson, op. cit., 72.

[57] Ibid.

[58] McGrath, op. cit., 48–49.

[59] Johnson, op. cit., 73.

[60] We must be careful at this point to distinguish between high realism and moderate realism. High realism, associated with Platonic philosophy, asserted that universals—"the eternal ideas"—are the *only* truly existing realities. Particular things are transitory manifestations of the universal ideas. That which is real is not "this man" or "that man" but the universal idea "man." The scholastic realists, such as Thomas Aquinas and Duns Scotus,

existence and the necessity of "universals." Many of them argued that universals were simply *names*, thus "nominalism." "Redness," they would argue, exists *only* in particular things.[61] Realism dominated Christian thinking in the early scholastic period (ca. 1200–1350), while nominalism dominated in the later scholastic period (ca. 1350–1500).[62]

The rediscovery of the writings of Aristotle in the late twelfth and early thirteenth centuries also impacted the development of the Church's understanding of reason and revelation. Christian thinkers such as Duns Scotus and Thomas Aquinas helped establish the conviction that the philosophy of Arisistotle was the best means by which Christianity could be both systematized and defended. This view, although initially welcomed in the Church, was eventually questioned, as Aristotelian philosophical presuppositions were seen to negatively influence theological discussion.

SCHOLASTICISM AND HUMANISM

Realism and nominalism developed within the medieval movement known as scholasticism. This movement derived its name from the *Scholastici*—the Schoolmen who taught in the cathedral schools and in the universities in the later Middle Ages.[63] It was a term coined by sixteenth-century humanists to belittle what they saw as a tedious and uninteresting theological movement.[64] Some of the Christian thinkers whose names are commonly associated with scholasticism are Anselm of Canterbury, Peter Abelard, Hugh of St. Victor, Peter the Lombard, Albert the Great, Thomas Aquinas, John Duns Scotus and William of Ockham. Alister McGrath provides a good working definition of the term:

---

were not high realists. Their position may be termed "moderate realism." While the universal ideas are certainly real, according to the moderate realists, they exist in particulars giving them their identity. Our perception of those universals occurs as we abstract the essence from the mass of particulars.

[61] McGrath, *Reformed Theology*, 71–73. Although it is obscure, a grasp of the realist/nominalist debate is important for an understanding of medieval scholasticism.

[62] Ibid., 71.

[63] Previte-Orton, op. cit., I:627.

[64] McGrath, *Christian Theology*, 33.

Scholasticism is best regarded as the medieval movement, flour-
ishing in the period 1200–1500, which placed emphasis upon the
rational justification of religious belief, and the systematic presentation of those beliefs. "Scholasticism" thus does not refer to
a *specific system of beliefs,* but to a *particular way of organizing theology*
—a highly developed method of presenting material, making
fine distinctions, and attempting to achieve a comprehensive
view of theology.[65]

It has already been noted that the early scholastic period was
dominated by realism while the later scholastic period was dominated by nominalism. Each of these theories of knowledge affected scholastic Christian thinkers. In the early scholastic period
there were two major schools characterized by a "realist" epistemology. The *via Thomae* or "Thomism" was a realist school characterized by its adherence to the writings of Thomas Aquinas.
Scotism was a realist school which followed the writings of Duns
Scotus.[66] In the later scholastic period nominalist epistemology
dominated and was also represented by two "schools" of thought
—the *via moderna*—"the modern way" and the *schola Augustiniana
moderna*—"the modern Augustinian school." While both of these
schools agreed in their rejection of universals, they agreed on little else.[67]

A second intellectual movement of the Middle Ages which
must be noted for its influence is humanism.[68] While in modern
times the term "humanism" has come to mean a secular or atheis-
tic worldview, it meant nothing of the kind in the later Middle
Ages. "Humanism," as McGrath observes, "was essentially a cultural program, which appealed to classical antiquity as a model of

---

[65] Ibid., 33–34.

[66] The moderate realism characterized by the Thomists and Scotists is sometimes
termed the *via antiqua* or "antique way."

[67] For an excellent discussion of these two types of scholasticism and their significance, see McGrath, *The Intellectual Origins of the European Reformation,* (Oxford: Blackwell Publishers, 1987), 70–93.

[68] For an in-depth history of Renaissance humanism, see Bard Thompson, *Humanists
& Reformers: A History of the Renaissance and Reformation,* (Grand Rapids: Wm. B. Eerdmans
Publishing Co., 1996).

eloquence."[69] This emphasis on classical antiquity had tremendous effects on biblical study and marked a major turning point in the history of hermeneutics.[70] McGrath lists some of these contributions of humanism to the study of Scripture:[71]

1. The emphasis on a return *ad fontes,* "to the sources."
2. The emphasis on studying the original languages.
3. The production of printed texts of Scripture in the original languages and the production of linguistic tools enabling scholars to learn those original languages.
4. The development of textual criticism.
5. The belief that the use of proper literary methods could enable Christians to recapture the vitality of apostolic Christianity.
6. The emphasis on the need for a literate laity.

Many humanists were believers who truly desired the revival of the Church. Their goals were summarized by the slogan *Christianismus renascens*—"Christianity being born again."[72] In many ways their work paved the way for the Reformation of the sixteenth century.

SCRIPTURE AND TRADITION IN THE MIDDLE AGES

Having outlined some of the more important historical and theological developments of the Middle Ages, the focus must be turned to the development of the medieval concept of Scripture and tradition. Both Tradition I and an undeveloped form of Tradition II had medieval adherents, but Tradition I remained dominant until the late Middle Ages. For most medieval theologians, as McGrath notes, "Scripture was the materially sufficient source of Christian doctrine."[73]

---

[69] McGrath, *Christian Theology,* 38.
[70] Muller, op. cit., 47–48.
[71] McGrath, *Reformation Thought,* 138–39.
[72] McGrath, *Christian Theology,* 38–42.
[73] McGrath, *Reformation Thought,* 135.

Heiko Oberman is careful to note that the concepts of Tradition I and Tradition II are obviously somewhat artificial constructs since there were in reality a number of subtly differentiated views on the subject of Scripture and tradition in the Middle Ages.[74] In general, however, most of these views would fall under one of these two general concepts. Having seen a brief description of Tradition I and Tradition II, a more detailed definition is necessary at this point. Oberman provides us with the definitions involved. He observes that the typical way in which the debate is framed is misleading. In defining Tradition I, he notes,

> Closer consideration, however, proves the impossibility of forcing medieval theologians into the straight jacket of the alternatives of Scripture or Tradition. We are, rather, confronted with the encounter of two general notions about Tradition. In the first case the sole authority of Holy Scripture is upheld as the canon, or standard, of revealed truth in such a way that Scripture is not contrasted with Tradition. Scripture, it is argued, can be understood only within the Church and has been understood within the Church by the great doctors specifically committed to the task of interpretation of Scripture and especially endowed with the gift of understanding this unique source of truth. The history of obedient interpretation is the Tradition of the Church.[75]

He continues with a detailed definition of the concept of Tradition II:

> In the second case Tradition is a wider concept. It is argued that the Apostles did not commit everything to writing, usually on the grounds that the scriptural authors reported what Christ said and did during His lifetime but not what Christ taught His disciples in the period between the resurrection and the ascension. During these forty days an oral Tradition originated which is to

---

[74] Heiko Oberman, *Forerunners of the Reformation: The Shape of Late Medieval Thought*, trans. Paul L. Nyhus, (London: Lutterworth Press, 1967), 60.
[75] Ibid., 54; Cf. Muller, op. cit., 39.

be regarded as a complement to Holy Scripture, handed down to the Church of later times as a second source of revelation. In the first case Tradition was seen as the instrumental vehicle of Scripture which brings the contents of Holy Scripture to life in a constant dialogue between the doctors of Scripture and the Church; in the second case Tradition was seen as the authoritative vehicle of divine truth, embedded in Scripture but overflowing in extra-scriptural apostolic tradition handed down through episcopal succession.[76]

Given these definitions, how did these two views develop and progress?

THE CANON LAWYERS

The first possible evidence of major development occurs in the twelfth century. For most of the early Middle Ages, Tradition I was the prevalent position in the Church. Oberman argues that this consensus started to disintegrate when twelfth- and thirteenth-century canon lawyers began to develop a two-source theory of revelation—"Tradition II." He claims that Tradition II is evident as early as Ivo of Chartres (d. 1116) who insisted that equal reverence and obedience be given to scriptural revelation as well as oral revelation. When Gratian of Bologna (d. 1158) copied the passage from Ivo into his influential *Decretum*, an undeveloped Tradition II officially found its way into the textbooks of later canon lawyers and theologians.[77] Oberman observes that Basil of Caesarea is cited by the canonists as the source of Tradition II.

Alister McGrath concurs with the fact of a medieval two-source theory of revelation, but disagrees that it was originated by the canon lawyers. He argues that what the twelfth-century canon lawyers were actually dealing with was the need for a final court of appeal in disputes over doctrine. Gratian, for example, insists upon the doctrinal authority of Scripture but also upon the

---

[76] Ibid., 54–55; Cf. Muller, op. cit., 39–40.
[77] Ibid., 55; Cf. *Harvest of Medieval Theology*, 369–371.

judicial authority of the pope. McGrath points out that some of those cited by Oberman as supporters of Tradition II were actually positing one source of revelation while conceding to the pope an interpretive authority in doctrinal matters.[78] The pope's authority, according to the canonists, was as an interpreter of scriptural revelation, not as a source of extra-scriptural revelation. McGrath also notes that the canonists idea of "unwritten tradition" tended to be used primarily in the areas of Christian rites such as extreme unction and the consecration of the chalice. It was not used to establish such things as the novel Mariological doctrines that were beginning to develop in the Middle Ages.[79]

Oberman argues that one cannot make such a neat distinction between doctrinal truths and liturgical practices. He observes that "here too, the life of prayer (*lex orandi*) proves to be the form of faith (*lex credendi*), and devotion proves to be the highway to doctrine and hence to dogma."[80] In other words, it has often been the practice of the Church to which the Church appealed in defense of her dogma. Recent research, however, indicates that McGrath is correct in his evaluation of the intention of the canonists. As Tierney notes, "Canonistic teaching throughout the twelfth and thirteenth centuries was entirely consistent with the doctrines commonly taught by the theologians of that age—that sacred Scripture contained implicitly or explicitly all the revealed truths of Christian faith."[81] In spite of this fact, it cannot be denied that the particular emphases of the canonists watered the seeds of Tradition II, which had been inadvertently planted by Basil.

THE THEOLOGIANS

Oberman argues that the canon lawyers were not the only ones responsible for the development of Tradition II. He argues that the medieval theologians also bear some of the responsibility.

---

[78] McGrath, *Intellectual Origins of the European Reformation*, 142–148.
[79] Ibid., 147.
[80] Oberman, *Forerunners of the Reformation*, 57.
[81] Tierney, op. cit., 18.

We have observed that in the twelfth century, with the rediscovery of Aristotle, there was a gradual move away from the allegorical method of scriptural interpretation towards a more literal and grammatical hermeneutic. One of the results of this hermeneutical shift was that theologians began to notice an increasing number of doctrines about which the Holy Scripture said nothing.[82] Unlike the canon lawyers, however, the scholastic doctors were more subtle in their development of a doctrine of oral tradition.

> In theory the material sufficiency of Holy Scripture is upheld long after it has been given up in practice. The key term of this development is the word "implicit," and the history of this term is one of increasing loss of content. When finally the two propositions, "Holy Scripture implicitly says" and "Holy Scripture silently says," are equated, the exegetical concept of Tradition I has fully developed into what we have called Tradition II and the Basilean passage borrowed from canon law provides the rational and patristic authority.[83]

It is actually doubtful whether what we find in these theologians at this point in history is a "fully developed" version of Tradition II, but in the work of the theologians we do see, at the very least, continuing evidence of its development.

THOMAS AQUINAS (1225–1274)

In the thirteenth century there arose two of the greatest thinkers of the scholastic era—Thomas Aquinas and Duns Scotus. Thomas, who was born near Aquino, Italy, in 1225 and lived until 1274, wrote over ninety separate works, the most influential being the *Summa Theologiae*, a systematic and philosophical presentation of Christian theology. In 1879, his system was declared by Pope Leo XIII to be the official teaching of the Catholic church. Because of his influence it is imperative to get some idea of his

---

[82] Oberman, *Dawn of the Reformation*, 281–82.
[83] Oberman, *Forerunners of the Reformation*, 59.

position on Scripture and tradition. Richard Muller summarizes Aquinas' view on this subject:

> Like the majority of the scholastic teachers of the thirteenth and fourteenth centuries, Thomas Aquinas did not develop a separate question or article dealing with the doctrine of Scripture. He did, however, make a major contribution to the medieval doctrine of Scripture and included an extended comment on the sources and grounds of sacred theology in the first question of the *Summa*. There, he clearly argues what Alexander [of Hales] stated by implication: that Scripture by its very nature is the ground or foundation of necessary argument in theology— whereas other sources, such as the church's normative tradition, yield up only "probable" arguments.[84]

In the first question of the *Summa Theologica*, Aquinas writes,

> Yet holy teaching employs such authorities [e.g., human reason, philosophy] only in order to provide as it were extraneous arguments from probability. Its own proper authorities are those of canonical Scripture, and these it applied with convincing force. It has other proper authorities, the doctors of the Church, and these it looks to as its own, but for arguments that carry no more than probability. For our faith rests on the revelation made to the Prophets and Apostles who wrote the canonical books, not on a revelation, if such there be, made to any other teacher.[85]

Aquinas, it appears, stands in the line of Tradition I advocating Scripture as the single source of revelation to be interpreted in and by the Church.[86]

DUNS SCOTUS (1266–1308)

John Duns Scotus was born in Scotland in 1266 and was educated at the Universities of Oxford and Paris. According to

---

[84] Muller, op. cit., 22; Cf. J. Van der Ploeg, "The Place of Holy Scripture in the Theology of St. Thomas," *Thomist* 10 (1947): 417–419.

[85] Aquinas, *Summa Theologiae*, Question I, art. 8.

[86] See "The *Summa* and the Bible," Appendix 11 in the Blackfriars edition of the *Summa Theologiae*.

Muller, it is Duns Scotus who "must be credited with the development of a clearly defined doctrine of Scripture, the basic divisions and arguments of which provided a structural and doctrinal foundation for the arguments of later theologians, including the Protestant orthodox."[87] His position on Scripture and tradition is set forth in his *Ordinatio*. He affirms there that "theology does not concern anything except what is contained in scripture, and what may be drawn (*elici*) from this."[88] Responding to arguments that the Scriptures are insufficient, "Scotus poses simply the statement of Augustine, that the canonical Scriptures are authoritative for faith 'in those things of which we must not be ignorant, but which we cannot know of our selves.'"[89] Scotus also believed that Holy Scripture was to be interpreted by the Church in the context of the *regula fidei*.[90] As Muller notes, "it was the assumption of the theologians of the thirteenth and fourteenth centuries that Scripture was the materially sufficient 'source and norm' for all theological formulation, granting the inspiration and resulting authority of the text."[91]

WILLIAM OF OCKHAM (CA. 1280–1349)

The work of the Franciscan William of Ockham marks a decisive turning point in the history of the doctrine of tradition. Because of the difficulty of his style, scholars have come to different conclusions about his views on this subject, but recent research indicates that he was one of the principle inspirers of Tradition II.[92] He clearly embraces this position in his work, the *Dialogus*. One fascinating point to note is the motivation behind Ockham's development and refinement of Tradition II. Brian Tierney explains,

---

[87] Muller, op. cit., 32.

[88] Scotus, *Ordinatio*, praefatio, cited by McGrath, *Intellectual Origins of the European Reformation*, 140.

[89] Scotus, *Ordinatio*, prol., II, q. 1, cited by Muller, op. cit., 34.

[90] Muller, op. cit., 36.

[91] Ibid., 30.

[92] Oberman, *Harvest of Medieval Theology*, 375; Tierney, op. cit., 220–222.

Ockham's purpose in raising the issue of the sources of faith in the *Dialogus* was the same as his purpose in writing the work as a whole—to expound in detail all the arguments that could be useful to the Michaelist Franciscans in their feud against the pope. Ever since the days of Bonaventure an emphasis on the church as a source of divine revelation had been associated with the defense of the "new tradition" of St. Francis against the enemies of the Franciscan Order; and Ockham's whole intention in breaking with John XXII was still to defend the authenticity of Francis' teaching. . . . Moreover, the assertion that the church as well as Scripture provided a certain guide to the truths of faith had been of particular importance in the Michaelist case against Pope John XXII (who consistently affirmed that Scripture alone was the source of immutable articles of faith).[93]

Ironically, like the historically unprecedented doctrine of papal infallibility, Tradition II originally finds its strongest support in the radical Franciscan enemies of the pope in the late thirteenth and early fourteenth century. Although not widely accepted during Ockham's lifetime, his view of tradition would later prove to be useful to Rome. As Tierney observes, "In the course of the fifteenth and sixteenth centuries, Ockham's 'two-sources' theory of revelation came to be accepted as Catholic doctrine principally in order to refute the *sola scriptura* principle as it was presented by Wyclif and later by Luther."[94]

THE LATE MIDDLE AGES

As the fourteenth and fifteenth centuries progressed, we find exponents of both Tradition I and Tradition II. In addition to Ockham, other prominent nominalist thinkers such as Jean Gerson (1363–1429), Johannes Breviscoxa, Pierre d'Ailly and Gabriel Biel (1420–1495) strongly advocate Tradition II.[95] Others such as John Wyclif (ca. 1330–1384), John Hus (ca. 1372–1415)

---

[93] Tierney, op. cit., 222.
[94] Ibid., 270.
[95] Oberman, *Harvest of Medieval Theology*, 373.

and Wessel Gansfort argue for Tradition I.[96] What we find in the teaching of men such as John Wyclif is not a pitting of Scripture against tradition. Instead, as Muller explains, Wyclif identified "the norm of doctrinal truth with 'Scripture and its traditional and catholic interpretation'. . . . Wyclif was able to reject contemporary churchly teachings without rejecting a close association of Scripture with tradition—indeed, on the assumption of a coherence of traditionary interpretation with its theologically and soteriologically sufficient scriptural foundation."[97] In other words, Wyclif was arguing for Tradition I.

By the end of the fifteenth century, a number of rival authorities to Scripture had emerged which obscured the original tradition of the Church. There were claims to post-apostolic revelation, claims of an oral tradition, aggressive theological claims by the canonists.[98] In addition, there were at least three recognizable positions regarding the relationship between Scripture and the Church. The Franciscans continued to advocate a strong version of Tradition II. The Thomists combined Aquinas' Tradition I with developing views of papal supremacy. And finally the *schola Augustiniana moderna*, identified with Giles of Rome and Gregory of Rimini, emphasized what Oberman terms Tradition I.[99] Finally, as a result of the gradual movement away from the allegorical *quadriga* towards a more literal and grammatical hermeneutic, there was at this point in history "an increasing separation between the canonical text and the postcanonical tradition."[100]

---

[96] Oberman, *Dawn of the Reformation*, 282; Cf. *Forerunners to the Reformation*, 59.

[97] Muller, op. cit., 39.

[98] John M. Headley, *Luther's View of Church History*, (New Haven: Yale University Press, 1963), 78.

[99] Alister McGrath, *Intellectual Origins of the European Reformation*, 148–149.

[100] Muller, op. cit., 43.

SUMMARY

This survey of the Middle Ages reveals that the consensus of the early Church continued throughout most of the middle ages, with most theologians adhering to Tradition I. In the changing environment of the twelfth century, the beginnings of a real movement towards a two-source theory can be discerned in the writings of the canon lawyers. The shift reaches a turning point in the work of William of Ockham in the early fourteenth century. He is one of the first, if not the first, medieval theologian to clearly and explicitly embrace a two-source theory of revelation. From the fourteenth century onward, then, we see the parallel development of two concepts of tradition. There are those who continue to maintain the position of the early Church by insisting that, although the Scriptures must be interpreted by the Church and in the Church according to the rule of faith, they are the sole source of authoritative revelation—"Tradition I." And there are those who maintain the existence of extra-scriptural sources of revelation equally as authoritative as Scripture—"Tradition II." In addition there were numerous political, ecclesiatical, philosophical, and hermeneutical shifts occurring throughout the Western Church and Western Europe. As the late medieval Roman church continued to degenerate into an extreme form of worldliness, all of these factors combined to pave the way for the intense debates of the sixteenth century.

3

Martin Luther and John Calvin

The Protestant Reformation was one element in a complex of events that shook medieval Christendom to its core.[1] Virtually every aspect of life in Western Europe experienced upheaval in the sixteenth century, the likes of which had not been seen since the fall of Rome. The Renaissance was changing the way men thought about themselves and the world. The political structure of Europe was painfully shifting under the weight of an emerging nationalism. The economy was gradually transforming from the old guild system to a nascent capitalism. The discovery and exploration of the new world was expanding man's geographical horizons. The use of the printing press was expanding his intellectual horizons. In the midst of this were heard cries for reform in the Church, cries which could not and would not be ignored.[2]

Within the Church itself a crisis of authority had been simmering since the rise of the Avignon papacy in the early fourteenth century. The intensity of this crisis had been increased by certain scholastic theologians, such as Ockham, who had denied the pope the right to legislate in matters of faith, and the ensuing debate had not abated. The Great Schism (1378–1417), during which time there had simultaneously been two and ultimately three popes, called into question the very institution of the Church

---

[1] For a good introduction to the history of the Reformation, see Owen Chadwick, *The Reformation*, (London: Penguin Books, 1972); Roland H. Bainton, *The Reformation of the Sixteenth Century*, (Boston: Beacon Press, 1952).

[2] See Roland H. Bainton, op. cit., 3.

itself. For forty years, there was no certain direction to turn for an authoritative statement of faith—and this during a period of unprecedented doctrinal speculation and diversity.[3] A number of factors contributed to this doctrinal diversity including: the emergence of several different theological schools of thought; disagreements on the sources of theology and their inter-relationships; disagreements concerning theological methodol-ogy; the rise of lay piety; and general confusion regarding the official teaching of the Church on certain doctrines—most nota-bly the doctrine of justification.[4]

One debate that flared up again during the sixteenth-century Reformation concerned the source and norm of the Church's doctrine and practice. Oberman observes that, "traditionally this is described as the clash of the *sola scriptura*-principle with the Scripture *and* tradition-principle."[5] This common misunder-standing continues to this day and is found in the works of both Protestant and Catholic scholars. Martin Luther and the Protes-tant Reformers are repeatedly portrayed as the inventors of an absolutely unheard of doctrine of scriptural authority. Yet this is demonstrably untrue. Unfortunately, endless repetition in the context of heated polemical debates seems to have caused an his-torically untenable proposition to be regarded as a fact. But as Pelikan rightly notes,

> In Luther's day there were several theories of biblical inspiration being taught by various theologians, and the doctrine of the su-preme authority, if not the sole authority, of the Scriptures was widely acknowledged by medieval scholastic theologians. The church did not need a Luther to tell it that the Bible was true.[6]

[3] Cf. Alister McGrath, *The Intellectual Origins of the European Reformation*, (Oxford: Blackwell Publishers, 1987), 12–28.

[4] Ibid., 16; cf. McGrath, *Iustitia Dei: A History of the Christian Doctrine of Justification*, 2 vols. (Cambridge: Cambridge University Press, 1986).

[5] Heiko Oberman, *The Dawn of the Reformation*, (Edinburgh: T&T Clark, Ltd., 1986), 270.

[6] Jaroslav Pelikan, *Obedient Rebels: Catholic Substance and Protestant Principle in Luther's Reformation*, (London: SCM Press, Ltd., 1964), 21. Cf. Richard Muller, *Post-Reformation Reformed Dogmatics*, Vol. 2, (Grand Rapids: Baker Book House, 1993), 67.

As several recent scholars have noted, the real issue did not concern the status of Scripture as much as it concerned the interpretation of Scripture.[7] In fact, the position the magisterial Reformers maintained was essentially that which was held in the early Church and throughout most of the medieval Church—that Scripture was the sole source of revelation; that it was the final authoritative norm of doctrine and practice; that it was to be interpreted in and by the Church; and that it was to be interpreted according to the *regula fidei*. In other words, the case can be made that the Reformers adhered to Tradition I.

Their desire was not to reject the Church or the apostolic faith; their desire was to remove the obvious accretions and abuses that had come to cripple the Church and obscure that faith. The Reformers were convinced that the Church must be reformed, not by being created from scratch, but by returning to her ancient beliefs and practices—including her ancient belief about the place of Scripture.[8] As G.C. Berkouwer notes,

> The decisive question that the Reformers considered and answered in the affirmative was as follows: Had not tradition in the Roman Catholic Church become an independent and in fact a normative authority, valid in itself, through a gradual historical process? The Reformers wished to protest against that independence and its range of influence. The sentiment was not that of an antihistorical revolt but that of a desire for preservation and continuity.[9]

As we have observed, there were, by the time of the Reformation, two main positions regarding Scripture and tradition. During the sixteenth century, however, these two views "became so associated with Protestantism on the one hand and Roman

---

[7] Alister McGrath, *Reformation Thought: An Introduction*, second edition, (Oxford: Blackwell Publishers, 1993), 140; Cf. John M. Headley, *Luther's View of Church History*, (New Haven: Yale University Press, 1963), 80.

[8] McGrath, op. cit., 21.

[9] G.C. Berkouwer, *Holy Scripture*, trans. Jack B. Rogers, (Grand Rapids: Wm. B. Eerdmans Publishing Co., 1975), 303.

Catholicism on the other that they could no longer exist within the same ecclesial and confessional body."[10] As Muller observes, "at the same time that the first great Protestant codifiers were formulating their doctrine of the priority of Scripture over tradition . . . Roman Catholic theologians were in the process of de-emphasizing the patristic and medieval tradition concerning the sufficiency of Scripture."[11] What we observe in the Reformation is not Scripture vs. tradition. Instead it is the inevitable clash between two mutually exclusive concepts of tradition: Tradition I and Tradition II.[12] The Reformers strongly asserted the position termed Tradition I, and in reaction Rome adopted, and eventually dogmatized, Tradition II.[13]

MARTIN LUTHER

If the early sixteenth century Western Church was in an unstable and volatile situation, Martin Luther was the catalyst that caused it to explode. His conflicts with Rome ignited what is called the Protestant Reformation. The concern here is with only one particular aspect of Luther's thought—his view of Scripture and tradition, but it is almost impossible to understand why Luther said and did the things he did without some understanding of his

---

[10] Muller, op. cit., 360.

[11] Muller, op. cit., 367–368.

[12] Oberman, op. cit., 283.

[13] McGrath, *Intellectual Origins of the European Reformation*, 150. Oberman's thesis has been countered by A.N.S. Lane, who argues for a fourfold categorization of the historical views of tradition in "Scripture, Tradition & Church: An Historical Survey," *Vox Evangelica* 9 (1975), 37–55. Lane distinguishes between the Coincidence view (tradition coincides with the content of Scripture); the Supplementary view (tradition is a second source of revelation); the Ancillary view (tradition is an aid for interpreting Scripture); and the Unfolding view (tradition is the process by which the meaning of the apostolic doctrine is gradually unfolded). The first view he identifies with the church of the first three centuries; the second with Tridentine Rome; the third with the Reformation; and the fourth with modern Roman Catholicism. He believes it is incorrect to see continuity between the Coincidence view and the Ancillary view. The reason that his criticism fails, however, is simply due to the fact that the early Church's view contained elements of the "ancillary" view, and the Reformers' position contained elements of the "coincidence" view. The broader categories suggested by Oberman are more helpful and accurate.

personal background and the social and ecclesiastical context in which he found himself.[14]

In July of 1505, as a twenty-one-year-old student at the University of Erfurt, Luther was returning to school from home when a sudden bolt of lightning nearby threw him to the ground. In terror, he vowed to become a monk. He had been acutely depressed over the prospect of death since his youth, and since monasticism was considered by many at that time to be the surest way to escape hell, he did what thousands of others had done. Two weeks after his terrifying experience, he became a novice at an Augustinian monastery.

Luther's second spiritual crisis occurred in the year after his probationary period had ended. Having been selected and ordained to the priesthood, Luther was prepared to celebrate his first mass on May 2, 1507. As he began to recite the first words of the mass, terror struck him as he realized his unworthiness to stand before the infinitely holy God. The word Luther used to describe this inner fear was *Anfechtung*. As Roland Bainton notes, there is no exact English equivalent.

> It may be a trial sent by God to test man, or an assault by the Devil to destroy man. It is all the doubt, turmoil, pang, tremor, panic, despair, desolation, and desperation which invade the spirit of man.[15]

Despite this Luther pulled himself together and continued to perform those duties which were assigned. As a priest who stood daily at the altar in the presence of the living and holy God, he determined to pursue holiness. Whatever good works he could do, he attempted—fasting, vigils, prayers, self-deprivation and constant confession. In 1510 the opportunity to travel to Rome

---

[14] For good introductory biographies of Luther, see Roland H. Bainton, *Here I Stand: A Life of Martin Luther*, (Nashville: Abingdon Press, 1950), and Heiko A. Oberman, *Luther: Man Between God and the Devil*, trans. Eileen Walliser-Schwarzbart, (New Haven: Yale University Press, 1989).

[15] Bainton, op. cit., 31.

presented him with another opportunity. The medieval popes had specified that the merits of the saints could be dispensed to those who visited their relics, and Rome held more relics than any other single location on earth. The Church had determined the exact reduction in the amount of time spent in purgatory that could be obtained by viewing these relics, and Luther was determined to see every holy relic in the city.[16]

After his return from Rome, Luther was transferred to Wittenberg to teach in the new university and came under the spiritual guidance of Johann von Staupitz. His anguished spirit continued to trouble him and he sought relief in the sacraments of the Church—especially penance. He would confess his sins daily—sometimes for periods as long as six hours, but his torment continued. Staupitz eventually decided to try a radical spiritual cure for this young monk. He informed Luther that he should study for his doctorate, begin preaching, and assume the chair of professor of Bible at the university. Luther assumed the tasks and in 1513 began lecturing on the book of Psalms.

Luther's third spiritual crisis occurred while studying for his lectures. While studying the Psalms, Luther gradually came to understand what it meant for Christ to take upon Himself all of our sins and iniquities on the cross. He finally resolved the remaining problem of the justice of God while studying Romans. He wrote of the experience,

> I greatly longed to understand Paul's Epistle to the Romans and nothing stood in the way but that one expression, "the justice of God," because I took it to mean that justice whereby God is just and deals justly in punishing the unjust. My situation was that, although an impeccable monk, I stood before God as a sinner troubled in conscience, and I had no confidence that my merit would assuage him. Therefore I did not love a just and angry God, but rather hated and murmured against him. Yet I clung to the dear Paul and had a great yearning to know what he meant.
>
> Night and day I pondered until I saw the connection between

16 Ibid., 36–38.

the justice of God and the statement that "the just shall live by his faith." Then I grasped that the justice of God is that righteousness by which through grace and sheer mercy God justifies us through faith. Thereupon I felt myself to be reborn and to have gone through open doors into paradise. The whole of Scripture took on a new meaning, and whereas before the "justice of God" had filled me with hate, now it became to me inexpressibly sweet in greater love. This passage of Paul became to me a gate to heaven. . . .

If you have a true faith that Christ is your Savior, then at once you have a gracious God, for faith leads you in and opens up God's heart and will, that you should see pure grace and over-flowing love. This it is to behold God in faith that you should look upon his fatherly, friendly heart, in which there is no anger nor ungraciousness. He who sees God as angry does not see him rightly but looks only on a curtain, as if a dark cloud had been drawn across his face.[17]

These insights were lectured upon and clarified between 1513 and 1516 at the university. As Bainton notes, "What came after was but commentary and sharpening to obviate misconstruction."

The center about which all the petals clustered was the affirma-tion of the forgiveness of sins through the utterly unmerited grace of God made possible by the cross of Christ, which recon-ciled wrath and mercy, routed the hosts of hell, triumphed over sin and death, and by the resurrection manifested the power which enables man to die to sin and rise to newness of life.[18]

Martin Luther, who had been tormented since youth by his sin-fulness in the presence of the living and holy God, had finally dis-covered good news. His spirit found its rest in Christ and Him crucified. It is important to realize this as we examine the subse-quent conflicts between Luther and the Roman church.

Initially, Luther's ideas of reform were simple and not very controversial. He wanted theological education to focus more on

[17] Cited in Bainton, op. cit., 49–50.
[18] Ibid., 51.

the Bible and less on the speculations of the canon lawyers and the scholastics. There was a practice of the Roman church, however, which eventually drew Luther's angry attention—the dispensing of indulgences. Technically indulgences are defined as "a remission before God of the temporal punishment for sin the guilt of which is already forgiven."[19] Eternal punishment is said to be removed when the repentant sinner receives absolution from the priest after confession. Temporal punishment, however, remains but can be removed if the Church grants an indulgence to cover all or part of that punishment. The Church is said to have access to a treasury of merits which may be applied to sinners by means of the granting of the indulgence. The practice readily lent itself to abuses. As Catholic theologian Richard McBrien notes,

> Plenary indulgences, i.e., the remission of all temporal punishment due to sin, had come into prominence during the Crusades in the eleventh century when the crusaders were promised complete remission of punishment in return for their military service (Pope Urban II, d. 1099). Indulgences for the dead began to be granted from the middle of the fifteenth century. Their connection with almsgiving was established as early as the eleventh century. In the later Middle Ages, however, they became a convenient source of income for the Church and, as such, were multiplied to scandalous proportions. Simony (i.e., buying and selling spiritual goods) was not unknown. Some preached indulgences in a theologically unsound and exaggerated way. The Council of Trent condemned such practices in its *Decree on Indulgences* (1563), but perhaps too late, since those very abuses were among the proximate causes of the Reformation.[20]

McBrien's comments are actually an understatement. By the time Luther came upon the scene, indulgences had proven to be a very lucrative method for the Roman church to raise revenues. Roland Bainton calls indulgences "the bingo of the sixteenth

---

[19] Richard P. McBrien, *Catholicism*, revised edition, (San Francisco: HarperCollins Publishers, 1994), 1169.
[20] Ibid., 1170.

century."[21] They were used to raise money for every conceivable enterprise. They were used to finance the construction of churches, cathedrals, monasteries, bridges, and hospitals, among other things.

It has already been noted that the pope at this time was Leo X (1513–1521), whose reign was one of the most worldly in the history of the papacy. His avarice and greed are evident in the rampant simony that he not only allowed but encouraged. When he sold a third bishopric to Albert of Brandenburg, another inadvertent step towards the Reformation was taken. Because the pope was raising money to rebuild St. Peter's in Rome and because Albert now had a large amount of money he owed the Fugger bankers, Leo granted him the exclusive right to sell a new indulgence in the territories of Mainz and Brandenburg for a period of eight years. Half of the revenues would go to the coffers of the pope, and half would go to Albert to enable him to repay his debt. Albert chose a young Dominican, John Tetzel, to publish this indulgence. Bainton observes how Albert handled this responsibility:

> In briefing the vendors Albert reached the pinnacle of pretensions as to the spiritual benefits to be conferred by indulgences. He made no reference whatever to the repayment of his debt to the Fuggers. The instructions declared that a plenary indulgence had been issued by His Holiness Pope Leo X to defray the expenses of remedying the sad state of the blessed apostles Peter and Paul and the innumerable martyrs and saints whose bones lay moldering, subject to constant desecration from rain and hail. Subscribers would enjoy a plenary and perfect remission of all sins. They would be restored to the state of innocence which they enjoyed in baptism and would be relieved of all the pains of purgatory, including those incurred by an offense to the Divine Majesty. Those securing indulgences on behalf of the dead already in purgatory need not themselves be contrite and confess their sins.[22]

[21] Bainton, op. cit., 54.
[22] Ibid., 58.

Tetzel was not able to preach in Wittenberg, but he was close enough that the parishioners entrusted to the pastoral care of Luther were able to go and buy these pardons from sin for themselves and for their departed loved ones who were suffering in purgatory. Luther was angered and responded on October 31, 1517 by nailing to the door of the Castle Church ninety-five theses on indulgences. In Luther's day this was the accepted way of inviting scholars to debate. There were three primary objections expressed in the theses. First, Luther objected to German money being sent to Rome to be spent on St. Peter's basilica. Second, he objected to the doctrine that the pope had any power over purgatory or that there was any treasury of merits. Finally he objected that indulgences were positively harmful to the spiritual state of the Christian because they prevented the believer from giving that money to the poor and because they provided a false sense of security and complacency. Luther made no attempt to publish these ninety-five theses. Others, however, translated the theses into German. Soon they were everywhere.

Luther had sent a copy of the ninety-five theses to Albert of Mainz who promptly forwarded them to the pope. Had a more godly man been reigning in Rome, perhaps the abuses would have been immediately addressed and corrected, and few today would have heard of Martin Luther. But Leo was not a godly man, and he was not about to allow anyone to threaten one of his most valuable sources of income. He set about to silence Luther. The situation gradually worsened as Luther attempted to publicly defend his theses and was met by increased Roman resistance. Eventually he was excommunicated by the pope for his views. What is interesting about the excommunication of Luther, observes Jaroslav Pelikan, is that

> there seems to have been room in the Roman Church for almost anyone and anything except Luther and the gospel he was proclaiming. In the very Italy from which Pope Leo X issued his decree of excommunication there were men whose skepticism

denied basic Christian tenets; but they were not excommunicated.[23]

So why was Luther excommunicated when these others were tolerated? Pelikan continues,

> The answer to that question is exceedingly complex. Its roots lie in the situation of imperial and papal politics in the first half of the sixteenth century, and in that triangle of pope, emperor, and princes that is the framework for so much of Luther's Reformation. In addition, there is a theological answer to the question, lying at the very foundation of Reformation theology. Irritating and troublesome as these other men and movements may have been to the Roman Church, the Reformation alone constituted a basic threat to the medieval theological and ecclesiastical system. For the Reformation had as its central Protestant principle the doctrine of justification by faith alone, the uselessness of human or ecclesiastical merit in the process of salvation, the free forgiveness of sins for the sake of Jesus Christ. If all this were true, then the traffic in merit and grace dispensed by the hierarchy was worse than useless. This was the threat of the Protestant principle to the ecclesiastical establishment, and against this threat the pope reacted when he excommunicated Luther.[24]

In other words, Luther's doctrine was seen as a threat to both the pomp and pocketbook of the papacy. Leo, who adored both, had to remove this thorn in his side. Everything Luther said concerning the role of Scripture, tradition, and the teaching authority of the Church must be understood within this historical context in which he found himself.

Luther's writings are not ivory-tower speculations. They are tracts, sermons, and treatises written by a man of conscience in the midst of a heated battle with a pope who is almost universally recognized to have been a wicked, power-hungry and avaricious

---

[23] Pelikan, op. cit., 17.
[24] Ibid., 17–18.

man. Such a context does not lend itself to polite and polished theological treatises. With this in mind, we shall proceed to examine what Luther actually taught about the role of Scripture and tradition.

Perhaps Luther's assertions and his criticisms of Rome may be understood better in light of what Rome herself was saying. Heiko Oberman provides an example:

> In early June 1520 a tract written in 1519—the *Epitoma responsionis ad Lutherum*—claiming to be a concise refutation of all Luther's fundamental errors, reached Wittenberg. Luther was well acquainted with the author of this *Refutation*, the Dominican and highest-ranking curial theologian Silvester Prieras. . . . The crucial theological argument upon which Prieras' 1519 response to Luther hinged was . . . the Church means the Church of Rome, headed by the pope, who is infallible and thus more authoritative than councils and even the Holy Scriptures themselves. There is no authority higher than the pope; and he cannot be deposed, "even if he were to give so much offense as to cause people in multitudes . . . to go to the Devil in Hell," as Prieras quoted from canon law.[25]

For Luther, teachings such as this clearly proved that the pope was more concerned about power than about the sheep entrusted to his care. He was so distressed at Prieras' doctrine that he wrote in frustration to his friend Spalatin, "I think that everyone in Rome has gone crazy; they are ravingly mad, and have become inane fools and devils."[26] But such was the state of the Roman church at this time that these comments could be made by the most prominent curial theologian without any fear of reproof.

There exists a common and superficial interpretation of the Reformation which sees Luther as a "schismatic, who was willing

---

[25] Oberman, *Luther*, 42.

[26] Cited in Ibid., 43. It must also be remembered that only four months before reading this response by Prieras, Luther had read Valla's published demonstration that the Donation of Constantine was a forgery. From his perspective, in the midst of this conflict, Rome was obviously founded on lies.

to divide the church in order to retain his private notions."[27] A number of factors clearly indicate that this was not the case. Pelikan notes, for example, the reluctance with which Luther protested against Rome and his efforts to stay with the Church. He also notes Luther's constant willingness to discuss specific points of doctrine and to consider reunion even after the split.[28] Luther voiced his criticisms as a member of the Church to other members of the Church because his calling as a theologian and pastor compelled him to speak out. Luther believed in apostolic succession, but as Kung points out, in the context of an extremely corrupt church, Luther had a choice between holding to a succession of the apostolic office or to a succession of the apostolic life.[29] Luther chose apostolic life. As Pelikan notes, "Martin Luther was the first Protestant, and yet he was more Catholic than many of his Roman Catholic opponents."[30]

We find the first public hints of Luther's concept of *sola scriptura* at the Leipzig debate between himself and John Eck. At this debate Luther defended the proposition that Scripture was the supreme authority—above the pope and above councils. It was at the Diet of Worms, however, where Luther made his most famous statement regarding the authority of Scripture. After being challenged by the magistrates to repudiate his books and recant his views, Luther said,

> Since then Your Majesty and your lordships desire a simple reply, I will answer without horns and without teeth. Unless I am convicted by Scripture and plain reason—I do not accept the authority of popes and councils, for they have contradicted each other—my conscience is captive to the Word of God. I cannot and will not recant anything, for to go against conscience is neither right nor safe. God help me. Amen.[31]

---

[27] Pelikan, op. cit., 20.

[28] Ibid., 20–21.

[29] Hans Kung, *Structures of the Church*, trans. Salvator Attanasio, (New York: Thomas Nelson & Sons, 1964), 127.

[30] Pelikan, op. cit., 11.

[31] Cited in Bainton, op cit., 144.

We must ask at this point whether Luther's view was and is consistent with Tradition I or whether he came up with a completely new and different concept of scriptural authority. If the statement made at Worms is considered alone, it is possible to see an altogether new position. However, this was not all that Luther had to say on the subject. When his teaching is taken as a whole, an entirely different conclusion is reached.

The fact that Luther operated within the context of a Tradition I concept of authority may be gathered from several sources. In Luther's Larger Catechism, for example, Luther expounds on the nature and purpose of the Church:

> Learn, then, to understand this article most clearly. If you are asked: What do you mean by the words: I believe in the Holy Ghost? you can answer: I believe that the Holy Ghost makes me holy, as His name implies. But whereby does He accomplish this, or what are His method and means to this end? Answer: By the Christian Church, the forgiveness of sins, the resurrection of the body, and the life everlasting. For, in the first place, He has a peculiar congregation in the world, which is the mother that begets and bears every Christian through the Word of God, which He reveals and preaches, [and through which] He illumines and enkindles hearts, that they understand, accept it, cling to it, and persevere in it.

In other words, the Holy Spirit's work is accomplished through the Word *and* in the Church. In his conflicts with the Anabaptists, Luther said,

> We do not act fanatically as the sectarian spirits. We do not reject everything that is under the dominion of the Pope. For in that event we should also reject the Christian Church. . . . Much Christian good, nay, all Christian good, is to be found in the papacy and from there it descended to us.[32]

---

[32] Cited in Oberman, *Dawn of the Reformation*, 285.

As Oberman explains, for Luther, there "are not two sources for the Christian faith, but two modes in which it reaches the Church in every generation: Holy Scripture and the *viva vox evangelii.*"[33] He continues,

> This position would not be restricted to that of Luther, but would form a constitutive part of the "heritage of the Reformation." The Calvinistic *Confessio Helvetica posterior* (1562) would succinctly formulate this with the words: "praedicatio verbi dei est verbum dei": The preaching of the word of God is *the* word of God.[34]

When Luther's understanding of "tradition" is examined, it must be kept in mind that Luther did not reject the true Catholic tradition; he rejected certain traditions. In the sixteenth century the plural term "traditions" was universally used to refer to customs and ceremonies.[35] Luther's attack on these traditions must not be confused with an attack on the Church.

Luther's criticisms of the Church were directed at one particular view of the Church—the view which identified the Church with the Roman ecclesiastical institution with the pope as its head. According to the Reformed confessions,

> this doctrine of the church had its source in a rationalization of the politico-ecclesiastical situation rather than in a primarily theological concern. It was intended to provide divine validation for the political involvement of the Roman bishop, and the exegetical and doctrinal support for it was supplied after the fact. The theory of papal sovereignty had appeared in its most extreme form during the medieval controversies between church and state. It was at times like these that the papacy had defined the church as a "supreme outward monarchy of the whole world in which the Roman pontiff must have unlimited power beyond question or censure. . . . Therefore the pope must be lord of the

[33] Ibid., 286.
[34] Ibid.
[35] Headley, op. cit., 88.

whole world, of all the kingdoms of the world, and must have . . . both swords, the temporal and the spiritual." Characterizing this desire for organizational prestige and power as the source for the Roman Catholic doctrine of the church, Luther explained sarcastically that "the holy see of Rome came to the aid of the poor church," and he accused the papacy of having drawn its viewpoints "from the imperial, pagan law."[36]

This view of her own power caused Rome to absolutize her own interpretation of her history to the degree that evidence was found where none existed and historical criticism was essentially ruled out *a priori*. In other words, Rome's view of herself removed the heavy burden of accountability from the shoulders of the papacy.

Luther was writing at a time when the papacy was vigorously reasserting her authority over against the conciliarists who taught the superior authority of an ecumenical council over the pope. The Council of Constance (1414–1418) had been convened only a century earlier to heal the Great Schism. Because of the confusion that existed with three popes reigning simultaneously, the council was called by Sigismund, who would eventually be crowned Holy Roman Emperor. The Council deposed the popes John XXIII and Benedict XIII, and Pope Gregory XII resigned. The council then selected Cardinal Oddone Colonna to be pope, and he took the title of Martin V. The council also sought to prevent future problems by taking practical steps to implement the conciliar theory. The very fact that it had taken a council to finally end the Schism and select one pope was seen by many as an obvious vindication of the conciliar theory. However, soon after being elected, Martin V took it upon himself to restore the power, prestige and supremacy of the papacy. Martin's successor, Eugene IV, completed the task of placing the councils back under the sovereignty of the popes. The conflict did not immediately end, however, and conciliarists continued to argue their case into

---

[36] Pelikan, op. cit., 29.

the following centuries.[37] Therefore, when Luther responded to Prieras, Eck, and the Diet of Worms by denying the supreme and infallible authority of the pope, he was not attacking the authority of the Church itself. He was doing what numerous theologians had been doing for over a century. He was attacking a hotly contested theory of the papacy which happened to be the one held at that point in history by the pope himself and the Roman curia.

Luther's assertion that Scripture was the only infallible authority in matters of faith and his historical criticisms of the papacy and certain traditions did not mean that he advocated a rejection of the communion of saints and the *regula fidei*.[38] Instead Luther attempted to distinguish Scripture from the multitudes of conflicting authorities that existed in the Church.[39] His main complaint was directed against the view that "Scripture can be properly understood only by a few and must not be interpreted by its own Spirit."[40] As Headley observes, "Such a principle leads to the burial of Scripture and theology's immersion in the commentaries of men, where the sophists seek not the substance of Scripture but what they may notice in it."[41] As noted before, in the late Middle Ages, the text of Scripture was almost universally published with the text of the Gloss and comments upon that Gloss by other interpreters.

> By asserting the principle that Scripture is its own simplest, most certain, and direct interpreter, Luther sought to reverse this process and extract Scripture from the wrappings of commentaries and interpreters. The scriptures can be understood only through the Holy Spirit by whom they were written and this Spirit is nowhere to be found more living and present than in His own sacred writings.[42]

[37] For an overview of the conciliar movement, see Brian Tierney, *Foundations of Conciliar Theory*, (Cambridge: Cambridge University Press, 1955).

[38] McGrath, *Intellectual Origins of the European Reformation*, 149.

[39] Headley, op. cit., 81.

[40] Ibid., 82.

[41] Ibid.

[42] Ibid., 82–83.

And yet Luther did not equate this principle with a radical individualism. Luther taught that the Spirit accomplishes His work in the Church. The Spirit-inspired Word of God and the Spirit-indwelt people of God must be distinguished, but they cannot be artificially separated. Luther's view is Tradition I as stated within the context of a heated battle with proponents of Tradition II. Regarding Luther's position, Pelikan observes,

> As a Protestant, he subjected the authority of church councils to the authority of the word of God; as a Catholic he interpreted the word of God in conformity with the dogmas of the councils and in this sense made the councils normative. This attitude was an inconsistency according to both the traditionalists and the iconoclasts; for neither of them could see that Catholic substance and Protestant principle belong together, not only in Luther's Reformation, but in the life of the church and indeed in the very message of the New Testament.[43]

Luther's understanding of Church councils is most clearly set forth in his work *On the Councils and the Church*. In this work, Luther argues that although Rome claims the authority of the fathers and the councils, her views are actually at odds with those of the early councils and fathers. He appeals to Rome to let him join her in Church reform based upon the councils and the fathers. He argues, as Pelikan notes, that the "genuine defenders of the councils and of their Catholic substance . . . were not those who claimed supreme authority for the councils, but those who, like the fathers at the councils themselves, subjected the authority of the councils to the authority of the Scripture."[44] In his study of church history, Luther observed that every council was convoked to deal with one principle issue. He concluded: "The decrees of the genuine councils must remain in force permanently,

---

[43] Pelikan, op. cit., 76.

[44] Ibid., 62; cf. David C. Steinmetz, "Luther and Calvin on Church and Tradition" in *Articles on Calvin and Calvinism*, vol. 10, ed. Richard C. Gamble, (New York: Garland Publishing, Inc., 1992), 6–7.

just as they have always been in force, especially the primary concerns for whose sake they are councils and are called such."[45] Other secondary issues, such as disciplinary canons and decrees, were temporary and binding only when and where the conditions necessitating them still existed. On the Council of Ephesus, for example, Luther wrote, "The Council of Ephesus condemned the Nestorian heresy; its other decrees have to do with temporal matters. . . . These we ignore."[46] Jaroslav Pelikan notes that what emerged from the Reformation was the existence of three distinct attitudes towards history and tradition:[47]

1. Authoritarian Reverence—Roman Catholicism
2. Critical Reverence—Reformed Catholicism or Protestantism
3. Utter Contempt—Radical Reformers

The radical Reformers will be examined in the following chapter, but here the emphasis is that Luther rejected both the autonomy and the radical individualism that instilled in those men the idea that each individual is his own final authority in doctrinal matters.[48]

Finally a word must be said about Luther's statement at Worms: "[M]y conscience is captive to the Word of God." Some have detected here in Martin Luther's appeal to "conscience" the seeds of subjectivity and thus the rejection of Tradition I.[49] However, as Kung has pointed out,

The classic theological and canonical view is that a Christian should not be deterred from following the dictates of his conscience even by the threat of excommunication. As a believing Christian anyone who found himself involved in such a tragic

[45] Cited in Pelikan, op. cit., 75.
[46] Ibid.
[47] Ibid., 40.
[48] Ibid., 33.
[49] E.g., Robert Fastiggi, "What did the Protestant Reformers Teach about *Sola Scriptura?*" in *Not by Scripture Alone*, ed. Robert A. Sungenis, (Santa Barbara: Queenship Publishing Company, 1997), 327–328.

conflict would have in a spirit of faith to bear the excommunication, however hard his loyalty to the Church made this. The answer was given long ago by Innocent III, relying on the words of St. Paul that are always rightly quoted in such cases: "Every act done in bad faith is sin," said Innocent, "and whatever is done contrary to conscience leads to hell . . . as in this matter no one must obey a judge against God, but rather humbly bear the excommunication." Sebastian Merkle . . . writes: "St. Thomas, the greatest doctor of the Order of Preachers, and with him a number of other scholastics, accordingly taught that an individual excommunicated for erroneous reasons ought rather to die under the interdict than obey superior orders he knew to be mistaken. 'For that would be contrary to the truth (*contra veritatem vitae*) which is not to be sacrificed even on account of possible scandal.'" Even at the time of the Counter-Reformation, when there was much more rigidity on this question, Cardinal Bellarmine, for all his emphasis on papal authority, admitted that "just as it would be legitimate for a man to resist the Pope if he physically assaulted him, so, if the Pope made an assault on souls, if he sowed confusion in the State, and particularly if he set out to destroy the Church, would passive resistance be legitimate, in the form of refraining from carrying out his orders, and also active resistance, by preventing him from carrying out his will."[50]

Again this is a case in which Luther is more truly Catholic than many of his opponents, men such as Prieras who counseled unquestioned subservience to the will of the papacy even if the pope's will necessitated the destruction of his flock. In opposition to a papacy intent upon increasing her earthly power and releasing herself from any accountability to a higher authority, Martin Luther stood with those who, through the centuries, had advocated the apostolic concept of authority.

---

[50] Hans Kung, *Infallible? An Enquiry*, trans. Eric Mosbacher, (London: William Collins Sons & Co, Ltd, 1971), 39.

JOHN CALVIN

John Calvin was born on July 10, 1509 in Noyon, France. He began his education and training for the priesthood at the University of Paris, but when his father decided that he should become a lawyer, he was sent to Orleans. Because of the lack of clear written testimony, there is much scholarly debate over the exact date of Calvin's conversion to Protestantism. But be that as it may, we do know that he did convert, and because the situation in France was very precarious for Protestants, Calvin left for Switzerland. Soon after Calvin left, many French Protestants, including a close friend, were imprisoned, tortured and put to death. With another friend, Louis du Tillet, he found his way to Metz, Strasbourg and finally Basel. While there he heard of the sufferings of his fellow Protestants in France and decided to write a book vindicating their faith. In 1536, the first edition of the *Institutes of the Christian Religion* was published in Basel.[51]

While traveling to the Protestant city of Strasbourg, Calvin stopped in Geneva and was ultimately persuaded by the Reformer William Farel to stay and assist in the work of reformation in that city. In 1538 both Calvin and Farel were exiled from Geneva. Calvin spent three years in Strasbourg during his exile, but after being recalled to the city in 1541, he stayed for the remainder of his life, preaching and teaching the Reformed faith. The city of Geneva became a model for many exiled Reformers, such as John Knox, who while living there in 1556 referred to it as "the most perfect school of Christ that ever was in the earth since the days of the Apostles."[52]

In order to determine Calvin's understanding of the authority of Scripture, tradition and the Church, we must examine his relevant works. The 1559 edition of the *Institutes of the Christian*

---

[51] For an introduction to the life of John Calvin, see T.H.L. Parker, *John Calvin: A Biography*, (Philadelphia: The Westminster Press, 1975); and Alister McGrath, *A Life of John Calvin*, (Oxford: Basil Blackwell, 1990).

[52] Cited in John T. McNeill, *The History and Character of Calvinism*, (Oxford: Oxford University Press, 1954), 178.

Religion contain the theology of the mature Calvin.[53] Book One of the *Institutes* is devoted to the doctrine of the knowledge of God, and several chapters are devoted to the nature and authority of the Holy Scripture. Calvin begins by explaining the purpose of Scripture. God gave his people Scripture "in order that truth might abide forever in the world with a continuing succession of teaching and survive through all ages, the same oracles he had given to the patriarchs it was his pleasure to have recorded, as it were, on public tablets."[54] But why was it necessary to put His revelation into writing?

> Suppose we ponder how slippery is the fall of the human mind into forgetfulness of God, how great the tendency to every kind of error, how great the lust to fashion constantly new and artificial religions. Then we may perceive how necessary was such written proof of the heavenly doctrine, that it should neither perish through forgetfulness nor vanish through error nor be corrupted by the audacity of men.[55]

In chapter seven, Calvin explains that the authority of Scripture derives from the nature of the One whose Word it is, namely almighty God. Its authority is not established upon the decision of the Church.

> When that which is set forth is acknowledged to be the Word of God, there is no one so deplorably insolent—unless devoid also both of common sense and of humanity itself—as to dare impugn the credibility of Him who speaks. . . . Hence the Scriptures obtain full authority among believers only when men regard them as having sprung from heaven, as if there the living words of God were heard. . . . But a most pernicious error widely prevails that Scripture has only so much weight as is conceded to it by the consent of the church. As if the eternal and inviolable truth of God depended upon the decision of men.

[53] All citations from the *Institutes* are taken from the Ford Lewis Battles translation, edited by John T. McNeill, (Philadelphia: The Westminster Press, 1960).
[54] Ibid., I.vi.2.
[55] Ibid., I.vi.3.

. . . What reverence is due Scripture and what books ought to be reckoned within its canon depend, they say, upon the determination of the church.[56]

Calvin proceeds to refute this claim, demonstrating that the Church is in fact established and dependent upon the Word of God.

[S]uch wranglers are neatly refuted by just one word of the apostle. He testifies that the church is "built upon the foundation of the prophets and apostles" [Eph. 2:20]. If the teaching of the prophets and apostles is the foundation, this must have had authority before the church began to exist. Groundless, too, is their subtle objection that, although the church took its beginning here, the writings to be attributed to the prophets and apostles nevertheless remain in doubt until decided by the church. For if the Christian church was from the beginning founded upon the writings of the prophets and the preaching of the apostles, wherever this doctrine is found, the acceptance of it— without which the church itself would never have existed— must certainly have preceded the church. It is utterly vain, then, to pretend that the power of judging Scripture so lies with the church that its certainty depends upon churchly assent. Thus, while the church receives and gives its seal of approval to the Scriptures, it does not thereby render authentic what is otherwise doubtful or controversial. But because the church recognizes Scripture to be the truth of its own God, as a pious duty it unhesitatingly venerates Scripture. As to their question—How can we be assured that this has sprung from God unless we have recourse to the decree of the church?—it is as if someone asked: Whence will we learn to distinguish light from darkness, white from black, sweet from bitter? Indeed, Scripture exhibits fully as clear evidence of its own truth as white and black things do of their color, or sweet and bitter things do of their taste.[57]

When God speaks, His Word—by definition—is authoritative prior to any hearing of that Word or assent to it. When Jesus

---

[56] Ibid., I.vii.1.
[57] Ibid., I.vii.2.

spoke to the multitudes, the people did not have to wait for Peter and the other disciples to authenticate or verify His Word. His Word is authoritative because of Who He is. The authority of God's Word in Scripture, therefore, does not rest upon the Church's assent to it. The authority of God's Word rests solely upon the authority of the One speaking—God Himself.

Calvin continues with an explanation of the inward witness of the Holy Spirit to His own Word in Scripture.

> We ought to remember what I said a bit ago [I.vii.1]: credibility of doctrine is not established until we are persuaded beyond doubt that God is its Author. Thus, the highest proof of Scripture derives in general from the fact that God in person speaks in it. The prophets and apostles do not boast either of their keenness or of anything that obtains credit for them as they speak; nor do they dwell upon rational proofs. Rather they bring forward God's holy name, that by it the whole world may be brought into obedience to him. Now we ought to see how apparent it is not only by plausible opinion but by clear truth that they do not call upon God's name heedlessly or falsely. If we desire to provide in the best way for our consciences—that they may not be perpetually beset by the instability of doubt or vacillation, and that they may not also boggle at the smallest quibbles—we ought to seek our conviction in a higher place than human reasons, judgments, or conjectures, that is, in the secret testimony of the Spirit. . . . If we turn pure eyes and upright senses toward it, the majesty of God will immediately come to view, subdue our bold rejection, and compel us to obey.[58]

Over against those who would establish the veracity and authority of God's Word upon human testimony, arguments and proofs, Calvin argues that the witness of the Holy Spirit is the highest proof. He continues,

> They who strive to build up firm faith in Scripture through disputation are doing things backwards. . . . [because] even if

---

[58] Ibid., I.vii.4.

anyone clears God's Sacred Word from man's evil speaking, he will not at once imprint upon their hearts that certainty which piety requires. Since for unbelieving men religion seems to stand by opinion alone, they, in order not to believe anything foolishly or lightly, both wish and demand rational proof that Moses and the prophets spoke divinely. But I reply: the testimony of the Spirit is more excellent than all reason. For as God alone is a fit witness of himself in his Word, so also the Word will not find acceptance in men's hearts before it is sealed by the inward testimony of the Spirit. The same Spirit, therefore, who has spoken through the mouths of the prophets must penetrate into our hearts to persuade us that they faithfully proclaimed what had been divinely commanded.[59]

Calvin concludes his discussion of the inherent authority of Holy Scripture by summing up his previous comments,

Let this point therefore stand: that those whom the Holy Spirit has inwardly taught truly rest upon Scripture, and that Scripture indeed is self-authenticated; hence, it is not right to subject it to proof and reasoning. And the certainty it deserves with us, it attains by the testimony of the Spirit. . . . We seek no proofs, no marks of genuineness upon which our judgment may lean; but we subject our judgment and wit to it as a thing far beyond any guesswork. . . . God, therefore, very rightly proclaims through Isaiah that the prophets, together with the whole people are witnesses to him; for they, instructed by prophecies, unhesitatingly held that God has spoken without deceit or ambiguity [Isa. 43:10]. Such then is a conviction that requires no reasons; such, a knowledge with which the best reason agrees—in which the mind truly reposes more securely and constantly than in any reasons; such, finally, a feeling that can be born only of heavenly revelation. I speak of nothing other than what each believer experiences within himself—though my words fall far beneath a just explanation of the matter.[60]

[59] Ibid., I.vii.4.
[60] Ibid., I.vii.5.

There is nothing in Calvin's argument thus far that contradicts the early Church's understanding of Scripture. All Calvin has done to this point is state the obvious: God and what He says is the ultimate and final authority. Since the Word of God is the Word *of God*, it is what God Himself says, and therefore it is the ultimate authority. The authority of the Word of God is the authority of God Himself, and that authority does not depend upon the assent or verification of anyone or anything, including the Roman church.

In Book Four, Calvin turns to a lengthy discussion of the Church. Here we see how he conceives of the relationship between scriptural authority and Church authority. Like many before and after him, Calvin states that those for whom God is Father must have the Church as their Mother.[61] With the fathers, Calvin stands in asserting that outside of the Church there is no salvation.[62] Those who would separate themselves from the ministry of the Church he refers to as "fanatics." Since these schismatics "do their utmost to sever or break the sacred bond of unity, no one escapes the just penalty of this unholy separation without bewitching himself with pestilent errors and foulest delusions."[63]

Turning to the question of how one may recognize the true Church, Calvin answers by listing the distinguishing marks of the Church. He argues that "we recognize as members of the church those who, by confession of faith, by example of life, and by partaking of the sacraments, profess the same God and Christ with us."[64] The Christian may not forsake a church bearing these marks.

> However it may be, where the preaching of the gospel is reverently heard and the sacraments are not neglected, there for the time being no deceitful or ambiguous form of the church is seen; and no one is permitted to spurn its authority, flout its warnings,

---

[61] Ibid., IV.i.1.
[62] Ibid., IV.i.4; Cf. Cyprian, *Epistles*, 73.21.
[63] *Institutes*, IV.i.5.
[64] Ibid., IV.i.8.

resist its counsels, or make light of its chastisements—much less to desert it and break its unity. For the Lord esteems the communion of his church so highly that he counts as a traitor and apostate from Christianity anyone who arrogantly leaves any Christian society, provided it cherishes the true ministry of Word and sacraments.[65]

It is very clear that Calvin has a very high view of the Church, but he does not believe that perfection is required in order for a church to be a true Church.[66] It should also be noted that he does not advocate any kind of radical individualism regarding the judgment of truth and falsehood. He writes, "even if the church be slack in its duty, still each and every individual has not the right at once to take it upon himself the decision to separate."[67] Of course, all of his comments on this subject beg the question of whether Rome was a true Church. If so then he stands condemned by his own words.

Calvin realizes this and devotes a fair amount of space to explaining why the forsaking of the Roman communion is not only justified in light of his previous comments but absolutely necessary. If the ministry of Word and sacraments are the marks of a true Church, then "as soon as falsehood breaks into the citadel of religion and the sum of necessary doctrine is overturned and the use of the sacraments is destroyed, surely the death of the church follows. . . . If the foundation of the church is the teaching of the prophets and apostles, which bids believers entrust their salvation to Christ alone—then take away that teaching, and how will the building continue to stand?"[68]

It is important to note here the distinction Calvin makes between necessary doctrines and nonessentials. A church can be a true Church and be mistaken in nonessentials. It cannot, however, remain a true church if the essentials of Christianity have

---

[65] Ibid., IV.i.10.
[66] Ibid., IV.i.10–29.
[67] Ibid., IV.i.15.
[68] Ibid., IV.ii.1.

been destroyed, or forsaken. It is Calvin's contention that the state of the Roman church at this time is such that it no longer remains a true Church. He argues that the ministry of both Word and sacrament have been destroyed by Roman abuses. He argues that Rome has completely abandoned the faith and practice of the early Church despite her claims to apostolic "succession."[69]

Because of the centrality of this assertion, Calvin devotes several lengthy arguments to proving that Rome is no longer a true Church. Rome's argument from unbroken episcopal succession is invalidated by her claim that the Greeks, who also enjoy unbroken episcopal succession, are schismatics. Rome would like to have it both ways when succession is considered. But succession is only valid, Calvin observes, if it preserves and protects the truth.[70] He uses a number of examples from the Old Testament to demonstrate that an unbroken succession of the priesthood does not automatically guarantee preservation of truth (cf. Jer. 7; Ezek. 10; Mal. 2:1–9).[71]

Calvin proceeds to argue that Rome's claim to valid episcopal succession is also invalidated by its actual practice of episcopal selection. He points out that, more often than not, morally reprobate men are chosen to be bishops—drunkards and fornicators who know nothing of Scripture or of Christian doctrine. Even boys as young as ten years old are granted the office of bishop with the pope's blessing. Worst of all, these offices are bought and sold.

> I contend that nowadays in the papacy scarcely one benifice in a hundred is conferred without simony—as the ancients defined simony. I do not say that all buy them at a price, but show me one out of twenty who comes to a benefice without some indirect commendation. Some are advanced by kinship or affinity; others, by parental influence; still others obsequiously curry favor for themselves. In short, priestly livings are conferred for this

[69] Ibid., IV.ii. 2.
[70] Ibid.
[71] Ibid., IV.ii. 3, 7–11.

purpose: not to benefit the churches but those men who receive them.[72]

Any pretense to a true apostolic succession is obviously invalidated, according to Calvin, if the holders of those offices presumed to purchase them.

Calvin continues by turning his attention to the papacy itself. He begins by arguing that it is utterly absurd to claim that any primacy Peter may or may not have had could be perpetually tied to a particular city simply because Peter died there. If Rome is granted this special dignity by virtue of the fact that Peter died there, then Jerusalem should be granted much more dignity since the Lord Jesus died there.[73] He then points out the incongruity of Roman claims with admitted historical facts. Since Peter's first see was in Antioch, why is Antioch not granted the first place of honor? If it is because the Petrine see was transferred to Rome, why is Antioch not second?

> Paul names three disciples who seem to be pillars, James, Peter, and John [Gal. 2:9]; if in Peter's honor first place is assigned to the Roman see, do not the churches of Ephesus and Jerusalem deserve second and third place, where John and James presided? Yet among the patriarchates Jerusalem of old had last place; Ephesus could not even cling to the last corner. . . . Let them either confess that order was preposterous; or grant us it is not a perpetual principle that to each church is due the same degree of honor as to its founder.[74]

From a consideration of these "childish follies" Calvin moves to an examination of the office of the pope himself.

---

[72] Ibid., IV.v.6.

[73] Ibid., IV.vi.11.

[74] Ibid., IV.vi.13. The reason the five patriarchates (Rome, Constantinople, Alexandria, Antioch, and Jerusalem) were ordered as they were was simply because the first four were the four most important cities in the ancient Roman empire. Jerusalem was granted a place because it was where Jesus had been crucified. (cf. Timothy Ware, *The Orthodox Church*, New Ed., (London: Penguin Books, 1993), 26).

He begins by pointing out the deplorable state of the theology found in Rome, including blasphemous denials of central doctrines.[75] John T. McNeill has pointed out a comment made by Erasmus after visiting Rome. Erasmus wrote,

> It may be that in Germany there are those who do not shrink from blasphemies against God; but they are corrected with the severest penalties. But at Rome I have heard with these ears some who raged in abominable blasphemies against Christ and his apostles, in my presence and that of many, and that with impunity.[76]

Calvin notes this type of Roman doctrinal apostasy and then proceeds to critique the basis for Rome's papal claims. He points out the claim being made by many at the time that popes cannot err because Jesus had said to Peter, "I have prayed for you that your faith may not fail" (Luke 22:32). He counters that this argument is hardly worth considering.

> Yet of itself this claim is also so childish it needs no answer. For if they wish to apply to Peter's successors everything that was said to Peter, it will follow that they are all Satans, since the Lord also said this to Peter: "Get behind me, Satan! You are a hindrance to me" [Matt. 16:23]. Indeed, it will be as easy for us to turn back this latter saying upon them as for them to cast the other against us.[77]

After a lengthy critique of the Roman theory of authority, Calvin proceeds to explain the relationship between the authority of the Word and the authority of the Church. "The power of the church," he says, "resides partly in individual bishops, and partly in councils, either provincial or general." This authority, however, is not unconditional. "The power of the church is therefore to be not grudgingly manifested but yet kept within definite

---

[75] *Institutes*, IV.vii.27–28.
[76] Cited by McNeill in Ibid., vol. 2, p. 1146, note 57; Cf. Oberman, *Luther*, 149.
[77] *Institutes*, IV.vii.28.

limits, that it may not be drawn hither and thither according to men's whim."[78] He explains, "Accordingly, we must here remember that whatever authority and dignity the Spirit in Scripture accords to either priests or prophets, or apostles, or successors of apostles, it is wholly given not to the men personally, but to the ministry to which they have been appointed; or (to speak more briefly) to the Word, whose ministry is entrusted to them."[79] In the Bible priests, prophets, and apostles had authority—but that authority was to speak nothing but what God had given them to speak. What this means is that the "power of the church, therefore, is not infinite but subject to the Lord's Word and, as it were, enclosed within it."[80]

Just as the priests and teachers of ancient Israel were subject to the Scripture as the standard (Deut. 5:32), so too the apostles were subject to the Word of God (Matt. 28:19–20; 1 Pet. 4:11).[81] According to Calvin, the Holy Spirit, the Church, and the Word of God in Scripture are inseparably tied. This becomes clear when he describes the differences between Rome's understanding of infallibility and the Reformers' understanding of infallibility.

> Their statement that the church cannot err bears on this point, and this is how they interpret it—inasmuch as the church is governed by the Spirit of God, it can proceed safely without the Word; no matter where it may go, it can think or speak only what is true; accordingly, if it should ordain anything beyond or apart from God's Word, this must be taken as nothing but a sure oracle of God.
>
> If we grant the first point, that the church cannot err in matters necessary to salvation, here is what we mean by it: The statement is true in so far as the church, having forsaken all its own wisdom, allows itself to be taught by the Holy Spirit through God's Word. This, then, is the difference. Our

[78] Ibid., IV.viii.1.
[79] Ibid., IV.viii.2.
[80] Ibid., IV.viii.4.
[81] Ibid., IV.viii.6–9.

opponents locate the authority of the church outside God's
Word; but we insist that it be attached to the Word, and do not
allow it to be separated from it.

And what wonder if Christ's bride and pupil be subject to her
Spouse and Teacher, so that she pays constant and careful attention to his words! For this is the arrangement of a well-governed
house, that the wife obey the husband's authority. . . .

Now it is easy to conclude how wrongly our opponents act
when they boast of the Holy Spirit solely to commend with his
name strange doctrines foreign to God's Word—while the Spirit
wills to be conjoined with God's Word by an indissoluble bond,
and Christ professes this concerning him when he promises the
Spirit to his church. Assuredly this is so. That soberness which
the Lord once prescribed for his church [cf. 1 Pet. 1:13; 4:7;
5:8; etc.] he wills to be preserved forever. But he forbade anything to be added to his Word or taken away from it [Deut. 4:2;
cf. Rev. 22:18–19]. It is this inviolable decree of God and of the
Holy Spirit which our foes are trying to set aside when they pretend that the church is ruled by the Spirit apart from the
Word.[82]

There is nothing novel in this. Calvin expresses here the ancient
view that the Word of God is the final authority by which the
Church—a subordinate ministerial authority—is to live and
teach. Like the fathers of the first centuries, Calvin rejects extra-
scriptural revelation and its use as a foundation for so-called
"traditions."[83] Scripture, he says, is "the sole rule of perfect wisdom."[84]

In an examination of the authority of Church councils, Calvin
points out that councils have never been considered inherently
infallible simply because they conformed to all of the outward re-
quirements of a true council. He uses John 11:47 as an example
of an externally proper yet fallible council.

---

[82] Ibid., IV.viii.13.

[83] Ibid., IV.viii.14.

[84] Ibid., IV.ix.1; Cf. Francois Wendel, *Calvin: Origins and Development of His Religious Thought*, trans. Philip Mairet, (Durham, North Carolina: The Labyrinth Press, 1987), 306; Ronald S. Wallace, *Calvin's Doctrine of Word and Sacrament*, (Edinburgh: Oliver and Boyd Ltd., 1953), 99–100.

In that council which the high priests and Pharisees convened at Jerusalem against Christ [John 11:47], what was lacking as far as outward appearance is concerned? For unless a church then existed at Jerusalem, Christ would never have taken part in the sacrifices and other ceremonies. A solemn convocation takes place; the high priest presides; the whole priestly order is present. Yet Christ is there condemned, and his teaching cast away [Matt. 26:57ff.].[85]

Anticipating the objections of the Roman Catholic church, he proceeds to explain what it means to judge between true and false councils.

I am not arguing here either that all councils are to be condemned or the acts of all to be rescinded, and (as the saying goes) to be canceled at one stroke. But, you will say, you degrade everything, so that every man has the right to accept or reject what the councils decide. Not at all! But whenever a decree of any council is brought forward, I should like men first of all diligently to ponder at what time it was held, on what issue, and with what intention, what sort of men were present; then to examine by the standard of Scripture what it dealt with—and to do this in such a way that the definition of the council may have its weight and be like a provisional judgment, yet not hinder the examination which I have mentioned. . . . Thus councils would come to have the majesty that is their due; yet in the meantime Scripture would stand out in the higher place, with everything subject to its standard. In this way we willingly embrace and reverence as holy the early councils, such as those of Nicaea, Constantinople, Ephesus I, Chalcedon, and the like, which were concerned with refuting errors—in so far as they relate to the teachings of the faith. For they contain nothing but the pure and genuine exposition of Scripture, which the holy fathers applied with spiritual prudence to crush the enemies of religion who had then arisen.[86]

[85] *Institutes*, IV.ix.7.
[86] Ibid., IV.ix.8.

Although Calvin grants the councils subordinate authority, he does not grant that they are inherently infallible in everything they proclaim. To demonstrate that this view is not a novelty, he quotes Pope Leo, who declared the possibility that Chalcedon may have erred on matters not central to the Christian faith.[87]

In response to Roman claims that the councils must be obeyed without question simply because men are to obey their rulers, Calvin writes,

> They, therefore, will be our spiritual rulers who turn aside from the law of the Lord neither this way nor that. But if we must accept the teaching of all pastors whatever without any doubting, what was the point of the Lord's frequent admonitions to us not to heed the talk of false prophets? "Do not," he says through Jeremiah, "listen to the words of the prophets who prophesy to you; for they teach you vanity, and not from the mouth of the Lord" [Jer. 23:16]. Likewise: "Beware of false prophets, who come to you in sheep's clothing but inwardly are ravenous wolves" [Matt. 7:15]. John also would vainly exhort us "to test the spirits to see whether they are of God" [1 John 4:1]. Not even the angels are exempt from this judgment, much less Satan with his lies [Gal. 1:8]. . . . Does this not sufficiently declare that it is very important what sort of pastors should be heard, and that not all are to be heard indiscriminately?[88]

Does this mean that Calvin believes the Church has no authority to interpret Scripture? To the contrary, he concedes that, "if any discussion arises over doctrine, that the best and surest remedy is for a synod of true bishops to be convened, where the doctrine at issue may be examined."[89] This, he argues, was the method the Apostle Paul himself prescribed. What Calvin does not grant is that any council is given a gift of infallibility. The veracity of a council's decisions is not determined in advance simply because it meets a list of external criteria. In his debate with Cardinal

---

[87] Ibid., IV.ix.11; Cf. Leo, *Letters*, cv, cvi.
[88] *Institutes*, IV.ix.12.
[89] Ibid., IV.ix.13.

Sadoleto, Calvin explained, "For although we hold that the Word of God alone lies beyond the sphere of our judgment, and that fathers and Councils are of authority only in so far as they accord with the rule of the Word, we still give to Councils and fathers such rank and honor as it is meet for them to hold, under Christ."[90]

Calvin points out that the problem with Rome's claim is that she refers to contradictions with Scripture as interpretations of Scripture. He writes,

> But the Romanists aim at another goal when they teach that the power of interpreting Scripture belongs to councils, and without appeal. For, in calling everything ordained in councils "interpretation of Scripture," they misuse this as pretext. Not one syllable of purgatory, of intercession of saints, of auricular confession, and the like will be found in Scripture. But, because all these things have been sanctioned by the authority of the church, that is (to speak more accurately), received by opinion and use, every one will have to be taken as an interpretation of Scripture.[91]

He points out the fallacy of such reasoning by offering several examples. Christ bids all to drink of the cup (Matt. 26:27–28), yet the Council of Constance forbade the laity from receiving the cup. Paul refers to the prohibition of marriage as a demonic doctrine (1 Tim. 4:1–3), and elsewhere marriage is called holy (Heb. 13:4), yet priests are prohibited from marriage. But as Calvin points out, "If anyone dare open his mouth in opposition, he will be adjudged a heretic, because the decision of the church is without appeal; and it is unlawful to question whether its interpretation is true."[92]

That which Calvin is contending against is human traditions— not the apostolic Tradition. The apostolic Tradition is that which he is attempting to defend. He explains,

---

[90] John C. Olin, ed., *John Calvin & Jacopo Sadoleto: A Reformation Debate*, (New York: Harper & Row, Publishers, 1966), 92.

[91] *Institutes*, IV.ix.14.

[92] Ibid.

For this reason we freely inveigh against the tyranny of human tradition which is haughtily thrust upon us under the title of the church. For we do not scorn the church (as our adversaries, to heap spite upon us, unjustly and falsely assert); but we give the church the praise of obedience, than which it knows no greater. But grave injury is done to the church by those who make it obstinate against its Lord, when they pretend that it has gone beyond what is permitted by God's Word. . . . But, if, as is fitting, we are minded to agree with the church, it is more to the point to see and remember what the Lord has enjoined upon us and the church, that we may obey it with one consent. For there is no doubt that we shall agree very well with the church if we show ourselves in all things obedient to the Lord.

But to trace the origin of these traditions (with which the church has hitherto been oppressed) back to the apostles is pure deceit. For the whole doctrine of the apostles has this intent: not to burden consciences with new observances, or contaminate the worship of God with our own inventions. Again, if there is anything credible in the histories and ancient records, the apostles not only were ignorant of what the Romanists attribute to them but never even heard of it.[93]

When the historical and ecclesiastical context in which the Reformers lived and wrote is taken into consideration, it is evident that there was no intent or desire to break with the church.[94] They were convinced that Rome had become thoroughly apostate and could no longer even be considered a true Church. Luther and Calvin were attempting to preserve the continuity with the early Church which they believed had been abandoned by Rome. Steinmetz observes, "What the Protestants are attempting to do is to persuade the Church to abandon its fascination with the theological and disciplinary innovations of the later Middle Ages and to return to Scripture and the fathers, Scripture as the authoritative text and the fathers as helpful interpreters (not infallible but better by far than the scholastics)."[95] As

---

[93] Ibid., IV.x.18.
[94] Muller. op. cit., 51.
[95] Steinmetz, op. cit., 12.

Calvin explains to Cardinal Sadoleto, "You know. . . not only that our agreement with antiquity is far closer than yours, but that all we have attempted has been to renew that ancient form of the Church, which, at first sullied and distorted by illiterate men of indifferent character, was afterward flagitiously mangled and almost destroyed by the Roman pontiff and his faction."[96]

Calvin's *Institutes* itself is a testimony to the fact that he believed Scripture should be interpreted according to the *regula fidei* and in light of the early fathers doctrine. The letter to King Francis I that forms the preface to the *Institutes* is written with this very thing in mind. As T.H.L. Parker notes concerning this preface, "The presupposition to Calvin's argument is that . . . the Christian religion was the adherence to the Nicaeno-Constantinopolitan Creed."[97] The entire letter to the King is an apologetic and defense of the thesis that it is the Reformers who are the true heirs of the faith of the fathers and that it is actually Rome which has introduced a novel gospel.

Regarding the Reformers' desire that Scripture be interpreted in and by the Church according to the rule of faith, McGrath notes,

> Although it is often suggested that the reformers had no place for tradition in their theological deliberations, this judgment is clearly incorrect. While the notion of tradition as an extra-scriptural source of revelation is excluded, the classic concept of tradition as a particular way of reading and interpreting scripture is retained. Scripture, tradition and the *kerygma* are regarded as essentially coinherent, and as being transmitted, propagated and safeguarded by the community of faith. There is thus a strongly communal dimension to the magisterial reformers' understanding of the interpretation of scripture, which is to be interpreted and proclaimed within an ecclesiological matrix. It must be stressed that the suggestion that the Reformation represented the triumph of individualism and the total rejection of

---

[96] Olin, op. cit., 62.

[97] T.H.L. Parker, *John Calvin: A Biography*, (Philadelphia: The Westminster Press, 1975), 35.

tradition is a deliberate fiction propagated by the image-makers of the Enlightenment.[98]

What this means is that Calvin, like Luther, held to Tradition I against any who would introduce higher sources of authority than God's own revealed Word.

SUMMARY

Martin Luther and John Calvin did not formulate a novel doctrine of scriptural and ecclesiastical authority. Like the ancient fathers before them, they asserted the Scripture as the sole source of revelation and denied the existence of equally authoritative extra-scriptural revelation. They asserted that Scripture was to be interpreted in and by the Church and that it was to be interpreted according to the ancient apostolic teaching of the Church—the *regula fidei*. Their complaint arose because the Roman church had completely forsaken the apostolic life and doctrine and had also theologically insulated itself against the possibility of ever being corrected by submitting itself to a higher standard of truth. By declaring herself to be infallible, Rome had, in effect, become autonomous—a law unto herself. The classical Reformation doctrine of *sola scriptura* is not a novel doctrine of scriptural authority. Its distinctiveness arises instead from the fact that it is the doctrine of Tradition I as expressed within the historical context of debate with an almost universally apostate and autonomous church.

Until the sixteenth century the ancient doctrine of Tradition I and the newer doctrine of Tradition II were both found within the Western church. Tradition I had been the only position for the first three centuries of the Church and the predominant position for the next thousand years. But when, in the light of

---

[98] Alister McGrath, *The Genesis of Doctrine: A Study in the Foundations of Doctrinal Criticism*, (Oxford: Basil Blackwell, 1990), 130.

ecclesiastical tyranny and apostasy, men such as Luther and Calvin asserted Tradition I (in terms of *sola scriptura*), Rome reacted by defending and later, officially adopting Tradition II. At the same time that these debates were raging, other more radical Reformers adopted a completely new concept of scriptural authority which has shaped much Protestant thinking to this day.

4

The Radical Reformation, the Counter-Reformation, and Post-Reformation Developments

The ancient concept of Scripture, tradition, and ecclesiastical authority advocated by magisterial Reformers such as Martin Luther and John Calvin was not embraced by every segment of Western Christendom. At one end of the spectrum were those Roman Catholics who advocated Tradition II—a two-source theory of tradition that had become commonplace only in the later Middle Ages. But during the early sixteenth century, as Tradition I became more and more identified with the Protestants, Tradition II by default became more and more identified as the position of those loyal to Rome.

At the other end of the spectrum were those who responded to the current Roman Catholic concept of tradition—not by adopting the early Church's concept of tradition—but by rejecting tradition altogether. These Radical Reformers insisted that not only was Scripture the sole infallible authority, but that it was the sole authority altogether. Secondary authorities such as the Church, the *regula fidei,* and the fathers were considered irrelevant at best. All that was necessary, according to these men, was the individual and his Bible. Each individual had the right to interpret the Scripture by himself and for himself.

The magisterial Reformers and their heirs were, therefore, faced with a battle on two fronts—against the Roman exaltation of the Church and against the radicals' exaltation of the individual. This chapter examines the concepts of Scripture and tradition advocated by the radical Reformers, by the Roman Catholics in the counter-Reformation, and by the heirs of the magisterial Reformers.

THE RADICAL REFORMATION

It is difficult to accurately describe the Radical Reformation in only a few introductory sentences.[1] The term itself is rather broad and is often used to describe a variety of men and movements of the sixteenth century whose beliefs varied considerably. The earliest "radical Reformers" were probably the Anabaptist followers of Conrad Grebel in Zurich in the early 1520s.[2] Disappointed with Zwingli's allowance of magisterial influence over the Church, Grebel started a new fellowship in 1525. Their more distinctive beliefs included the rejection of infant baptism and insistence on believer's baptism (thus the name Anabaptists—or "re-baptizers"), rejection of civil oaths, strict pacifism, religious toleration of dissenters, and a doctrine of scriptural authority generally disconnected from ecclesiastical tradition of any kind. In 1527, Michael Sattler consolidated the beliefs of the Swiss Anabaptists in the Schleitheim Articles.

In South Germany, mystical Anabaptists such as Thomas Muntzer advocated revolution while pacifistic mystics such as Hans Denck advocated the transformation of the inward spirit rather than the transformation of the world. Jacob Hutter founded a communion whose distinctive mark was shared community goods. His followers, the Hutterites, have survived until this day. In the Low Countries an apocalyptic form of Anabaptism arose under the leadership of Melchoir Hofmann who believed that God's Kingdom would soon begin, thereby releasing God's

---

[1] For a more thorough history of a broad spectrum of radical reform movements, see George Huntston Williams, *The Radical Reformation*, (Philadelphia: The Westminster Press, 1962).

[2] For a helpful introduction to the Anabaptist movement, see William R. Estep, *The Anabaptist Story*, third edition, (Grand Rapids: Wm. B. Eerdmans, 1996).

vengeance upon the wicked. His views spawned two radically divergent branches of "Melchoirites." The Peace Wing was pacifistic, believing that the righteous would participate in God's vengeance upon the wicked only as witnesses. This branch was later continued by Menno Simons and his followers the Mennonites. The Revolutionaries were the other branch, and under the leadership of Jan Matthys they set up a theocracy in Munster. In their understanding, they themselves were to carry out God's vengeance upon the wicked with the sword. Their rebellion was forcefully put down, and many of the leaders were executed.

Another group identified as part of the Radical Reformation was that referred to as "spiritualists." Men such as Caspar Schenkfeld rejected all external forms, ceremonies, and rites. He believed that neither baptism nor the Lord's Supper had been observed properly since apostolic times and even suggested that the Lord's Supper not be celebrated until the proper observation was once again determined. Sebastian Franck completely rejected the idea of a visible Church with visible ceremonies, insisting that the true Church is invisible and scattered until the Lord returns.

Finally a word must be said about the rationalist wing of the Radical Reformation. There were a number of men at this time who so elevated the role of reason and the right of the individual to interpret Scripture apart from the communion of saints and the ancient rule of faith that they rejected several aspects of traditional orthodox theology. Faustus Socinus, for example, rejected the doctrines of the deity of Christ, the Trinity, the atonement, original sin, predestination, and the resurrection of the body.

It would certainly be an oversimplification to argue that all of these various men and movements shared a common understanding of scriptural authority. It would be grossly unfair, for example, to suggest that either Conrad Grebel or Menno Simons shared the theological views of Socinus or Servetus. Not all of these men were anti-Trinitarians. And not all of these men were apocalyptic revolutionaries. What they did have in common, although to varying degrees, was a radicalization of the principle of *sola scriptura* and a rejection of tradition in any form. As McGrath explains, the magisterial Reformers adopted a positive approach to tradition, particularly the *testimonia patrum,* whereas the radicals adopted a generally negative approach. To most of the radicals, the fathers were an irrelevance: every individual had the unfettered right to interpret scripture in whatever manner seemed right to him or her.[3]

Unlike the magisterial Reformers, who had sought to maintain a continuity with the ancient patristic Church, the radicals believed that they could do theology without reference to what the Church had confessed in the past.[4] They believed that the magisterial Reformers had not gone far enough in their use of the *sola scriptura* principle. According to the radicals, the magisterial Reformers may have done away with many of the scholastic theological accretions, but they wrongly insisted on adhering to the creedal formulations of ancient Christianity.[5]

Building on Oberman's terminology, Alister McGrath refers to the Anabaptist concept of Scripture and tradition as "Tradition 0"—a view which allows no role whatsoever to tradition. This is in contrast to "Tradition I", the position of the magisterial Reformers, a position which allowed for a traditional interpretation of Scripture.[6] He explains the radical view:

> For the radicals (or "fanatics," as Luther dubbed them), such as Thomas Muntzer and Caspar Schwenkfeld, every individual had the right to interpret Scripture as he pleased, subject to the guidance of the Holy Spirit. For the radical Sebastian Franck, the Bible "is a book sealed with seven seals which none can open unless he has the key of David, which is the illumination of the Spirit." The way was thus opened for individualism, with the private judgment of the individual raised above the corporate judgment of the church. Thus the radicals rejected the practice of infant

---

[3] Alister McGrath, *The Genesis of Doctrine: A Study in the Foundations of Doctrinal Criticism,* (Oxford: Basil Blackwell, 1990).

[4] Jaroslav Pelikan, *Obedient Rebels,* (London: SCM Press, Ltd., 1964), 36–38.

[5] Williams, op. cit., 240.

[6] Alister McGrath, *Reformation Thought: An Introduction,* second edition, (Oxford: Basil Blackwell, 1993), 144.

baptism (to which the magisterial Reformation remained committed) as nonscriptural. (There is no explicit reference to the practice in the New Testament). Similarly, doctrines such as the Trinity and the divinity of Christ were rejected as resting on inadequate scriptural foundations. "Tradition 0" placed the private judgment of the individual above the corporate judgment of the Christian church concerning the interpretation of Scripture. It was a recipe for anarchy—and, as the history of the radical Reformation sadly demonstrates, that anarchy was not slow to develop.[7]

One of the reasons for the theological conservatism of the magisterial Reformation was its reverence for the traditional patristic interpretation of Scripture. Their high regard for the fathers was due to their belief that the fathers were developing an explicitly biblical theology—attempting to build their theology upon the foundation of Scripture alone.

> This understanding of the *sola scriptura* principle allowed the [magisterial] reformers to criticize their opponents on both sides—on the one side the radicals, on the other the catholics. The catholics argued that the reformers elevated private judgment above the corporate judgment of the church. The reformers replied that they were doing nothing of the sort: they were simply restoring that corporate judgment to what it once was, by combating the doctrinal degeneration of the Middle Ages by an appeal to the corporate judgment of the patristic era. The radicals, however, had no place whatsoever for the "testimony of the Fathers." As Sebastian Franck wrote in 1530: "Foolish Ambrose, Augustine, Jerome, Gregory—of whom not one even knew the Lord, so help me God, nor was sent by God to teach. Rather, they were all apostles of Antichrist." Tradition 0 had no place for any traditional interpretation of Scripture. The magisterial reformers thus dismissed this radical understanding of the role of Scripture as pure individualism, a recipe for theological chaos.[8]

[7] Ibid., 144–145.
[8] Ibid., 145–146.

In its zeal to overturn all that was wrong with the Church, the Radical Reformation resulted in "a hyper-criticism which supposed that because it could discern the errors of the past, it had been released from the errors of the present and inoculated against the errors of the future."[9]

It is important to realize that there were two very different versions of the *sola scriptura* principle which were advanced during the sixteenth-century Reformation. The first concept, advocated by magisterial Reformers such as Luther and Calvin, insisted that Scripture was the sole source of revelation, the sole infallible authority, but that it was to be interpreted in and by the communion of saints according to the *regula fidei*. Tradition in the sense of the traditional interpretation of Scripture was not discarded. This is the view for which we are using the term "Tradition I." The second concept, advocated by many of the radical Reformers, insisted that Scripture was the sole authority altogether. Not only were medieval "traditions" disregarded, but tradition in the sense of the *regula fidei*, the testimony of the fathers, the traditional interpretation of Scripture, and the corporate judgment of the Church were discarded as well. The interpretation of Scripture, according to this concept, was a strictly individual matter. This is the concept for which we are using the term "Tradition 0." Unless these two positions are carefully and consciously distinguished, the kind of confusion that has prevailed in the debates of the last five hundred years will continue.

THE COUNCIL OF TRENT

The cries for reform within the Church and the increasing pressure of the Protestant movement led Rome to call a council in the mid-sixteenth century. The Council of Trent lasted from 1545–1563 and addressed a wide range of issues and doctrines including the relationship between Scripture and tradition. On April 8, 1546, after much debate, the Council issued its answer to the

---

[9] Pelikan, op. cit., 38.

Protestants. The decree concerning the Canonical Scriptures asserted,

> The holy, ecumenical and general Council of Trent, lawfully as-
> sembled in the Holy Ghost, the same three legates of the Apos-
> tolic See presiding, keeps this constantly in view, namely, that
> the purity of the Gospel may be preserved in the Church after
> the errors have been removed. This [Gospel], of old promised
> through the Prophets in the Holy Scriptures, our Lord Jesus
> Christ, the Son of God, promulgated first with His own mouth,
> and then commanded it to be preached by His Apostles to every
> creature as the source at once of all saving truth and rules of con-
> duct. It also clearly perceives that these truths and rules are con-
> tained *in the written books and in the unwritten traditions,* which,
> received by the Apostles from the mouth of Christ Himself, or
> from the Apostles themselves, the Holy Ghost dictating, have
> come down to us, transmitted as it were from hand to hand. Fol-
> lowing, then, the examples of the orthodox Fathers, it receives
> and venerates with a feeling of piety and reverence all the books
> both of the Old and New Testaments, since one God is the au-
> thor of both; *also the traditions,* whether they relate to faith or to
> morals, as having been dictated either orally by Christ or by the
> Holy Ghost, and preserved in the Catholic Church in unbroken
> succession. [10]

It is important to note that in the official decree, the Council used
the words "written books *and* unwritten traditions." During the
preliminary debates, an earlier draft of the decree was proposed
which stated that revelation came to the Church "partly" (*partim*)
through the Scriptures and "partly" (*partim*) through tradition.
This wording was rejected in favor of the simple conjunction
"and" (*et*). Much has been made of this change by modern Roman
Catholics who have argued that the simple word "and" allows for
a "one-source" view of revelation. [11] While this is certainly true

---

[10] John H. Leith, *Creeds of the Churches,* third edition, (Louisville: John Knox Press,
1982), 401–402. Emphasis mine.

[11] Cf. Joseph R. Geiselmann, "Scripture and Tradition in Catholic Theology," *Theology
Digest,* Vol. 6, 1958, pp. 73–78.

when considered outside of any historical context, the question of the council's intent remains. The contemporary Roman Catholic theologian Richard McBrien concedes that "the Council of Trent did speak of two sources of revelation, one written and the other unwritten."[12] In his massive study of the history of the concept of tradition, the Roman Catholic scholar Yves Congar, points out the almost incontrovertible fact that the Council itself intended to teach a "two-source" view of revelation. He notes that

> Contemporary witnesses . . . show that, although *partim* . . . *partim* . . . as a form of words was dropped, it is the *partim* . . . *partim* . . . theological position that the council wished to canonize. The correspondence of the legates shows that the council wanted to define, against the Reformation, the existence of unwritten apostolic traditions containing, possibly, dogmatic truths.[13]

He continues,

> [It is questionable that] . . . the post-Tridentine theologians, Canisius and Bellarmine in particular, misunderstood the council's intention in interpreting its text in the sense of *partim* . . . *partim* . . . and in admitting the existence of points of *doctrine* held by the Church on the basis of an oral tradition, and not Scripture. Moreover, the council itself appealed to an oral tradition in matters which were very definitely doctrinal. Theologians at the time made exactly the same assessment.[14]

In addition, as a study of the teachings of the Roman Catholic magisterium will reveal, the two-source interpretation was assumed to be the Council's position for almost three hundred

---

[12] Richard P. McBrien, *Catholicism*, Rev. Ed., (San Francisco: Harper Collins Publishers, 1994), 62.

[13] Yves Congar, *Tradition and Traditions: An Historical and a Theological Essay*, (New York: The MacMillan Company, 1967), 167.

[14] Ibid.

years. Until the nineteenth century, the magisterium consistently treats Scripture and tradition as two sources of divine revelation.[15] Pope Pius IX, for example, in the Bull *Ineffabilis* taught that "Scripture and tradition are the *fontes divinae revelationis* ["sources of divine revelation"—plural] and that the Church, the magisterium, is entrusted with the function of guarding and announcing the *dogmas contained in these sources* [plural].[16]

Heiko Oberman also argues that Trent intended to teach the two-source view. In addition to the arguments listed by Congar, Oberman notes the following facts:

> This conclusion [that the change from *partim . . . partim* to *et* was insignificant] is borne out by the statement of the cardinal legate Cervini who announces on 6th April 1546 after a night spent on the revision of the original draft that the final version is "in substance" the same. This would hardly seem compatible with the idea that the Council changed its mind.
>
> The energetic protest against the "partly-partly" formulation which. . . [is cited] as the cause for the alleged change proves to be limited to two representatives, Bonacci and Nacchianti, of which the first stands under suspicion of heresy on points related to Scripture and tradition and the second was once called "avid for novelties."
>
> The *Catechismus Romanus* (1566) quite clearly interprets "and" (*et*) as "partly-partly" (*partim-partim*) when it states that the Word of God is *distributed* over Scripture and tradition.[17]

Although vehemently denied by some Roman Catholics, the historical evidence indicates that the Council of Trent dogmatized Tradition II. As Oberman notes,

> In short, the Council of Trent clearly admits that not all doctrinal truths are to be found in Holy Scripture. Tradition is seen as a second doctrinal source which does not "simply" unfold the

[15] Ibid., 165–166.
[16] Ibid., 206.
[17] Oberman, *The Dawn of the Reformation*, (Edinburgh: T&T Clark, Ltd., 1986), 288.

contents of Scripture, as in Tradition I but adding its own substance complements Holy Scripture contentwise.[18]

Congar argues that although Trent obviously intended to teach a
two-source doctrine of Scripture and tradition, one may continue to hold the one-source view.[19] This requires, however,
completely ignoring the intent of the Council. Congar provides
an interesting explanation of how a faithful Roman Catholic may
hold to a one-source concept of tradition even though a council,
accepted as ecumenical and authoritative by Rome itself, intended to dogmatize a two-source theory.

> From the *theological* point of view, we must take the text of the
> Council of Trent as it stands. Nevertheless, the fact that the ex-
> pression *partim . . . partim* was removed has some meaning for us
> in the efforts we are making to understand better the relation be-
> tween Scripture and tradition. Why not a prophetic meaning go-
> ing beyond what the Fathers themselves could have had in mind?
> The completely human historicity of councils does not prevent a
> transcendent Moderator from realizing his intentions in them;
> rather does he use it as his *unconscious instrument* [emphasis mine].
> It may well be that the Fathers at Trent did not, after all, formu-
> late exactly what they *personally* had in mind. Did they not limit
> their decree to *apostolic* traditions (though without using the
> word), when many of them read a wider application into the ex-
> pression *traditiones?* It is undoubtedly true that a text of the mag-
> isterium ought to be interpreted according to the intentions of
> its author or authors, but it is also true that we are bound by the
> divine intention of the Holy Spirit, and not the human intention
> of men. The latter can in fact be transcended by the former,
> whose instrument it is and which, on the whole, it expresses.[20]

This type of argument is often used by modern Roman Catholic
apologists wishing to explain the differences between current

[18] Ibid.
[19] Congar, op. cit., 166.
[20] Ibid., 168–169.

Roman Catholic dogma and earlier Roman Catholic dogma, but it is a seriously flawed argument. Even if, for the sake of argument, we were to grant that the Council of Trent was supernaturally overseen by the Holy Spirit and that its decrees were in some sense His words, how else would we be able to discern *His* meaning than through the words of the men He used instrumentally to communicate that meaning? If it is possible that the meaning the Holy Spirit intends to communicate to the Church may be revealed, not only apart from the conscious understanding of the men involved but also in direct opposition to their own intention, then the interpretation of the Holy Spirit's meaning in any document is rendered impossible. If this is how the Holy Spirit works, then it could be argued that the Council of Trent actually allows for the Lutheran position on justification or the Anabaptist position on baptism. One could argue that the Lutheran doctrine or the Anabaptist doctrine was that which the Holy Spirit intended to communicate—albeit apart from the consciousness of the council fathers and against their own personal intentions. Obviously such is not the case, but if applied consistently, this dangerous argument used to justify modern Roman changes to earlier Roman dogmas relativizes everything God has ever communicated to man through the medium of human language.

POST-REFORMATION DEVELOPMENTS

ROMAN CATHOLIC DEVELOPMENTS

Much has happened in the Roman Catholic church since the Council of Trent officially elevated Tradition II to the status of dogma. Of special importance for our study is the gradual development of an even newer concept of tradition within the church. After Trent the two-source view was preserved for several centuries through the influence of the Roman Catechism and the influence of Peter Canisius and Robert Bellermine.[21] Heiko

---

[21] Oberman, op. cit., 289.

Oberman summarizes the developments in the Roman church since the nineteenth century.

> The two notions of living development and binding authority of the teaching office of the Church to which Cardinal Newman and systematic theologian Jos. Scheeben (d. 1888) contributed in the same century, together with the declaration of the dogmas (1854) of the immaculate conception of the Virgin Mary, of (1870) the definition of papal infallibility and of (1950) the pronouncement of the bodily assumption of the immaculate Virgin, have led in our time to a reconsideration of the relation of the *Magisterium* as active tradition to the so-called sources of Revelation as the objective tradition. Notwithstanding appearances the debate on the relation of Scripture and extra-biblical tradition has lost some of its former urgency. A Tradition III concept is in the process of being developed by those who tend to find in the teaching office of the Church the one and only source for revelation. Scripture and tradition are then not much more than historical monuments of the past.[22]

What this means is that Rome is moving towards a one-source concept of tradition, but that source is different than the one-source confessed by the apostolic Church. Rather than Scripture (and/or tradition), that single source of revelation is the present Roman Magisterium. As Oberman notes,

> *Humanii generis* declared in 1950 that it is the task of theology to show in what way a doctrine defined by the Church is contained in the sources of faith: Scripture and tradition. The task of the doctor, be he biblical scholar or Church historian, is to read the latest doctrinal decisions back into his sources. From the vantage point of medieval history, we may say that what first was the vital teaching office of the Doctor of Scripture, standing together with the Bishop as the custodian of the deposit of faith, has now been transformed into the office of the Apologete of the Teaching Office of the Church; the Doctor has become the *ancilla papae!*[23]

---

[22] Ibid., 289–290.
[23] Ibid., 292–293.

In practice this means that whatever the Roman church teaches now *is* tradition by definition. Theology is the task of demonstrating the scriptural and apostolic nature of a particular current doctrine after the fact. This is admitted by Roman Catholic theologians and historians. The Roman Catholic theologian Walter Burghardt explains the current Roman position on tradition in relation to the doctrine of the Assumption of Mary:

> A valid argument for a dogmatic tradition, for the Church's teaching in the past can be constructed from her teaching in the present. And that is actually the approach theology took to the definability of the assumption before 1st November 1950. It began with a fact: the current consensus, in the Church teaching and in the Church taught, that the Corporeal Assumption was revealed by God. If that is true, if that is the teaching of the magisterium of the moment, if that *is* the Church's tradition, then it was always part and parcel of the Church's teaching, part and parcel of tradition.[24]

It goes without saying that this view of tradition is a virtual declaration of autonomy on the part of the Roman church, and when it is combined with the doctrine of papal infallibility, it amounts to a Church for whom Scripture and tradition are essentially irrelevant. If whatever the Church teaches now is by definition the unadulterated apostolic faith, then finding support in Scripture or the fathers is really superfluous. With Tradition III Rome has, in effect, freed herself not only from Scripture but also from the burden of her own past authoritative doctrinal decisions.[25]

---

[24] Cited in Oberman, op. cit., 295.

[25] A perfect example of this may be seen in the dogmatic change that has taken place on the issue of salvation outside the Roman Catholic church. The papal bulls *Unam Sanctam* (1302) and *Cantate Domine* (1441) expressly state that there is absolutely no possibility of salvation for any man outside of visible union with the Roman Catholic church and subjection to the bishop of Rome. The decrees of Vatican II (1962–65), however, expressly allow for the possibility of salvation, not only for non-Roman Catholic Christians, but also for Jews, Muslims, pagans and even those without an "explicit knowledge of God." The issue is not which if either of these two positions is true. The issue is the fact that they cannot both be true, and the fact that the second cannot be seriously considered a "development" of the first. The bulls decree that "it is altogether necessary to salvation

PROTESTANT ORTHODOXY

In the years immediately following the Reformation, a number of Protestant theologians began the work of systematizing Reformation theology. Protestant orthodoxy closely followed the lead of the magisterial Reformers on the doctrine of Scripture.[26] Richard Muller observes that the "authority of Scripture *quoad nos* ["as far as us" i.e., "in respect of us"] is the central issue of the orthodox Protestant doctrine of Scripture."[27] The issue was "the authority of Scripture considered as a property of the written Word according to which the Word has a canonical, normative, or regulatory function in all debates concerning Christian doctrine."[28]

One of the first Protestants to comprehensively work through this issue and define the doctrine of Scripture was the Lutheran Matthias Flacius Illyricus. In 1567, he published the influential work *Clavis scripturae sacrae* in which he explains the relationship between the authority of Scripture and the authority of creeds. He writes, "Every understanding and exposition of Scripture is to be in agreement with the faith. . . . For everything that is said concerning Scripture or on the basis of Scripture must be in agreement with all that the catechism declares or that is taught by the articles of faith."[29] Muller explains, "Flacius . . . understands Scripture as the *norma normans theologiae* and the creeds and confessional writings of the church as *norma normata*: the creeds and confessions express the contents and general theological sense of Scripture and, this being the case, any interpretation that differs from that offered in the creeds and confessions must be a denial of

---

for every human creature to be subject to the Roman Pontiff" (*Unam Sanctam*). Vatican II decrees that it is *not* altogether necessary to salvation for every human creature to be subject to the Roman Pontiff; in fact it is not even necessary for salvation that a person be Christian. The two doctrines are in direct and complete contradiction with each other, and no amount of explanation can hide that plain fact.

[26] The most exhaustive study of the Post-Reformation Protestant doctrine of Scripture is Richard Muller, *Post Reformation Reformed Dogmatics*, Vol. 2, (Grand Rapids: Baker Book House, 1993).

[27] Ibid., 357.

[28] Ibid.

[29] Cited in Muller, op. cit., 100.

the true sense of Scripture."[30] In other words, Scripture must be interpreted according to a rule of faith, and that rule of faith is the apostolic faith.

This espousal of Tradition I was also expressed by Zwingli's successor, Heinrich Bullinger, in his *Decades* and in the *Confessio Helvetica Posterior* or Second Helvetic Confession, which he authored. Bullinger was very concerned with the role of tradition in his works. Muller notes that in all of his systematic works,

> Bullinger was intent upon demonstrating in both principle and specific doctrinal argument the continuity of the Reformation with the tradition of patristic interpretation and theology and, therefore, the catholicity of the Reformation. To that end he prefaced his *Decades* with an essay on the four general councils of the ancient church and with full quotations of their credal formulations and the rules of faith of several church fathers. Similarly the *Confessio* is prefaced by a quotation from the Imperial edict of A.D. 380—the code of Justinian—which defines orthodoxy and heresy in terms of adherence to and departure from the apostolic faith and the Nicene symbol.[31]

This is extremely significant, especially when we recall that the Second Helvetic Confession is "the most universal of Reformed creeds."[32] Charles Hodge writes, "The Second Helvetic Confession is, on some accounts, to be regarded as the most authoritative symbol of the Reformed Church, as it was more generally received than any other, and was sanctioned by different parties."[33] The fact that it was widely accepted across Europe during the sixteenth century demonstrates that the magisterial Reformation—Reformed Catholicism—did not involve a rejection of Tradition I. Instead it recaptured the early Church's position on

---

[30] Ibid. *Norma normata* means a "standardized norm." *Norma normans* means "the standardizing norm." The first is applied to confessions. The second is applied only to Scripture, which stands behind the confessions.

[31] Ibid., 61.

[32] Leith, op. cit., 131.

[33] Charles Hodge, *Systematic Theology*, (Grand Rapids: Wm. B. Eerdmans Publishing Co., 1989), 3:634.

Scripture and tradition. Muller summarizes the Protestant orthodox systematization of the doctrine of Scripture.

> The Reformation itself was rooted in the question of authority,
> which it answered with the language of *sola Scriptura* and of the
> priority of Scripture as the ultimate norm of doctrine over all
> other grounds of authority. The Protestant orthodox doctrine of
> Scripture is a codification of this answer—and the focus of the
> entire doctrinal exposition is clearly the character of Scripture as
> rule or norm and the way in which Scripture ought to be consid-
> ered as prior to the church and its traditions. This issue, in other
> words, is the underlying reason for the form taken by the Prot-
> estant doctrine of Scripture in its development from the Refor-
> mation through the era of orthodoxy.[34]

THE WESTMINSTER CONFESSION OF FAITH

In the middle of the seventeenth century another highly influential Reformed confession of faith was written in England. The
Westminster Assembly was convoked by the English Parliament
in 1643 for the purpose of restructuring the Anglican church.
The Assembly produced several documents, but the most
influential was the Westminster Confession of Faith, which was
completed in 1646. The entire first chapter of the Westminster
Confession is devoted to the doctrine of Scripture. Paragraph one
explains the necessity of Scripture. Paragraph two lists all of the
books of the Old and New Testaments while paragraph three
states the Reformed understanding of the Apocrypha. The fourth
and fifth paragraphs, in a manner reminiscent of Calvin, explain
that the authority of Scripture depends upon God and not upon
the testimony of men. In the sixth paragraph, the Assembly sets
forth its understanding of the sufficiency of Scripture:

> The whole counsel of God, concerning all things necessary for
> his own glory, man's salvation, faith, and life, is either expressly
> set down in Scripture, or by good and necessary consequence

---

[34] Muller, op. cit., 358.

may be deduced from Scripture: unto which nothing at any time is to be added, whether by new revelations of the Spirit, or traditions of men (WCF, 1:6).

In other words, Scripture is the sole source of revelation and it is sufficient. This sufficiency is a logical corollary of the necessity of Scripture. Scripture was given by God for a purpose—the complete revelation of His will. And unless we are willing to ascribe incompetence to God, it is unreasonable to suppose that Scripture is insufficient to accomplish that for which God intended it.

The seventh paragraph briefly describes the perspicuity of Scripture, explaining that the primary message of Scripture is clear enough for all to comprehend. Paragraph eight claims that the original scriptural documents in Hebrew and Greek were immediately inspired by God and are therefore the authoritative standard. However, because not all know the original languages, they are to be translated into the native languages of all men. The ninth paragraph speaks briefly of the interpretation of Scripture:

> The infallible rule of Scripture is the Scripture itself; and therefore, when there is a question about the true and full sense of any Scripture (which is not manifold, but one), it must be searched and known by other places that speak more clearly (WCF, 1:9).

Finally, in paragraph ten, the Confession states the Assembly's doctrine of the unique authority of Scripture:

> The Supreme Judge, by which all *controversies of religion are to be determined,* and all decrees of councils, opinions of ancient writers, doctrines of men, and private spirits, are to be examined, and in whose sentence we are to rest, can be no other but the Holy Spirit speaking in Scripture (WCF, 1:10—emphasis mine).

What the Assembly is here confessing is something that should be self-evident to any believing Christian. The Holy Spirit, God Himself, is the Supreme Judge. Since the voice of Almighty God —the Word of God—is the ultimate authority, and since Holy Scripture is the inspired (*theopneustos*) Word of God, Holy

Scripture is our ultimate authority. No word of any man or group of men can stand on the same level of authority as the Word of the Living God.

In order to guard this statement of the doctrine of Scripture against the possibility of an anabaptistic type of individualistic interpretation, the Assembly went on to explain how the Scripture is to be used in the judgment of controversies:

> It belongeth to synods and councils, ministerially, *to determine controversies of faith,* and cases of conscience; to set down rules and directions for the better ordering of the public worship of God, and government of his Church; to receive complaints in cases of maladministration, and authoritatively to determine the same: which decrees are to be received with reverence and submission, not only for their agreement with the Word, but also for the power whereby they are made, as being an ordinance of God, appointed thereunto in his Word (WCF, xxxi, 2—emphasis mine).

We see then that according to the Westminster Divines the Holy Spirit speaking in Scripture is the Supreme Judge "by which all controversies of religion are to be determined," *and* that "It belongeth to synods and councils, ministerially, to determine controversies of faith." In other words, the authority of Scripture is the final authority which inherently resides in the Word of the Living God, but that authority must be applied *ministerially* by the Church. The Scripture must be read and interpreted by the Church in order to judge anything, and in cases of doctrinal controversy that ministerial authority belongs to the synods and councils of the Church. The sole infallible authority of Scripture and the interpretive ministerial authority of the Church must be distinguished, but they cannot be separated.

THE ENLIGHTENMENT

The centuries following the Reformation witnessed numerous philosophical developments. The seventeenth century witnessed the rise of philosophical rationalism in the works of men such as

Rene Descartes (1596–1650), Benedict de Spinoza (1632–1677), and G.W. Leibniz (1646–1716).[35] The rationalist philosophers differed among themselves on a number of details, but the one belief they shared in common was that the universe was rational and that man could grasp it through the use of his reason. In Great Britain, during the late seventeenth and early eighteenth century, a philosophy known as empiricism was advocated by philosophers such as John Locke (1632–1704), George Berkeley (1685–1753), and David Hume (1711–1776). Colin Brown observes,

> In contrast with the rationalists who tried to erect philosophical systems by means of reasoning on the basis of self-evident truths, the empiricists stressed the part played by experience in knowledge. They argued that we have no ideas at all other than those derived from experience which comes to us via our senses. Statements (apart from those of pure logic) can be known to be true or false only by testing them in experience.[36]

The eighteenth century has often been described as the Age of Enlightenment. In 1784, Immanuel Kant (1724–1804) wrote an article answering the question "What is Enlightenment?" He wrote the following as an answer,

> Enlightenment is man's release from his self-incurred tutelage. Tutelage is man's inability to make use of his understanding without direction from another. Self-incurred is the tutelage when its cause lies not in lack of reason but in lack of resolution and courage to use it without direction from another. *Sapere aude!* "Have courage to use your own reason!" That is the motto of enlightenment.[37]

---

[35] For a good summary of the thought of the rationalist philosophers, see Colin Brown, *Philosophy and the Christian Faith*, (Downers Grove: InterVarsity Press, 1968), 48–58.

[36] Brown, op. cit., 60–61.

[37] Cited in Colin Brown, *Christianity & Western Thought*, Vol. I, *From the Ancient World to the Age of Enlightenment*, (Downers Grove: InterVarsity Press, 1990), 285–286.

Reason, for the Enlightenment philosophers, was not to be hampered in any way by outside authorities or any traditions of the past.

> The motto of enlightenment was: dare to use your own understanding. This applies especially to religion. No generation should be bound by the creeds and dogmas of bygone generations.[38]

This rejection of the past and exaltation of the abilities of the individual originated in the skeptical, rationalist thought of Descartes, and it became the fundamental tenet of Enlightenment thought across the European continent. In an important work on the Enlightenment, James Byrne notes, "That this activity of doubting and the search for a clear and distinct foundation for knowledge is carried on by the lone individual, independent of all authority or coercion, is one of the most innovative things in Descartes' thought; it influenced not only the major philosophers after Descartes but also the popular assumption in the West that each of us must search out and determine the truth for ourselves."[39] As we will see, this Enlightenment view also had a major impact upon Christianity and especially upon much of modern evangelicalism's notion of scriptural authority.

AMERICAN CHRISTIANITY

The birth of the United States of America occurred in the middle of the Age of Enlightenment, and the founding fathers of this new nation were sons of the Enlightenment. Many of the idiosyncrasies of modern American evangelicalism can be traced back to the currents of thought popular at this time. In a definitive work on the subject Nathan Hatch has described the effects of the War of Independence upon the American population:

[38] Brown, *Philosophy and the Christian Faith*, 91.
[39] James M. Byrne, *Religion and the Enlightenment: From Descartes to Kant*, (Louisville: Westminster John Knox Press, 1997), 57.

Above all, the [American] Revolution dramatically expanded the circle of people who considered themselves capable of thinking for themselves about issues of freedom, equality, sovereignty, and representation. Respect for authority, tradition, station, and education eroded.[40]

He continues by describing the effects of this democratic spirit upon American Christianity: "In a culture that increasingly balked at vested interests, symbols of hierarchy, and timeless authorities, a remarkable number of people awoke one morning to find it self-evident that the priesthood of all believers meant just that—religion of, by, and for the people."[41] This new Americanized popular religion of the people soon gave birth to a number of distinctly American Christian groups. One of these was called the Christian Movement. Hatch describes their religious innovations:

> Taking seriously the mandate of liberty and equality, the Christians [The Christian Movement] espoused reform in three areas. First, they called for a revolution within the church to place laity and clergy on an equal footing and to exalt the conscience of the individual over the collective will of any congregation or church organization. Second, they rejected the traditions of learned theology altogether and called for a new view of history that welcomed inquiry and innovation. Finally, they called for a populist hermeneutic premised on the inalienable right of every person to understand the New Testament for him or herself.[42]

He continues,

> The Christians also illustrate the exaltation of public opinion as a primary religious authority. They called for common folk to read the New Testament as if mortal man had never seen it

---

[40] Nathan O. Hatch, *The Democratization of American Christianity*, (New Haven: Yale University Press, 1989), 6.

[41] Ibid., 69.

[42] Ibid., 71–73.

before. People were expected to discover the self-evident message of the Bible without any mediation from creeds, theologians, or clergymen not of their own choosing. This explicit faith that biblical authority could emerge from below, from the will of the people, was the most enduring legacy of the Christian movement.[43]

We see then that this peculiar combination of Enlightenment rationalism and democratic populism gave birth to a radically new understanding of scriptural authority in the minds of many Americans. Unlike the Reformers, who claimed that Scripture was the only infallible authority but who did not separate scriptural authority from legitimate ecclesiastical authority, these men and women claimed that Scripture was the only authority at all. We read this again and again in the claims of those who were rejecting some or all of orthodox Christianity.[44]

In religious faith we have but one Father and one Master, and the Bible, *the Bible,* is our only acknowledged creed book—(A.B. Grosh, Universalist minister).

I have endeavored to read the scriptures as though no one had read them before me, and I am as much on my guard against reading them to-day, through the medium of my own views yesterday, or a week ago, as I am against being influenced by any foreign name, authority, or system whatever—(Alexander Campbell, founder of the Disciples of Christ).

Why may I not go to the Bible to learn the doctrines of Christianity as well as the Assembly of Divines?—(Jeremy Belknap, Liberal Boston clergyman).

Lay aside all attachment to human systems, all partiality to names, councils and churches, and honestly inquire, "what saith the scriptures"—(Simeon Howard, Liberal clergyman).

The whole is written from the scripture account of the thing and not from any human scheme—(Charles Chauncy, on his published defense of universalism).

[43] Ibid., 81.
[44] All the following cited in Hatch, op. cit., 179–182.

The Unitarian Noah Worchester argued that Christians would reject the doctrine of the Trinity if they would simply study the Scriptures apart from the creeds of the Church. In the same vein the Liberal Charles Beecher denounced "creed-power" and called for "the Bible, the whole Bible, and nothing but the Bible."[45] This phenomenon caused the Reformed Princeton theologian Samuel Miller to remark in 1839 "that the most zealous opposers [of creeds] have generally been latitudinarians and heretics."[46]

Essentially what we see in eighteenth-century America is the wholesale adoption of an extreme version of Tradition 0. The doctrine of Scripture and tradition espoused by the Reformers (Tradition I) was completely rejected in favor of a radically individualized doctrine of scriptural authority. These men and women retained the Reformation slogan *sola scriptura*, but their doctrine was far removed from the doctrine of Martin Luther and John Calvin. Unfortunately, it is this eighteenth-century populist doctrine of Scripture which is often confused with the Reformation doctrine of *sola scriptura*. The simple fact of the matter is that the doctrine commonly held today has much more in common with Enlightenment rationalism than with Reformation theology.

Not all American Christians adopted Tradition 0. Some, such as the great nineteenth-century Reformed theologian Charles Hodge (1797–1878), followed the magisterial Reformers in maintaining *sola scriptura* in terms of Tradition I. Hodge taught biblical literature at Princeton Seminary from 1822 to 1840 and theology from 1840 to 1878. Having educated thousands of future ministers in over fifty years of teaching, he was easily the most influential Reformed theologian in America in the nineteenth century. Hodge's doctrinal views are set forth in his three-volume *Systematic Theology*. That he advocated the Tradition I position may be demonstrated by an examination of the relevant portions of this work.

---

[45] Cited in Hatch, op. cit., 182.

[46] Samuel Miller, *The Utility and Importance of Creeds and Confessions*, (Greenville: A Press, 1991), 15.

In a discussion of the Protestant rule of faith, Hodge explains that "the word of God, as contained in the Scriptures of the Old and New Testaments, is the only infallible rule of faith and practice."[47] Because Scripture alone is the infallible and inspired Word of the living God, only the Scriptures can inherently bind the consciences of men.[48] And because it does not contradict itself, Scripture must interpret Scripture.[49] He explains what this oft-caricatured doctrine means,

> If a passage admits of different interpretations, that only can be the true one which agrees with what the Bible teaches elsewhere on the same subject. If the Scriptures teach that the Son is the same in substance and equal in power and glory with the Father, then when the Son says, "The Father is greater than I," the superiority must be understood in a manner consistent with this equality. . . . This rule of interpretation is sometimes called the analogy of Scripture, and sometimes the analogy of faith.[50]

In his explanation of the perspicuity of Scripture, Hodge hints at his concept of tradition. He writes,

> If the Scriptures be a plain book, and the Spirit performs the functions of a teacher to all the children of God, it follows inevitably that they must agree in all essential matters in their interpretation of the Bible. And from that fact it follows that for an individual Christian to dissent from the faith of the universal Church (i.e., the body of true believers), is tantamount to dissenting from the Scriptures themselves.[51]

This teaching will appear strange to those who identify the Tradition 0 position with the Reformation doctrine of *sola scriptura*, but Hodge explains the meaning of this in his discussion of the role of tradition in the Church:

[47] Hodge, op. cit., 1:151.
[48] Ibid., 1:183.
[49] Ibid., 1:187.
[50] Ibid.
[51] Ibid., 1:184.

Protestants admit that as there has been an uninterrupted tradition of truth from the protevangelium to the close of the Apocalypse, so there has been a stream of traditionary teaching flowing through the Christian Church from the day of Pentecost to the present time. *This tradition is so far a rule of faith that nothing contrary to it can be true.* Christians do not stand isolated, each holding his own creed. They constitute one body, having one common creed. Rejecting that creed, or any of its parts, is the rejection of the fellowship of Christians, incompatible with the communion of saints, or membership in the body of Christ. In other words, Protestants admit that *there is a common faith of the Church, which no man is at liberty to reject, and which no man can reject and be a Christian.* They acknowledge the authority of this common faith for two reasons. First, because what all the competent readers of a plain book take to be its meaning, must be its meaning. Secondly, because the Holy Spirit is promised to guide the people of God into the knowledge of the truth, and therefore that which they, under the teaching of the Spirit, agree in believing must be true. There are certain fixed doctrines among Christians, as there are among Jews and Mohammedans, which are no longer open questions. The doctrines of the Trinity; of the divinity and incarnation of the eternal Son of God; of the personality and divinity of the Holy Spirit; of the apostasy and sinfulness of the human race; the doctrines of the expiation of sin through the death of Christ and of salvation through his merits; of regeneration and sanctification by the Holy Ghost; of the forgiveness of sins, the resurrection of the body, and of the life everlasting, have always entered into the faith of every recognized historical church on the face of the earth, and cannot now be legitimately called into question by any pretending to be Christians.[52]

In other words, although Scripture is the sole infallible authority, it *must* be interpreted by the Church within the boundaries of the ancient rule of faith or *regula fidei*. According to the teaching of the early Church and of the magisterial Reformation, a rejection of this rule of faith as a hermeneutical boundary is a rejection of the perspicuity of Scripture; a rejection of the promise of Christ

[52] Ibid., 1:113–114. Emphasis mine.

that the Holy Spirit would teach the Church; and a rejection of the Christian faith.

Hodge explains what he means by common consent. "When Protestants speak of common consent of Christians, they understand by Christians the true people of God."[53] He adds, "The common consent for which Protestants plead concerns only essential doctrines; that is, doctrines which enter into the very nature of Christianity as a religion."[54] He also explains how the authority of this "common faith" is consistent with the sole infallible authority of Scripture.

> A still more important difference is, that the common faith of the Church for which Protestants contend, is faith in doctrines plainly revealed in Scripture. It does not extend beyond these doctrines. It owes its whole authority to the fact that it is a common understanding of the written word, attained and preserved under that teaching of the Spirit, which secures to believers a competent knowledge of the plan of salvation therein revealed.[55]

And finally, he adds,

> Protestants do not regard "common consent" either as an informant or as a ground of faith. With them the written word is the only source of knowledge of what God has revealed for our salvation, and his testimony therein is the only ground of our faith. Whereas, with Romanists, tradition is not only an informant of what is to be believed, but the witness on whose testimony faith is to be yielded. It is one thing to say that the fact that all the true people of God, under the guidance of the Spirit, believe that certain doctrines are taught in Scripture, is an unanswerable argument that they are really taught therein, and quite another thing to say that because an external society, composed of all sorts of men, to whom no promise of divine guidance has been given,

53 Ibid., 1:115.
54 Ibid.
55 Ibid., 1:116.

agree in holding certain doctrines, therefore we are bound to receive those doctrines as part of the revelation of God.[56]

What Hodge is pointing out here is an important distinction between Tradition I and Tradition II (and Tradition III). The Patristic and Reformation argument for the rule of faith as a necessary hermeneutical boundary is not the same thing as the Roman Catholic argument for a second source of revelation and an infallible teaching magisterium.

In our own day the confusion over the definition of *sola scriptura* is astounding. The majority of evangelicalism has adopted Tradition 0 and convinced itself that this was the doctrine of the Reformers. The ideas of the rule of faith as a hermeneutical boundary or of the Church as a subordinate ministerial authority are virtually anathema in modern individualist evangelicalism. There are, however, some Protestants in our own day who have maintained the Reformation balance.[57] Michael Horton, for example, reminds evangelicals that, "Although the Reformation sought to purge the church of medieval superstitions and additions to apostolic Christianity, the Reformers staunchly defended the Nicene and Apostles' Creeds as *necessary* for a genuine Christian profession."[58] Elsewhere he writes,

> We have creeds, confessions, and catechisms not because we want to arrogantly assert ourselves above Scripture or other Christians, but for precisely the opposite reason: we are

---

[56] Ibid.

[57] In addition to the previously cited works of Alister McGrath, Heiko Oberman, and Richard Muller, see Douglas Jones, "*Sola*, Solo, or *Prima Scriptura?*" Audio tape, (Moscow, ID: Canon Press, 1997); Kenneth L. Gentry, "In Defense of Creedalism," *Penpoint*, Vol. 9, No. 4, Dec. 1998; Andrew Sandlin, "*Sola Scriptura* and Christian Orthodoxy," in *Keeping Our Sacred Trust: Biblical Authority, Creedal Orthodoxy, and Heresy*, Chalcedon Symposium Series, No. 1, (Vallecito, CA: Chalcedon Foundation, 1999), 161–167; Charles P. Arand, "The Church's Dogma and Biblical Theology," in Michael S. Horton, ed., *A Confessing Theology for Postmodern Times* (Wheaton: Crossway Books, 2000), 15-27.

[58] Michael Horton, *We Believe: Recovering the Essentials of the Apostles' Creed*, (Nashville: Word Publishing, 1998), 8. Emphasis mine.

convinced that such self-assertion is actually easiest for us when we presume to be going to Scripture alone and directly, without any presuppositions or expectations. With Isaiah, I must confess, "I am a man of unclean lips and I dwell among a people of unclean lips." As if my own ignorance and folly were not enough, I belong by divine providence to one of the most superficial, banal, and ungodly generations in history and am bound to be negatively shaped by my context in ways that are different from other saints in other times and places. Fearful of our own weaknesses in judgment and blind spots due to our own acculturation, we go to Scripture with the wider church, with those who have confessed the same faith for centuries.[59]

He adds the following explanation:

Nobody goes to the Bible alone, but carries with him or her a host of influences. It is infinitely easier to distort the Word of God when we cut ourselves off from the consensus of other Christians across time and place.[60]

In other words, the fact that Scripture alone is our infallible authority does not mean that we can interpret Scripture alone. The *sola scriptura* of Luther and Calvin is not the Reformation doctrine unless it is understood within the context of Tradition I. Scripture is the sole infallible authority and the sole source of revelation, but it must be interpreted in and by the Church within the hermeneutical boundaries of the rule of faith (Christian orthodoxy—as defined for example in the Nicene Creed). A doctrine of scriptural authority separated from its apostolic ecclesiastical and hermeneutical context is neither Reformational nor Christian.

---

[59] Michael Horton, "The *Sola's* of the Reformation," in *Here We Stand*, edited by James M. Boice and Benjamin Sasse, (Grand Rapids: Baker Book House, 1996), 107.
[60] Ibid.

SUMMARY

This brief historical survey has shown that for the first three centuries of the Church a general consensus existed on the subject of Scripture and tradition. The New Testament was the "inscripturisation" of the apostolic proclamation, and it together with the Old Testament was the sole source of revelation and the only doctrinal norm. The Scriptures were to be interpreted in and by the Church within the hermeneutical context of the *regula fidei*. Following Oberman, this has been referred to as Tradition I. In the fourth century the first hints of a two-source concept of tradition—Tradition II—are found in the writings of fathers such as Basil and Augustine. While it is questionable that either of them actually endorsed a two-source position, the language they used would later be interpreted as supporting such a position.

The consensus of the early Church continued throughout most of the Middle Ages with most theologians holding to Tradition I. In the twelfth century the first movements toward a real Tradition II position began. But it is in the early fourteenth century that we reach a turning point in the writings of William of Ockham. He is the first to clearly and explicitly teach a two-source concept of tradition. From this point onward there is a parallel development of these two concepts—Tradition I and Tradition II.

In the sixteenth-century Reformation, Martin Luther and John Calvin used Tradition I to battle the results of Tradition II within the Roman Catholic church. Their emphasis on Scripture as the sole source of revelation and as the sole infallible authority led them to argue for Tradition I using the slogan *sola scriptura*. It must be remembered, however, that they continued to teach that this authoritative Scripture must be interpreted in and by the Church within the hermeneutical context of the rule of faith. Because Tradition I was becoming identified with the Protestant position, Rome reacted by dogmatizing Tradition II at the Council of Trent. In recent centuries Rome's position has begun to develop into a Tradition III view in which the real source of revelation is neither Scripture nor tradition but instead is the living magisterium. Whatever Rome says today is the apostolic faith. Scripture and tradition are then interpreted by Rome to support whatever Rome teaches.

Many of the Radical Reformers of the sixteenth century not only rejected Tradition II but also Tradition I. They advocated Scripture not merely as the only infallible authority, but as the only authority altogether. The true authority of the rule of faith and of the Church was completely rejected by the radicals. According to this Tradition 0 position, there is no sense in which tradition of any kind has any true authority. The individual believer needs only the Holy Spirit and the Scripture.

In eighteenth-century America, this anabaptistic individualism combined with Enlightenment rationalism and democratic populism to create a radical version of Tradition 0, which has prevailed to this day. This doctrine has become the standard evangelical position on scriptural authority. Recognizing the many errors inherent in this doctrine, many evangelicals who wrongly believe it to be *the* Reformation doctrine of *sola scriptura* have left evangelical Protestantism for Roman Catholicism or Eastern Orthodoxy. Many others, including both liberals and professing evangelicals, have used this novel populist doctrine of Scripture to attack the rightful authority of the true Church and of the rule of faith as found summarized in the ecumenical creeds. From the Unitarian attack on the Christian doctrine of the Trinity to the hyper-preterist attack on the Christian doctrine of the resurrection of the body and the future return of Christ, no essential doctrine of Christianity has escaped fundamental revision or outright rejection by those who have rejected the hermeneutical boundaries of apostolic Christianity in favor of the self-proclaimed authority of their own individual minds.

Those who desire to maintain Tradition I (expressed by the Reformers in terms of *sola scriptura*) must fight a simultaneous battle for this precious truth on two fronts. On one front, we must continue to reject any two-source theory of tradition such as that dogmatized by Rome at the Council of Trent. Neither the older Roman doctrine of Tradition II nor the more recent Roman doctrine of Tradition III has any real scriptural or patristic support. On the other hand, we must also adamantly reject the modern evangelical doctrine of Tradition 0. Anarchy is not the cure for tyranny. The autonomy of the individual is equally as dangerous as the autonomy of the pope or of the Church. We must point out to both the advocates of Tradition 0 and to Roman Catholic and Eastern Orthodox opponents of the Reformation that Tradition 0 is *not* the Reformation doctrine. Those who advocate Tradition 0 under the banner of Martin Luther, John Calvin and the slogan *sola scriptura* do so either out of ignorance or dishonesty. Those who critique the Reformation doctrine of *sola scriptura* by equating it with Tradition 0 create an easily demolished strawman. The position of the classical Reformers and their heirs was and is Tradition I—the position of the apostolic Church.

If we are to maintain a sound Christian doctrine of authority we must, with the early fathers and with the magisterial Reformers, insist that Scripture is the sole source of revelation. We must insist that, by virtue of its absolutely unique character as the inspired Word of the living God, Scripture is the sole infallible authority for doctrine and practice. And we must also insist that Scripture is to be interpreted within the hermeneutical boundaries of the apostolic rule of faith in and by the communion of saints.

PART TWO:

THE WITNESS OF SCRIPTURE

5

Scripture on Scripture and Tradition

The debate over the relationship between the authority of Scripture and the authority of the Church has involved discussions of numerous passages of Scripture. It is well beyond the scope of this work to examine every one of these. There have, however, been certain passages and verses which have consistently surfaced in the works of those on each side of this debate. This chapter will examine some of the most important and controversial scriptural passages dealing with the nature of Scripture and tradition. The next chapter will examine some of the most important scriptural passages that deal with the authority of the Church.

The historical survey showed that the concept of Scripture and tradition which could most legitimately lay claim to being the doctrine of the early Church is that concept we have referred to as Tradition I. This was the consistent teaching of the early Church for at least the first three centuries of her existence. The question that should be asked at this point is whether this was the doctrine of the Apostles of Christ. It would be very easy to fall into any of a number of circular question-begging arguments. No one approaches Scripture without any preconceived notions or presuppositions, and if someone believes that he is able to do so, he has already implicitly adopted the position we have termed Tradition 0—which itself is a presupposition. It is perhaps unavoidable that a certain amount of circularity will be involved in any discussion of Scripture's doctrine of Scripture. Certain hermeneutical assumptions must be made by each of us before we can even begin to search the Scriptures to determine what hermeneutical presuppositions it demands of all of us. However, if Scripture is the Word of God, as those on every side of this debate would agree, and if Christ's sheep truly can hear His voice, it cannot be futile to open the Scriptures and prayerfully examine what is written, and all the following texts have been examined with the *regula fidei* as a guiding hermeneutical principle.

SCRIPTURE ON SCRIPTURE

A complete discussion of everything Scripture teaches us about itself is obviously beyond the scope of this book.[1] The majority of Evangelicals, Catholics, and Orthodox who are involved in the current debate agree, for example, that Scripture is the revelation of God and that it is inspired and infallible. Rather than arguing for truths upon which all sides already agree, the focus below will be upon a few of the most debated texts in the controversy concerning the relationship between Scripture, tradition, and the Church.[2]

THE BEREANS (ACTS 17:10–11)

Acts 17:10–11 is one of the most used and abused texts of Scripture in the ongoing debate. The text itself reads as follows:

> Then the brethren immediately sent Paul and Silas away by night to Berea. When they arrived, they went into the synagogue of the Jews. These were more fair-minded than those in Thessalonica, in that they received the word with all readiness, and searched the Scriptures daily to find out whether these things were so.

Paul's custom when entering a city was to go first to the Jewish synagogue to preach the gospel of Christ (Acts 17:2; cf. 9:20;

---

[1] There are a number of excellent works that have been written for this purpose. For a good introductory study, see E. J. Young, *Thy Word is Truth* (Grand Rapids: Wm. B. Eerdmans Publishing Co., 1957).

[2] Because of the importance of the issue of the canon in this debate, it shall be discussed separately, in more detail, in Part Four.

13:5; 14; 14:1). He does the same in Berea. In order to understand what happens in Berea, it is important to grasp the surrounding context of this passage. In 17:1, Paul, Silas and Timothy arrive in Thessalonica. For three Sabbaths, Paul reasons with the Jews in the synagogue. From the Old Testament he explains and demonstrates "that the Christ had to suffer and rise again from the dead" (cf. Luke 24:25–26, 44–46; Acts 3:18; 26:22–23; 1 Cor. 15:3–4; 1 Pet. 1:10–11). He declares to them that Jesus, since He has fulfilled these conditions, is the Christ, the Messiah of Israel.

When we recall the difficulty Jesus' own disciples had grasping the fact that He must suffer and die (e.g., Matt. 16:21–22), it is not surprising that this message came as news to other Jews as well. They expected the coming of the Messiah and His kingdom to be cataclysmic. The Messiah was to destroy Israel's enemies and restore her to a place of prominence. When Paul enters the synagogue and begins to show them from the Old Testament that the Messiah had to suffer and die, this is something contrary to the traditional Jewish interpretation of the Old Testament. When he tells them that the Messiah had in fact come, that He had suffered and died, and that this had been at the hands of His own people, we can only imagine their shock.

In 17:4, we are told that some of the Jews were persuaded along with a great number of the devout Greeks and numerous leading women. The reaction of the majority of the Jews, however, was envy (v. 5). Instead of continuing to examine and reason from the Old Testament, these Jews incite a mob and start a riot. They drag some of the Christians to the city rulers accusing them of treason saying, "these are all acting contrary to the decrees of Caesar, saying there is another king—Jesus" (v. 7). The brethren, fearing for the safety of Paul, Timothy and Silas, help them escape under cover of darkness, and they leave for Berea. When they arrive, they go immediately to the synagogue of the Jews (v. 10).

This is where the text begins. We are told first in verse eleven that these Jews were more fair-minded, or noble, than the

Thessalonican Jews. The reason given is that the Berean Jews "received the word with all readiness, and searched the Scriptures daily to find out whether these things were so." Unlike the emotional and irrational response of the Thessalonican Jews, the Berean Jews were open to discovering if what Paul was saying was true. What are "these things" that they were trying to verify from the Old Testament? They were trying to verify the same things Paul preached to the Thessalonican Jews, "that the Christ [Messiah] had to suffer and rise again from the dead" and that "this Jesus whom I preach to you is the Christ" (cf. 17:3). The Old Testament, Paul proclaims, prophesies that the Messiah must suffer and die and be resurrected from the dead. This is not something that he is inventing. What is not in the Old Testament is the name of the Messiah. Paul declares unto them that the Messiah foretold in the Old Testament has come in the person of Jesus of Nazareth. Unlike what happened at Thessalonica, many of the Berean Jews were persuaded and believed (v. 12).

Roman Catholic apologist Robert Sungenis overstates the case that can be made from Paul's new revelation that Jesus of Nazareth is the Old Testament Messiah. He writes,

> Everyone believed Scripture's prophecy about the coming Messiah. But the information that the Christ was "Jesus" who had recently suffered and died at the hands of the Jews was something Paul was getting from another source outside Scripture. This new information would, of course, correlate with Scripture but it would nonetheless be in addition to Scripture.[3]

He explains at a later point that "we have seen from our comparison of the Jews in Berea with the Jews in Thessalonica that Luke considered the former noble not because they merely examined Scripture, but mainly because they believed Paul's *oral revelation* that the Christ of the Old Testament was the Jesus of the New."[4]

---

[3] Robert Sungenis, "Does Scripture Teach *Sola Scriptura?*" in *Not By Scripture Alone*, ed. Robert A. Sungenis, (Santa Barbara: Queenship Publishing Company, 1997), 133.
    [4] Ibid., 136.

Sungenis is correct when he says Paul's declaration that Jesus of Nazareth is the Messiah is a new revelation not found in the Old Testament. Nobody denies this. But Sungenis is implying that because the Apostle Paul's oral proclamation of the gospel of Jesus Christ was as authoritative as the Old Testament at that time, we must agree that oral revelation "in addition to Scripture" is as authoritative as Scripture *today*. The error in this argument is the failure to distinguish between an era in which God's revelation was still being communicated to His people and an era in which it has been completed. Paul was living when God's final revelation was being completed, and he was a chosen instrument of that revelation. We do not live in a period of continuing revelation. This is not simply a Protestant doctrine. Vatican II states that, "no new public revelation is to be expected before the glorious manifestation of our Lord, Jesus Christ."[5]

A second problem with Sungenis's explanation of this text is that he anachronistically reads a later debate into the passage. When he asserts that the Bereans were considered noble because "they believed Paul's *oral revelation*," he emphasizes "oral" presumably to distinguish it from "written." But again, this is irrelevant when we consider when this revelation occurred. It does not follow that because the Bereans accepted oral revelation spoken by an Apostle before God's revelation ceased, we must accept oral revelation which cannot be demonstrated to have come from an Apostle.

The difficulty with Sungenis's argument is that he is arguing from the standpoint of Tradition II (or possibly Tradition III) against those who adhere to Tradition 0. He assumes that by demonstrating that Paul's oral teaching was as authoritative as Scripture that he has overturned the Protestant position. However, we must remember the concept we referred to as Tradition I, the teaching of the early Church and many of the classical Reformers. According to this concept, Scripture is to be interpreted according to the apostolic rule of faith—the apostolic revelation. And

---

[5] *Dei Verbum*, 4.

this is exactly what happens in Acts 17 at Berea. Paul's message *is* the apostolic revelation. He is bringing the apostolic revelation to bear upon the Old Testament Scriptures.

Contrary to those evangelicals who advocate Tradition 0, there is nothing in this passage which warrants a radically individualized concept of solo *scriptura* apart from the apostolic rule of faith. The Scriptures were read, examined, and debated by the Bereans day by day in community with an Apostle of Christ present. Paul does not come to Berea and tell them that he wants each of them to go home and determine for himself and by himself the true interpretation of Scripture. Nor does Acts 17:10–11 imply that the revelation in the Old Testament Scriptures was more authoritative than the apostolic revelation brought to Berea by Paul. The Bereans were not judging Paul's apostolic revelation by a *higher standard* of truth. The Divine revelation given to Paul was as authoritative as the Divine revelation found in the written Old Testament. The source of both was God. What the Bereans were attempting to determine was whether Paul's message was in fact revelation from God. To do this they had to first establish its consistency with what they already knew to be revelation from God.

The situation the Bereans found themselves in cannot be strictly paralleled with our own situation in a post-revelational era, but it is significant that Paul did appeal to consistency with the known revelation—Old Testament Scripture—as a touchstone for the validity of his own revelation. In a post-revelational era, this is even more important. We now have the known revelation of the Old and New Testament. If equally authoritative revelation was to be tested against the known revelation, then certainly that which is admittedly less than inspired revelation must be measured against this touchstone.

ALL SCRIPTURE IS GOD-BREATHED (2 TIMOTHY 3:16–17)

One of the most frequently cited texts in the debate over the authority of Scripture is 2 Timothy 3:16–17. In this text Paul tells Timothy,

All Scripture is given by inspiration of God, and is profitable for doctrine, for reproof, for correction, for instruction in righteousness, that the man of God may be complete, thoroughly equipped for every good work.

Like Acts 17, 2 Timothy 3:16 has been at the center of much debate. Unfortunately, much of this debate has been wasted discussing issues of secondary importance. Page after page has been written attempting to either defend or refute the thesis that 2 Timothy 3:16–17 teaches the sufficiency of Scripture. This is done because of the mistaken notion that the doctrine of sufficiency is virtually all that is involved in the doctrine of *sola scriptura*. Robert Sungenis, for example, spends the bulk of his discussion of 2 Timothy 3:16–17 discussing and critiquing the notion of sufficiency.[6]

The teaching of this text that has much more direct bearing on this discussion is its assertion that Scripture is "inspired." The Greek word translated "inspired" in most English translations of the Bible is *theopneustos*. A literal translation would be "God-breathed." The word indicates that Scripture's source is God's "breath." This is the essential characteristic of Scripture. It is Divine revelation. It is the very Word of God Himself (cf. John 10:35). We see proof of this fact elsewhere in the New Testament when the words "God says" are used to refer to Old Testament passages of Scripture even if the words of that passage were not words originally spoken by God Himself.[7] The fact that Scripture is Divine revelation is not debated by those conservative participants in the current debate.

The failure to carefully distinguish between Tradition 0,

---

[6] Ibid., 109–129; This is not entirely the fault of Sungenis. In several recent Protestant works on *sola scriptura* various authors have defined *sola scriptura* in a number of confusing ways, often reducing it to nothing more than a matter of sufficiency. This confusion is due in large part to a failure to differentiate between Tradition I and Tradition 0. The fallacy of strictly identifying *sola scriptura* with sufficiency will be discussed in Part Three.

[7] For a good discussion of this phenomenon, see B.B. Warfield, *The Inspiration and Authority of the Bible*, (Philadelphia: Presbyterian and Reformed Publishing Co., 1948), 299–348.

Tradition I, and Tradition II, however, has led to much needless confusion in the discussion of 2 Timothy 3:16—17. Sungenis, for example, in his discussion of this passage, attempts to find support for the concept of Tradition II. He first points out that the immediate context of 2 Timothy 1–3 refers several times to the authoritative oral teaching of Paul.[8] He reminds us that Paul's apostolic instruction was equally authoritative whether given orally or in writing (cf. 2 Thess. 2:15). Sungenis summarizes his argument as follows:

> since Paul did command the first Christians to preserve and obey oral revelation, the Catholic Church has always taught that oral revelation serves as an additional source of revelation alongside the written word. Therefore Scripture is not our sole authority.[9]

This argument contains several ambiguities and errors. First, as pointed out in the first four chapters, it is simply false to state that the Catholic church has "always" taught a two-source theory of revelation.[10] Second, note again that the Christians alive during the lifetime of the Apostles were in a unique situation. We no longer have Apostles who are being given inspired revelation from God. So oral revelation no longer "serves as an additional source of revelation alongside the written word." The Roman Catholic church affirms this when it teaches that inspired revelation ceased with the death of the last Apostle, but Sungenis's argument distorts this agreed-upon fact. In one footnote, for example, he criticizes James White for raising this point:

---

[8] Sungenis, op. cit., 126.

[9] Ibid., 127.

[10] As our discussion of these texts proceeds, the reason for beginning this book with a historical survey will become increasingly evident. Too many times, unfounded historical assertions are simply inserted into discussions of particular texts lending a particular interpretation more credibility than it would otherwise have. The statement ". . . the Catholic church has always taught that oral revelation serves as an additional source of revelation alongside the written word" is simply false. There is not even a hint of this idea for the first three hundred years of the Church's existence. See Chapter One for a complete discussion of this issue.

By this admission, White has unwittingly proven that Scripture does not teach sola scriptura, for if it cannot be a "valid concept during time of revelation," how can Scripture teach such a doctrine since scripture was written precisely when divine oral revelation was still being produced? Scripture cannot contradict itself. Since both the 1st century Christian and the 21st century Christian cannot extract differing interpretations from the same verse, thus, whatever was true about Scripture then must also be true today.[11]

This argument makes very little sense. First of all, it ignores the Catholic church's own teaching that the apostolic era was a unique era in redemptive history. Second, if whatever was strictly true about Scripture at that moment in history is strictly true about Scripture now, then we can only use the term Scripture to refer to the Old Testament. Sungenis's argument here for a second source of revelation would also be an argument for a Bible without a New Testament. In his zeal to overcome Tradition 0, Sungenis makes assertions that are simply unfounded and irrelevant to the real issue.

Sungenis's argument depends upon extending into our own day a situation that was historically unique. Because Paul communicated the revelation God gave him both orally and in written form Sungenis concludes, "Therefore Scripture is not our sole authority." Taking the position of Tradition II, Sungenis concludes that Tradition 0 cannot be true. This, however, is a false dilemma because it neglects to mention the oldest Christian position on the subject—Tradition I. As shown earlier, Tradition I does not deny the existence and necessity of the Church as a subordinate authority. Nor does it deny the necessity of the apostolic rule of faith as the hermeneutical context of Scripture. But according to Tradition I, Scripture is our sole *God-breathed* authority, and this makes it our *sole* inherently infallible authority.[12]

---

[11] Sungenis, op. cit., 128; note 24.

[12] The idea of "infallibility" is central to the debate over authority in the Church and will be discussed at length in Part Three.

It is this "God-breathed" nature of Scripture that is significant to the discussion of 2 Timothy 3:16–17. Its importance lies in the fact that today, in the post-apostolic age, this is an attribute that belongs uniquely to Scripture. What proof do we have for this assertion? 2 Timothy 3:16 does say all Scripture is "God-breathed," but it doesn't specifically say *only* Scripture is God-breathed. First, note that this attribute obviously applies to all God-given special revelation and that this revelation was ongoing at the time 2 Timothy was originally written. Any word from God is by definition God-breathed whether communicated in writing or orally. Second, however, it is granted by Rome that inspired divine revelation ceased with the last of the Apostles.

We still have the Scriptures which all admit are God-breathed. But we do not have access today to an inspired Apostle. Even the gift or "charism" of infallibility which Rome teaches is given to the pope under special circumstances is not identical to inspiration. Only divine revelation from God can be termed "inspired" or "God-breathed." The gift of infallibility is, in fact, distinguished from inspired divine revelation in the *Catechism of the Catholic Church*.[13]

This leaves only one question. Does any of the "God-breathed" oral revelation communicated by the Apostles to the Church survive today outside Scripture? Those who advocate Tradition 0 say no, but this is difficult for them to conclusively prove using nothing more than the New Testament. Those who advocate Tradition I say "yes" in the specific sense that the apostolic rule of faith remains the hermeneutical context of Scripture, but "no" in the sense that this rule of faith is not a second source of revelation "outside" or "apart from" Scripture.[14] Roman Catholic proponents of Tradition II say "yes" in the sense that a number of customs and practices were handed down from the Apostles. These

---

[13] Paragraph 2035.

[14] As we pointed out in our discussion of the early fathers, since the apostolic rule of faith and the content of Scripture are coinherent, this "rule of faith" is not, strictly speaking, a "second" source of revelation.

"traditions" are said to be as binding and authoritative as Scripture and are often described as a second source of revelation. This is usually based upon the words of Basil, which we examined in detail in chapter one.

An important problem for Tradition II is the fact that it finds no support in the witness of the earliest church fathers. For centuries, the view the fathers held was Tradition I—Scripture is the sole source of revelation which is to be interpreted in and by the Church within the context of the rule of faith. If there were a second source of divine revelation alongside Scripture in the post-apostolic church, the silence of the early Church to that fact and its explicit statements denying that possibility are weighty objections. The problem is that Tradition II itself is a novel doctrine.

A second problem with this position is the fact that Rome has never been able to definitively indicate to anyone exactly what all of these supposed unwritten traditions are. If they exist and are authoritative and binding on all Christians, then it is imperative that all Christians be made aware of all of them. But Rome has never definitively provided a "canon" of the "God-breathed" and authoritatively binding unwritten traditions. It is simply irrational to assert that God would give all Christians binding traditions and not provide them with any clear definition of those traditions. Since the statements of the Church are not "God-breathed," and since there are no surviving "God-breathed" unwritten traditions to which one can point with any certainty, the Scripture is the only place to which any of us can turn for authoritative "God-breathed" revelation. Because it is the only "God-breathed" revelation to which we have access, it is the sole final authority to which the Church must turn.

NO PROPHECY OF SCRIPTURE IS OF ANY PRIVATE INTERPRETATION (2 PETER 1:19–21)

In his second epistle, Peter makes some important comments on the nature of Scripture which read as follows:

> We also have the prophetic word made more sure, which you do
> well to heed as a light that shines in a dark place, until the day
> dawns and the morning star rises in your hearts; knowing this
> first, that no prophecy of Scripture is of any private interpreta-
> tion, for prophecy never came by the will of man, but holy men
> of God spoke as they were moved by the Holy Spirit.

This passage is important because of its statements regarding
the origin of the Scriptures, but it is also important because of
what it teaches us within its own context. The Second Epistle of
Peter is a short letter comprised essentially of three major sec-
tions. In chapter 1, Peter exhorts his readers toward spiritual
growth. In chapter 2, he warns them of the teachings and practices
of false prophets, and in chapter 3, he gives them teaching on the
Day of the Lord. The immediate context of our passage is chapter
1, verses 6–21. In this two-part section, Peter testifies to his readers of the truthfulness of the gospel message. In verses 16–18, he
provides them with the testimony of an eyewitness. In verses 19–
21, he adds the testimony of the Old Testament Scriptures.

In verse 19, Peter writes, "We also have the prophetic word
made more sure." The Greek words translated "prophetic word"
are *ton prophetikon logon*. As Richard Baukham points out, "All
other known occurrences of the phrase refer to OT Scripture,
except 2 *Clem.* 11:2. . . . It seems in fact to be interchangeable
with the term 'Scripture.'"[15] What does it mean, however, for Peter to say that we have this word "made more sure"? There are debates over the interpretation, but the linguistic and contextual
evidence favors the view that Peter is appealing to the Scriptures
to confirm his witness. This is what Paul repeatedly did ·in the
synagogues (cf. Acts 17:10–11). Michael Green summarizes Peter's point quite well:

> [A]s for the apostles, it is hard to overemphasize their regard for
> the Old Testament. One of their most powerful arguments for
> the truth of Christianity was the argument from prophecy (see

---

[15] Richard Bauckham, *Jude, 2 Peter*, (Waco: Word Books, Publisher, 1983), 224.

the speeches in Acts, Rom. xv, I Pet. ii, or the whole of Heb. or
Rev.). In the word of God written, they sought absolute assurance, like their Master, for whom "it is written" sufficed to clinch
an argument. . . . He is saying "If you don't believe me, go to the
Scriptures." "The question," says Calvin, "is not whether the
prophets are more trustworthy than the gospel." It is simply that
"since the Jews were in no doubt that everything that the prophets taught came from God, it is no wonder that Peter says that
their word is more sure."[16]

In 1:20, Peter indicates something of profound importance to his
readers telling them that "no prophecy of Scripture is of any private interpretation." Commentators have proposed two primary
meanings of this phrase because of the ambiguity of the word
translated "interpretation." According to some, the clause refers
to the interpretation of Scripture. According to others it refers to
the origin of Scripture. The first proposed reading would mean
that Scripture is not to be interpreted privately and individually.
The second proposed reading would mean that the origin of
Scripture is God.

In support of the first position is the fact that elsewhere in the
epistle, Peter does deal extensively with false teachers who are
misinterpreting Scripture (cf. 2:1; 3:16). The second position is
supported by the fact that the immediate context is dealing specifically with the origin of Scripture. It is difficult to explain the relevance of verse 21 if verse 20 is referring to the interpretation of
Scripture rather than the origin of Scripture.[17] The point of verse
20, then, is that Scripture does not find its origin in the minds of
individuals.[18] Verse 21 explains what the actual origin of Scripture is.

According to verse 21, "prophecy never came by the will of

---

[16] Michael Green, *The Second Epistle of Peter and the Epistle of Jude*, (Grand Rapids: Wm.
B. Eerdmans Publishing Company, 1968), 87.

[17] For a detailed survey of the evidence for each position, see Bauckham, op. cit.,
229–233.

[18] It should be noted that although the available evidence supports the "origin" position on verse 20, the "interpretation" position is not contrary to Tradition I.

man, but holy men of God spoke as they were moved by the Holy Spirit." The teaching of this text directly parallels 2 Timothy 3:16. Both teach that God is the direct source of the words of Scripture. Peter adds some intriguing comments about the holy men who were instrumentally used by God in the process of inspiration. While Peter does not explain exactly how this inspiration of Scripture is accomplished, he does assert it as a fact.

Peter makes an additional interesting comment later in his epistle. The entirety of chapter 2 is devoted to a warning against the doctrines of false teachers. Having warned his readers of this peril, Peter encourages his readers to "be mindful of the words which were spoken before by the holy prophets, and of the commandment of us, the apostles of the Lord and Savior" (3:2). Peter places the words of the apostles, himself included, on an equal level with the Old Testament prophets. He appeals to the same two authorities to which he appealed in 1:16–21—prophets and apostles. Both are authoritative because the direct source of the words of both is the Lord. We have here an implicit testimony to the unique authority of the Old Testament—"the holy prophets," and the New Testament—"the apostles." They are unique in their direct divine origin, and it is to the teaching of these unique revelations that Peter expects his readers to turn to guard against false doctrine.

Do not Add or Take Away from the Words of this Book (Revelation 22:18–19)

Revelation 22:18–19 is another text that is at the center of much discussion in the ongoing *sola scriptura* debate. The text itself reads,

> For I testify to everyone who hears the words of the prophecy of this book: If anyone adds to these things, God will add to him the plagues that are written in this book; and if anyone takes away from the words of the book of this prophecy, God shall take away his part from the Book of Life, from the holy city, and from the things which are written in this book.

First, the warning refers specifically to "this book," the book of Revelation. John is not speaking explicitly of the entire Scripture. Second, the allusions to Deuteronomy are striking. The same kind of warnings about "adding to" or "taking away from" the Word are found in Deuteronomy 4:2 and 12:32, and the curses John mentions are paralleled in Deuteronomy 29:19–20. Finally, by placing this warning where he did, John implicitly claims a status for the book of Revelation equal to the canonical status of the Old Testament law.

What then does John mean by warning against "adding to" or "taking away from" the words of the book? At a minimum, this is a warning against willfully distorting the message of the book. If the parallel with Deuteronomy is theological as well as linguistic, the thrust of the warning would be against adding to or taking away from God's revealed law.[19] The principle would therefore be applicable to more than simply the book of Revelation. It would apply to all of revealed Scripture.

Robert Sungenis argues,

> Attempts to use such passages as Revelation 22:18–19, Deuteronomy 4:2; 12:32 or Proverbs 30:6 to support sola scriptura are really quite naïve. . . . It is futile. . . to accuse those who believe in authoritative Tradition of disregarding these verses if, as is indeed true, Scripture itself commands its readers to obey and preserve oral tradition (2 Thess. 2:15; 2 Tim. 1:13–2:2). In verses such as Deut. 4:2 and Rev. 22:18, the sacred authors are merely condemning any attempt by man, whether from "tradition" or from a document which is claimed as inspired but is not, to add to God's inspired word. They cannot add their own words to God's and claim that they are divinely authorized, nor can they subtract from God's word claiming that some of it is not inspired. . . . Invariably, throughout Christian history, men have claimed to be "inspired" by God to give additional revelation in contradiction to the Church's clear statement that God's inspired revelation has ceased.[20]

---

[19] G.K. Beale, *The Book of Revelation*, NIGTC, (Grand Rapids: Wm. B. Eerdmans Publishing Co., 1999), 1151.

[20] Sungenis, op. cit., 233–234.

Once again we see Sungenis unnecessarily confusing the issue. First, his criticisms are directed solely at Tradition 0.[21] The passages on tradition to which he refers will be discussed below. Suffice it to say here that Tradition I does not reject the scriptural and patristic concept of tradition. Sungenis argues that simply because Revelation 22:18–19 prohibits added ongoing revelation, it does not prohibit obedience to and preservation of oral tradition. This is true. A major problem, again, is that Rome has never been able to provide anyone with any complete and definite statement of what all of these necessary oral traditions are which she claims to have preserved.

A second problem is that many individual doctrines and practices which she *has* declared to be preserved apostolic traditions cannot be found anywhere in the testimony of the early fathers. The Church cannot, by definition, receive a "new" apostolic tradition. If a tradition is truly apostolic, then it is not new. Yet, time and again, Rome declares something to be "apostolic" which is completely absent not only from the writings of the Apostles themselves but from the writings of the entire Church for centuries.[22]

Finally, by ignoring the parallel between Revelation 22 and Deuteronomy 4, Sungenis radically minimizes the significance of the warnings in both. We are told by Sungenis that Revelation 22:18–19 does not disallow oral revelation. As long as we define carefully what we mean by this, there is no problem. But John uses almost identical language as Moses, and when Moses wrote Deuteronomy, divine revelation was not complete. There were many more books of Scripture to be written. Ongoing revelation, therefore, cannot be the main danger against which either

---

[21] The entire book edited by Sungenis virtually ignores the existence of the concept of Tradition I. This obviously makes the Roman Catholic apologist's task easier since Tradition 0 is, as they repeatedly demonstrate, impossible to maintain scripturally, historically, or logically. Proving the falsity of Tradition 0, however, does not demand the validity of Tradition II. Both are relatively novel, a-historical concepts that diverge from the teaching of the early Church.

[22] We shall examine the thoroughly circular and arbitrary nature of the Roman Catholic claim in Part Three.

John or Moses is warning. It is much more likely that God is warning in both instances against the kind of thing Jesus speaks of in Mark 7:8–9, "laying aside" and "rejecting" the commandment of God for the sake of the "tradition of men."

We must remember what happened to the law of Moses in Israel. Because the Jews realized that Scripture must be interpreted and applied to later generations, an oral law, which is called "the tradition of the elders" in the New Testament, was gradually developed. As F.F. Bruce notes,

> As time went on the claim was made that this oral law, like the written law itself, was received by Moses on Sinai, and it was accorded much the same authority. From Moses, it was further claimed, it was handed down through a succession of tradents, until it was received by the leaders of the Shammite and Hillelite schools.[23]

The parallels with the claims made by Rome are striking. Both begin with a written law to which the warning against "adding to" or "taking away" is added. Both realize the necessity of interpretation. Both claim that their hermeneutical tradition was received in addition to the original written revelation. Both grant it authority equal to that of the written revelation. Both claim it has been faithfully preserved and handed down from generation to generation. Jesus says that the Jewish oral law was a human tradition that had resulted in the rejection of the inspired written law. It is not at all unlikely then that John is warning the Church not to make the same deadly mistake that Israel made.

The written Word is to be the norm to which nothing may be added and from which nothing may be taken away. Interpretation and application are legitimate, but by their very nature they are not identical to the written norm being interpreted and applied. When they are equated either through negligence or

23 F.F. Bruce, "Scripture in Relation to Tradition and Reason" in *Scripture, Tradition and Reason: A Study in the Criteria of Christian Doctrine*, Richard Bauckham and Benjamin Drewery, eds. (Edinburgh: T & T Clark, LTD., 1988), 44–45.

presumption, the warning of Deuteronomy and Revelation has been ignored.

SCRIPTURE ON TRADITION

Although this discussion has separated texts referring explicitly to Scripture from those addressing tradition and the Church, they are all related and bear witness to the same truth. The three passages to be examined below that highlight different aspects of the tradition are: Luke 1:1–4; Mark 7:5–13; and 2 Thess. 2:15.

THE WRITING OF THE TRADITION (LUKE 1:1–4)

The first text is not often referred to in discussions on this topic, but it does have some bearing upon the issues at hand. In Luke 1:1–4, we read,

> Inasmuch as many have taken in hand to set in order a narrative of those things which are most surely believed among us, just as those who from the beginning were eyewitnesses and ministers of the word delivered them to us, it seemed good to me also, having had perfect understanding of all things from the very first, to write to you an orderly account, most excellent Theophilus, that you may know the certainty of those things in which you were instructed.

Here, in the first sentence of Luke's Gospel, we have a significant statement regarding the purpose of a particular written text of Scripture—the Gospel of Luke itself. The earliest suggested date for the writing of the Gospel of Luke is approximately A.D. 59, almost thirty years after the death of Christ. But the Christian Church had not been without knowledge of the words and works of Jesus despite not having a written gospel for several decades. The Apostles who were eyewitnesses had faithfully declared unto them the gospel and at this point in time were still alive to continue bearing witness to the truth.

In verses 1 and 2, Luke explains that the things which the Church now believes (in A.D. 59 or thereabouts) were "delivered" to them by the eyewitnesses to the events. The word translated "delivered" is the verb *paradosan,* the aorist indicative of *paradidomi.* This verb literally means "to hand over, give (over), deliver, or entrust." It is related to the noun *paradosis* which is the Greek word meaning "tradition"—or that which is handed over. Literally, we could say that the Apostles "traditioned" the gospel "tradition" to the Church.

If the Church is in possession of the full apostolic tradition, then we must ask why Luke found it necessary to write down these "things believed among us," this "tradition." Luke tells Theophilus that he is putting the "tradition" to paper in order "that you [Theophilus] may know the certainty of those things in which you were instructed." Theophilus had already received the apostolic tradition through oral instruction according to Luke (v. 4). But this was deemed insufficient. Luke determines to gather all of the available information from all of the available reliable sources and put the oral tradition to writing. Luke tells Theophilus that compiling a complete and orderly account allows for more "certainty" regarding the tradition. Why? Because oral tradition is inherently unstable over any extended period of time and it cannot be independently verified if the one who originally gave the message is gone. When Luke wrote this Gospel, most of the Apostles were still alive. The extraordinary events were still fresh in their memory, and the Holy Spirit was keeping it alive in their minds (cf. John 14:26; 16:13). Although it might be difficult for some, it would not be impossible to find eyewitnesses who could verify an oral tradition. But this situation could not last forever. The Apostles would eventually die, and it would be necessary to have their witness preserved in a more stable form—the written Word.

Another interesting fact about this prologue to the Gospel of Luke is that Luke equates that which has been "handed down" or "traditioned" with what he will write in his Gospel. It is to be an orderly account of "all these things," not some of these things. It would defeat his own stated purpose for writing the book if he left out some necessary part of the gospel tradition. There is no reason, therefore, to suppose with Rome that Luke left out any secret teachings Jesus gave the Apostles.

TEACHING AS DOCTRINES
THE COMMANDMENTS OF MEN (MARK 7:5–13)

This text and the parallel passage in Matthew 15 indicate the degree to which a hermeneutical tradition can conflict with the inspired Scripture it claims to interpret. The text reads,

> Then the Pharisees and scribes asked Him, "Why do Your disciples not walk according to the tradition of the elders, but eat bread with unwashed hands?" He answered and said to them, "Well did Isaiah prophesy of you hypocrites, as it is written: 'This people honors Me with their lips, but their heart is far from Me. And in vain they worship Me, teaching as doctrines the commandments of men.' For laying aside the commandment of God, you hold the tradition of men—the washing of pitchers and cups, and many other such things you do." And He said to them, "All too well you reject the commandment of God, that you may keep your tradition. For Moses said, 'Honor your father and your mother'; and, 'He who curses father and mother, let him be put to death.' But you say, If a man says to his father or mother, "Whatever profit you might have received from me is Corban"'" (that is, dedicated to the temple); "and you no longer let him do anything for his father or his mother, making the word of God of no effect through your tradition which you have handed down. And many such things you do."

As noted above, the Jews had an oral tradition which had developed as the religious leaders sought to interpret and apply the Mosaic law. In his comments on the parallel passage in Matthew, D.A. Carson explains the meaning of the "tradition of the elders."

> The "tradition of the elders," the "tradition of men" (Mark 7:8; Col. 2:8), "your tradition" (Matt. 15:3, 6; Mark 7:9, 13), and the "tradition of the fathers" (Gal. 1:14) refer to the great corpus of oral teaching that commented on the law and interpreted it in detailed rules of conduct, often recording the diverse opinions of competing rabbis. This tradition in Jesus' time was largely oral and orally transmitted; but the Pharisees, though not the Sadducees, viewed it as having authority very nearly equal to the canon.[24]

---

[24] D.A. Carson, "Matthew" in *The Expositor's Bible Commentary*, Vol. 8, Frank E. Gaebelein, ed. (Grand Rapids: Zondervan Publishing House, 1984), 348.

The main point of this passage is the sharp contrast Jesus draws between the "tradition of the elders" and the Word of God. The "commandments of men" are being used by the Pharisees to set aside the "commandment of God."

This passage in Mark is dealt with by two authors in the Roman Catholic work *Not By Scripture Alone*. The way in which the passage is discussed by these two authors illustrates the confusion that surrounds any discussion of this topic. In his discussion of Mark 7, the Reverend Mitchell Pacwa writes, "In the controversy of Mark 7:1–23, Jesus takes on two issues: He attacks the Pharisees and Scribes for placing the oral tradition on the same level as the written Law, and He abrogates the dietary laws in Leviticus."[25] Sungenis, on the other hand, in his discussion finds no difficulty placing oral tradition on the same level as the written Law. He writes, "Tradition and Scripture stand as two witnesses verifying one truth."[26] Let us look briefly at Sungenis's argument.

He begins by setting up Tradition 0 as the Protestant position. Protestants, he says, claim that because Jesus condemns the tradition of the Pharisees, He therefore condemns all tradition. This may in fact be the argument of many Protestant proponents of Tradition 0, but it is not *the* Protestant position since many Protestants adhere to Tradition I. Sungenis writes, "It is not the idea of tradition, *per se*, that Jesus is condemning, but anything that is taught by men which is contrary to God's mandates."[27] But this is not an aspect of Jesus' teaching in this passage. As will be discussed below, there are passages of Scripture which speak of tradition in a positive light. However, what is meant by the word "tradition" in the different contexts is not the same.

Using Mark 7, Sungenis makes three basic observations about tradition to which we must briefly respond.[28] "First," he writes,

---

[25] Mitchell Pacwa, "Excursus on Matthew 15:1–20 and Mark 7:1–23," in *Not By Scripture Alone*, ed. Robert A. Sungenis, (Santa Barbara: Queenship Publishing Company, 1997), 555.

[26] Sungenis, op. cit., 167.

[27] Ibid., 163.

[28] Ibid., 165. Sungenis indicates that he is going to make four observations, but there are only three in the following pages.

"whether Catholic or Protestant, any teaching that purposely sets aside God's laws is condemnable."[29] This is a truism, and there is no disagreement on this point. Sungenis continues,

> Second, despite Protestant aversion to Catholic tradition, it remains an incontrovertible fact that the New Testament values oral tradition and commands the Church to preserve it (2 Thess. 2:15). No amount of exegetical contortions can dismiss this fact. No Protestant has ever shown where Paul's command to preserve oral tradition was ever rescinded in the New Testament. Hence, we must insist that when one studies Scripture's teaching on tradition, he must be willing to accept that there are two ways in which Scripture judges tradition—on the one hand, it highly praises tradition that it is divinely authentic, and on the other hand it castigates tradition that obscures or neutralizes divine teaching.[30]

First, obviously the Church has been commanded to preserve and hold fast to the apostolic tradition or *kerygma*. At the time 2 Thessalonians was written, this apostolic tradition was communicated by the Apostles both orally and in written form.[31] Second, the New Testament nowhere rescinds its repeated commands to preserve and hold to the apostolic tradition.[32] But, also, no Roman Catholic has ever proven that Rome *has* preserved any oral tradition. In fact, Rome cannot even tell us definitely what the content of this oral tradition is.

Sungenis's third observation on Mark 7 is that "the problem with the Pharisees was not tradition, *per se,* but their refusal to form a synthesis of Scripture and divine tradition that preserved the teaching of Scripture but allowed tradition to serve its main

---

[29] Ibid., 165.

[30] Ibid., 165–166.

[31] 2 Thess. 2:15 will be discussed in more detail below.

[32] Part of the difficulty in evaluating Sungenis's comments and arguments is that he repeatedly jumps from the use of "tradition" to refer to the apostolic *kerygma* to the use of "tradition" to refer to the Church's interpretation of that tradition or to the use of "tradition" to refer to ecclesiastical customs. He seldom specifies the precise definition he is using, and his arguments therefore continually fall into the fallacy of equivocation.

purpose, that is, to expound and enhance Scripture."[33] This, however, is precisely what Jesus condemned. The Pharisees had so tightly interwoven or "synthesized" the scriptural Torah with the halakhic formulations of the scribal oral law that they were for all practical purposes equated. Jesus, on the other hand, continually throughout this passage contrasts tradition to Scripture and subordinates tradition to Scripture. It cannot be any other way. Scripture cannot judge between authentic and inauthentic tradition, as Sungenis says it does, if tradition is placed on the same level with Scripture and "synthesized" with it.

The entire Roman Catholic argument depends upon the assumption that Rome could not do what Israel did. The problem is that in reality she has done exactly what Israel did. She has placed herself in precisely the same position that the Scribes and Pharisees found themselves in. Their oral law or tradition was so "synthesized" to the written Torah, that judgment of the validity of that unwritten law by means of the written law became an impossibility. Neither could judge the other because both were assumed to have originated with Moses. In the same way Rome has developed an unwritten tradition that she has synthesized with the written New Testament to the degree that it cannot be judged by that New Testament. If Mark 7 teaches us anything, it is that the two must not be "synthesized." The written Word of God must remain the unique norm.

HOLD THE TRADITIONS WHICH YOU WERE TAUGHT (2 THESSALONIANS 2:15)

Along with passages such as 1 Corinthians 11:2 and 2 Thessalonians 3:6, the next text provides a more positive evaluation of tradition. The text reads as follows:

Therefore, brethren, stand fast and hold the traditions which you were taught, whether by word or our epistle.

[33] Sungenis, op. cit., 166.

This command given by Paul to the church at Thessalonica is significant for our discussion. Proponents of Tradition 0 often ignore it, while it has become a key weapon in the arsenal of Tradition II adherents. Let us examine the context and try to discern what it is Paul is commanding.

The Thessalonian church has been troubled by some person or persons teaching them that the day of Christ had come (2:2–3). Paul reminds them that he had already taught them the true doctrine when he had been with them (2:5). He continues by providing them with a detailed description of what must occur before the Day of the Lord comes (2:3–12). He then reminds them, in the verse under discussion, to "stand fast and hold the traditions which you were taught, whether by word or our epistle." He is deliberately contrasting the apostolic teaching on the Day of the Lord that he gave them by means of word and epistle with the new teaching they had received "either by spirit or by word or by letter"(2:2).

Instead of being "shaken" by claims contrary to what they had learned, they are to "stand fast." They are to hold to the "traditions" (*paradoseis*) concerning the Day of the Lord which Paul had already taught them. Leon Morris comments on the meaning of the term *paradoseis*:

> "Traditions" is a word which points us to the fact that the Christian message is essentially derivative. It does not originate in men's fertile imaginations. It rests on the facts of the life, death, resurrection, and ascension of Jesus Christ. Paul disclaims originating these things, and expressly says that the things he passed on he had himself first received (1 Cor. 15:3).[34]

Charles Wanamaker offers further helpful explanation of the meaning of "traditions" in this specific context.

> If, as seems likely, we are to see v. 15 in terms of the broader context of chap. 2, then we probably have a reference specifically

---

[34] Leon Morris, *The First and Second Epistles to the Thessalonians*, (Grand Rapids: Wm. B. Eerdmans Publishing Co., 1959), 240.

to the kerygmatic traditions associated with the parousia of Christ. The fact that the command to keep these traditions represents an inference drawn from the discussion of salvation in vv. 13f. implies that nothing less than the salvation of the Thessalonians depended on their holding to these traditions. [35]

In other words, Paul is dealing here with the core apostolic tradition concerning essential elements of the Christian faith.

Significant to the discussion is the fact that Paul held up this apostolic tradition as a "rule of faith." Even if the Thessalonians receive a letter or message purporting to be from him (2:2), they are to stand fast holding to the original apostolic doctrine they received. This is similar to what Paul tells the Galatians when he warns them not to receive any other gospel than what has already been preached to them even if the new gospel is brought by an angel from heaven or from Paul himself (Gal. 1:8). Adherence to tradition in the sense of the rule of faith is not ruled out by this passage and is, in fact, explicitly affirmed and commanded. The Thessalonians were to measure anything—including other "traditions" claiming to be from Paul—against this original rule of faith.

There is no evidence that Paul is referring here to anything other than the apostolic tradition which is coinherent with the content of Scripture. To assert that Paul is referring here to those modern doctrines and practices of the Roman Catholic church simply begs the question. It is one thing to assert that Paul commanded the Church to hold fast to the "traditions." It is quite another to demonstrate that these are what Rome refers to when she speaks of her traditions. If Paul taught these first-century churches certain Roman ecclesiastical traditions, we would expect to find some evidence somewhere of early churches actually adhering to those practices. The fact that the vast bulk of what Rome refers to as her ecclesiastical traditions are devoid of any historical support is a strong testimony to the fact of their novelty.

[35] Charles A. Wanamaker, *The Epistles to the Thessalonians*, NIGTC, (Grand Rapids: William B. Eerdmans Publishing Company, 1990), 268.

SUMMARY

This chapter has not attempted to offer an exhaustive exposition of every scriptural text that has any bearing on the doctrine of Scripture. It has focused instead on certain texts that are repeatedly cited in discussions of this subject. There is no inconsistency between these texts and what we find in the teaching of the early Church. The early patristic concept of Tradition I finds ample support in these debated texts. Not surprisingly, we also find that apologists for conflicting positions will often read much more or much less into these texts than is actually there. To a certain degree this is unavoidable, but in interacting with these texts we must allow them to continually challenge and question the presuppositions we carry.

6

Scripture on the Church

In any study of the nature of authority in Christianity, the doctrine of the Church is central. The authority of the Church is understood differently by adherents of each of the positions we have discussed. The typical evangelical view, Tradition 0, does not allow for any real ecclesiastical authority. The Church as a communion of saints has no more authority than any individual. Scripture is described not merely as the sole final and infallible authority, but as the sole authority altogether. Tradition I—the view of the early Church and many of the classical Reformers, on the other hand—sees the Church as a subordinate authority with the responsibility of interpreting the sole final and infallible authority—Holy Scripture. The older Roman Catholic view, Tradition II, describes the Church as the infallible authoritative interpreter of the two sources of revelation and standards of truth—Scripture and tradition. The newer Roman Catholic position, Tradition III, sees the present Church as infallible and as the real authoritative standard of truth. According to Tradition III, whatever the Church teaches today is the Tradition whether evidence from Scripture or tradition can be found or not.

As in the previous chapter, the comments here will not attempt to be exhaustive but focused on key texts, namely, texts used to defend the claim of Rome's supremacy and infallibility, as well as some that contradict the modern evangelical denial of all ecclesiastical authority.

UPON THIS ROCK (MATTHEW 16:17–19)

Few passages of the New Testament have been the source of more discussion and debate in recent centuries than Matthew 16:17–19. Because it is used as a primary proof-text for the doctrine of Roman supremacy, it has been at the center of debate between Roman Catholics and Protestants. The text itself follows upon Peter's confession of Jesus as the Christ—the Messiah of Israel.

> Jesus answered and said to him, "Blessed are you, Simon Bar-Jonah, for flesh and blood has not revealed this to you, but My Father who is in heaven. And I also say to you that you are Peter, and on this rock I will build My church, and the gates of Hades shall not prevail against it, and I will give you the keys of the kingdom of heaven, and whatever you bind on earth will be bound in heaven, and whatever you loose on earth will be loosed in heaven."

Probably the most important observation that can be made about this text for the purposes of our study is the fact that before the Reformation of the sixteenth century, this passage was very rarely used to support papal claims. The simple reason for this is that most of the early and medieval Church interpreted the "rock" as Christ or as Peter's faith, not as Peter himself.[1] But why is this important? Vatican I and numerous other Roman Catholic decrees insist that no one may interpret Scripture contrary to the "unanimous consent" of the fathers. Aside from the fact that only on a handful of doctrines will one find anything approaching "unanimous consent," this rule contradicts the modern Roman

---

[1] Craig S. Keener, *A Commentary on the Gospel of Matthew*, (Grand Rapids: William B. Eerdmans Publishing Company, 1999), 426, n. 78. See also, Ulrich Luz, *Matthew in History: Interpretation, Influence, and Effects*, (Minneapolis: Fortress Press, 1994), 60, and John Bigane, *Faith, Christ or Peter: Matthew 16:18 in Sixteenth Century Roman Catholic Exegesis*, (Washington D.C.: University Press, 1981). The early Church's interpretation of the "rock" in Matthew 16:18 has been thoroughly documented in William Webster, *Peter and the Rock*, (Battle Ground, WA: Christian Resources, 1996), republished as *The Matthew 16 Controversy*.

Catholic interpretation of this text. First of all, there was no unanimous consent on the meaning of the "rock." Most interpreted it as Christ. Some interpreted it as Peter's faith. A few interpreted it as Peter.

Second, the strong patristic tendency toward interpreting the rock as Christ necessitates the falsity of the modern Roman Catholic interpretation. Why? Because if, as Rome claims, the papacy was established by Christ as a necessary constitutive element of his Church; and if, as Rome claims, Christ established Peter as "the rock," the supreme Apostle upon whom he would build his Church, then it is utterly inconceivable that most of the prominent leaders of this very Church would have failed to see that fact in this supposedly key passage until the middle ages. If support for the papacy is found in Matthew 16, why was it was missed by most of the early fathers? We are forced to ask why some, such as Augustine, go out of their way to assert that the "rock" is *not* Peter. Regardless of whether the patristic interpretation of this passage is correct or not, the fact that the fathers as a whole do not interpret it as Rome now claims it *must* be interpreted is decisive evidence against the Roman Catholic papal interpretation.[2] The most that can be positively asserted on the basis of patristic and medieval exegesis of this passage is that the interpretation of this passage has never been unanimous.

Ironically many Protestant commentators readily concede that Jesus may very well have been referring to Peter when He said, "Upon this rock." Rome's argument is not helped by this

[2] Of course it must be noted that because Rome considers herself infallible, a criticism such as this is completely irrelevant to her. Her "infallibility" renders her autonomous (a law unto herself), and renders her claims incapable of being subject to testing of any kind whether against Scripture or tradition. Even if every father and council explicitly contradicted Rome's current claims, they would have to be dismissed in order to maintain the current claim of infallibility. This is why it is not inaccurate to refer to Rome's modern Tradition III position as *sola ecclesia,* for in reality it is not Scripture and tradition which are the standards of truth for Rome; the standard of truth is whatever Rome currently teaches. When the claims of infallibility are combined with the novel theory of development proposed by Cardinal Newman in the nineteenth century, Rome can summarily dismiss any and every argument raised against her. We shall examine the unfounded basis for the Roman claim of infallibility more thoroughly in Part Three.

concession, however, because regardless of whether the "rock" refers to Peter, to Peter's faith or to Christ, Rome has read much more into the text than can be found there. While many Protestants have not allowed for the possibility that the "rock" is Peter because they believed that this would entail accepting the entire Roman Catholic argument, many Roman Catholics have assumed that if they can demonstrate that the "rock" is a reference to Peter then they have somehow proven that Christ established the Roman Catholic papacy in Matthew 16. The leap from "this rock" being a reference to Peter to the doctrine of the papacy, however, is textually groundless.

Let us assume that the "rock" does refer to Peter. What have we lost (if we are Protestant) or gained (if we are Roman Catholic)? Nothing. Because even if the passage is speaking of Peter, it says absolutely nothing about succession, infallibility, supreme jurisdiction or any other fundamental elements of the modern papacy.[3] As Carson points out, there are fundamental problems with the later Roman Catholic interpretation of this text. For example, if the Roman Catholic interpretation is correct, then when Peter died (ca. A.D. 68), his successor would have been in authority over a living Apostle—John, who did not die until the end of the first century.[4] Since the Apostles were gifted with unique authority, and since even Rome does not claim that the successors of Peter had the same unique authority as the Apostles, Rome's papal theory immediately falls into a self-contradiction when Peter dies.

If Jesus is referring to Peter as the "rock," the foundation of the Church, in this passage, it is reading into the text to assume that this implies the modern papacy. Other passages use the same metaphor by describing Christ (1 Cor. 3:11), and all of the Apostles and prophets (Eph. 2:20; Rev. 21:14) as the "foundation" of the Church. Stephen Ray, in his defense of the modern Roman Catholic interpretation of this text, attempts to get around this

---

[3] D.A. Carson, op. cit., 368.
[4] Ibid.

fact in order to prove the supremacy of Peter. He writes, "The Bible does not set up a dichotomy—*either* Jesus *or* Peter; rather, it presents us with *both* Jesus *and* Peter as foundation stones."[5] He fails to point out at this crucial point in his argument, however, that it also presents us with *all* of the prophets and Apostles as the foundation. It is not simply Jesus and Peter; it is Jesus, Peter, and all of the prophets and Apostles who are spoken of at various times as the foundation of the Church.

The remaining arguments presented in support of the Roman interpretation of this passage are no more substantive than the *non sequiturs* derived from the metaphor of the "rock." Consider some of the other details of the text. When Jesus asks the disciples who they say that He is, Peter answers, "You are the Christ, the Son of the living God" (v. 16). Jesus responds, by blessing Peter and telling him that this truth has been revealed to him by God. This hearkens back to Jesus' words in 11:25–27, in which He thanks the Father for hiding these things from the wise and revealing them to babes.

Jesus then says, "And I also say to you that you are Peter" (16:18). Some Roman Catholic commentators claim that Jesus is here changing Peter's name from Simon to Peter, and they make much of this supposed name change. Stephen Ray, for example, writes,

> Name changes held great weight in eastern cultures. Abraham's name change from Abram (father) to Abraham (father of nations) is a prime example. It signified a change of status or mission. Jesus changed Peter's name from Simon to Rock. Jesus is making it obvious that something important is taking place; Peter's status has changed for all time, and, as with Abraham, this change would have a continuing impact on the new covenant community. The fisherman was now the steward of a kingdom.[6]

[5] Stephen K. Ray, *Upon This Rock: St. Peter and the Primacy of Rome in Scripture and the Early Church*, (San Francisco: Ignatius Press, 1999), 36, n. 38.

[6] Ray, op. cit., 34, n. 36.

The problem with this interpretation is that there is no indication in the text itself that Jesus is changing Peter's name. As R.T. France observes, the name Peter "is not now given for the first time, for Matthew has used it throughout in preference to 'Simon' (which never occurs without 'Peter' until v. 17), and Mark 3:16 and John 1:42 indicate that it was given at an earlier stage."[7] Jesus is not changing Simon's name at this point. He is merely pointing out the significance of the name by means of a play on words.

Jesus continues, "And I also say to you that you are Peter (*petros*), and on this rock (*petra*) I will build my Church."[8] As discussed before, there is a lack of any patristic or medieval consensus on the interpretation of this word play. "This rock" has been variously interpreted as Peter himself, Peter's faith, and Christ. If we are to be honest with the text, none of these proposed interpretations should be ruled out *a priori*. As several Protestant commentators have pointed out, "this rock" may very well be a reference to Peter.[9] What they have also pointed out, however, is

[7] R.T. France, *The Gospel According to Matthew*, TNTC, (Grand Rapids: William B. Eerdmans Publishing Company, 1985), 254.

[8] Ray also places a lot of emphasis upon where Jesus was supposedly standing when he uttered this remark to Peter (Cf. *Upon This Rock*, p. 32–33, n. 32; p. 36, n. 37). Ray claims it to be a "fact" (p. 36) that Jesus is standing right in front of the massive rock that supported the temple to Caesar Augustus. Supposedly then, by saying to Peter, "You are *petros*," He is making a correlation with the massive stone in front of Him. Ray writes, "Then, after the correlation has been made, he looks at Peter *and* the massive rock and says, "And upon this Rock I will build my Church" (p. 36). Such sheer speculation would hardly be worth refuting were it not for the fact that Ray repeatedly emphasizes the importance of this geographical setting for his argument. In response, it must be pointed out that nowhere in Matthew 16:13–20 (or in the parallel passages in Mark 8:27ff. and Luke 9:18ff.) does the author indicate a specific location for this incident. All Matthew says is that Jesus and the disciples came into the "region" of Caesarea Philippi. Nothing is said about a specific location. Mark 8:27 says the discourse occurred on a "road" in the towns of Caesarea Philippi. Not only is Ray offering pure speculation as proof on this point, but one must ask how he could possibly know that Jesus looked at Peter *and* the massive rock? Where does the text say what or who Jesus was looking at when He made these comments? We can legitimately assume He looked at Peter since He was speaking to him. But to assert without *any* proof whatsoever that He also looked at a massive rock, which He may or may not have been anywhere near and to make all of this speculation a main point in one's argument is exegetically irresponsible.

[9] See Carson, op. cit., 367–369; Keener, op. cit., 426–427; France, op. cit., 254.

that this does not necessitate the Roman Catholic inferences based upon this play on words. As D.A. Carson observes,

> None of this requires that conservative Roman Catholic views be endorsed. . . . The text says nothing about Peter's successors, infallibility, or exclusive authority. . . . What the New Testament does show is that Peter is the first to make this formal confession and that his prominence continues in the earliest years of the Church (Acts 1–12). But he, along with John, can be sent by other Apostles (Acts 8:14); and he is held accountable for his actions by the Jerusalem church (Acts 11:1–18) and rebuked by Paul (Gal. 2:11–14). He is, in short, *primus inter pares* ("first among equals"); and on the foundation of such men (Eph 2:20), Jesus built his church.[10]

Carson continues by pointing out what the text does indicate about the place of Peter in the Church:

> In one sense Peter stands with the other disciples as fishers of men, as recipients of the Great Commission (notice in v. 20 that Jesus warns *all* his disciples, not just Peter, to tell no one). In that sense the disciples stand as paradigms for all believers during this period of redemptive history. But this does not exclude a special role for Peter or the Apostles. Peter was the foundation, the first stone laid: he enjoys this "salvation historical primacy," and on him others are laid. This results in certain special roles in the earliest years of the Christian church. But notions of hierarchy or sacerdotalism are simply irrelevant to the text.[11]

Jesus' reference to building His Church is paralleled in a number of passages which speak of the people of God in terms of building (cf. 2 Sam. 7:13–14; 1 Chron. 17:12–13; Ps. 28:5; Jer. 24:6; 31:4; 42:10; Amos 9:11; 1 Cor. 3:9; Eph. 2:20–22; 1 Pet. 2:5). As France points out, "The building metaphor is the natural one to use in connection with the name *Petros,* and does not demand

---

[10] Carson, op. cit., 368.
[11] Ibid., 373–374.

the idea of a full-blown hierarchical structure."[12] The word translated church is *ekklesia* and means literally "those who are called
out." It points to continuity with the faithful remnant of the Old
Testament people of God.

Jesus also promises that the "gates of Hades shall not prevail"
against His Church. There have been several interpretations of
this phrase. Some argue that it refers to the forces of Satan who
attack the Church. Some assert that it means death (Isa. 38:10; cf.
Job 17:16; 38:17; Ps. 9:13; 107:18). Still others believe it means
that Satan's defensive forces will not be able to resist the forward
march of the Church. Regardless of which specific interpretation
one takes, the main thrust is the same. The Church that Jesus
Christ is building cannot be completely overcome even by God's
greatest enemies (cf. 1 Cor. 15:25–26). It must be pointed out,
however, that this promise of ultimate victory does not entail infallibility. The two ideas are completely different concepts.

Finally, Jesus tells Peter, "and I will give you the keys of the
kingdom of heaven, and whatever you bind on earth will be
bound in heaven, and whatever you loose on earth will be loosed
in heaven" (v. 19). Several observations may be made about this
verse. First, Jesus gives Peter the "keys of the kingdom" not the
"keys of the Church." The two are different ideas, and light can be
shed on what Jesus meant by "the keys" by looking at Matthew
23:13 and Luke 11:52. The approach to Scripture taken by the
scribes and Pharisees shuts people out of the kingdom. D.A. Carson explains the significance of this metaphor as applied to Peter:

> In contrast [to the teachers of the law], Peter, on confessing Jesus
> as Messiah, is told he has received this confession by the Father's
> revelation and will be given the keys of the kingdom: i.e., by
> proclaiming "the good news of the kingdom" (4:23), which, by
> revelation he is increasingly understanding, he will open the
> kingdom to many and shut it against many. Fulfillments of this in
> Acts are not found in passages like 15:10 but in those like

---

[12] France, op. cit., 255.

2:14–39; 3:11–26, so that by this means the Lord added to the church those who were being saved (2:45), or, otherwise put, Jesus was building his church (Matt. 16:18). But the same gospel proclamation alienates and excludes men; so we also find Peter shutting up the kingdom from men (Acts 4:11–12; 8:20–23). The periphrastic future perfects [the tenses of "binding" and "loosing"] are then perfectly natural: Peter accomplishes this binding and loosing by proclaiming a gospel that has already been given and by making personal application on that basis (Simon Magus). Whatever he binds or looses will have been bound or loosed, so long as he adheres to that divinely disclosed gospel. He has no direct pipeline to heaven, still less do his decisions force heaven to comply; but he may be authoritative in binding and loosing because heaven has acted first (cf. Acts 18:9–10). Those he ushers in or excludes have already been bound or loosed by God according to the gospel which Peter, by confessing Jesus as the Messiah, has most clearly grasped.[13]

Second, although the authority to bind and loose is specifically addressed to Peter in this verse, the identical power is given to the disciples as a whole in Matthew 18:18. Peter was given this authority of the keys first, and the rest of the disciples are given this authority of the keys soon afterward. There simply is no support in Matthew 16 for the Roman Catholic papal doctrine.

JESUS PRAYS THAT PETER'S FAITH WILL NOT FAIL (LUKE 22:31–32)

Another text that is often used in support of the Roman doctrine of ecclesiastical authority, and specifically papal authority, is Luke 22:31–32. Jesus makes the following comments on the night of the Last Supper, after the disciples have had an argument over who will be greatest among them.

And the Lord said, "Simon, Simon! Indeed, Satan has asked for you, that he may sift you as wheat. But I have prayed for you, that your faith should not fail; and when you have returned to Me, strengthen your brethren."

[13] Carson, op. cit., 373.

In order to understand the significance of these verses for our study, we must note the use that has been made of them by Roman Catholic apologists. The comments of Stephen Ray are typical.

> Why does Jesus pray for Peter and not for the other eleven? The singular and plural pronouns in this passage are very telling. Jesus speaks directly to Simon, uttering his name twice for emphasis. Jesus tells Peter that Satan has demanded to sift them all as wheat, a passage reminiscent of Job 1:8–12. Jesus then tells Peter that He has prayed for him (singular, not the other eleven), that his faith will prevail, and that when he has gone through the trial, Peter should strengthen the other Apostles. "Strengthen" means to confirm, fix, establish, make stable, place firmly, and set fast. This is confirmation of the fact that Christ had made Peter the leader, the rock, and had invested him with the keys; Luke was not ignorant of the authority invested in Peter by our Lord. The whole apostolic band would be strengthened by the one for whom the Lord prayed—the one whom the Lord appointed as shepherd of His flock.[14]

Several observations may be made about the text in response to the claims of Rome. Ray asks why Jesus prays for Peter alone when He has just said that all of the disciples will be sifted by Satan. An examination of the parallel passage in the Gospel of Mark sheds light on that question. Mark tells us that after Jesus predicted that all of the Apostles would stumble, Peter said to Him, "Even if all are made to stumble, yet I will not be" (Mark 14:29). Mark then records Jesus' prediction of Peter's denial. Here in Mark, all of the Apostles are told they will stumble. Peter alone informs His Lord that He is wrong. Peter claims that even if everyone else falls away, he will not.[15] It is more likely, then, that the reason Jesus singled Peter out for a special prayer was because of Peter's special arrogance in this situation. Peter dramatically

---

[14] Ray, op. cit., 48, n. 63.

[15] Those claiming to be his successors have echoed Peter's erroneous thought down to the present.

overestimates his own faith despite Jesus' warning. That is an especially dangerous place for any believer to be, and therefore Jesus, because of His love for Peter, prays especially for him.

Ray also observes that Peter was the leader of the twelve. However, since this is not disputed no response is necessary. What neither Ray nor any Roman Catholic has demonstrated is that this text which involves a specific prayer for one specific man in one specific historical circumstance has anything to do with the modern Roman Catholic papacy. Jesus prays that Peter's faith will not fail during the temptation that is about to come that very night. There is absolutely nothing explicit or implicit in the text concerning the faith of potential successors of Peter. Nor is there anything in the text even remotely suggesting that Jesus' prayer involved the bestowal of any gift of infallibility upon either Peter or any successors. A prayer that Peter's faith will not fail in a specific coming test simply does not entail infallibility. This text in Luke 22 is a beautiful picture of our Lord's love and concern for Peter. It has absolutely no bearing on the question of the papacy.

HE WILL GUIDE YOU INTO ALL TRUTH (JOHN 16:12–15)

Another passage that is used to support the Roman Catholic position on the Church is John 16:12–15 which reads,

> I still have many things to say to you, but you cannot bear them now. However, when He, the Spirit of truth, has come, He will guide you into all truth; for He will not speak on His own authority, but whatever He hears He will speak; and He will tell you things to come. He will glorify Me, for He will take of what is Mine and declare it to you. All things that the Father has are Mine. Therefore I said that He will take of Mine and declare it to you.

The significance of John 16:12–15 lies in its use by Roman Catholic theologians as a textual support for the doctrine of papal infallibility.[16] The question remains, however, whether the text

16 See, for example, McBrien, op. cit., 761.

actually teaches any such doctrine. And it is quite clear that it does not. There is absolutely nothing in the text that refers to a supposed gift of infallibility. If by some eisegetical leap infallibility is read into the words "all truth," it would have to be observed that omniscience could be read into the same words with a lot less difficulty. It must also be noted that there is nothing in the text limiting what is said to Peter. The words are spoken to all of the disciples present with Jesus at that time. There is little by way of refutation that may be offered to the Roman use of this text because it is not based upon any real exegesis of the text. Instead it is simply based on a bare assertion.

FEED MY SHEEP (JOHN 21:15–17)

If there is any text outside of Matthew 16 that is considered by Roman Catholicism to be a virtual proof-text of her ecclesiastical authority, it is John 21:15–17, which reads as follows:

> So when they had eaten breakfast, Jesus said to Simon Peter, "Simon, son of Jonah, do you love Me more than these?" He said to Him, "Yes, Lord; You know that I love You." He said to Him, "Feed my lambs." He said to him again a second time, "Simon, son of Jonah, do you love Me?" He said to Him, "Yes, Lord; You know that I love You." He said to him, "Tend My sheep." He said to him the third time, "Simon, son of Jonah, do you love Me?" Peter was grieved because He said to him the third time, "Do you love Me?" And he said to Him, "Lord, You know all things; You know that I love You." Jesus said to him, "Feed My sheep."

The Roman Catholic understanding of this text is explained by Stephen Ray. He writes of the significance of the text,

> After rising from the dead, Jesus spends forty days with His Apostles, teaching them about the kingdom of God and His Church (Acts 1:3; Mt. 28:18–20). He invests Peter with a singular and special commission. Peter is to be the shepherd over Jesus' sheep—a visible, recognizable leader. . . . Jesus appoints Peter the universal shepherd of His whole flock.[17]

---

[17] Ray, op. cit., 49, n. 65.

Before proceeding further, it is important to note that Protestants do not necessarily deny that Peter was the leader of the Apostles. What is disputed is whether or not his role as leader of the Apostles was transferred to any successor and whether that role entails the claims of the modern papacy to be the leader of the entire Church.

It is helpful to begin by examining what the early church fathers said regarding this text of Scripture. Interestingly, in the collected writings of the Ante-Nicene fathers which span the first three hundred years of the Church, there are apparently only two explicit references to this passage. Both are by Cyprian (ca. 200–258). The first asserts nothing more than the fact that the three-fold commission to feed the sheep was related to Peter's threefold denial of Christ.[18] In the second reference, he asserts that although it was to Peter alone that Jesus spoke these words, all of the Apostles received equal power from Christ.[19] In the fourth century, Augustine also connects this threefold commission to Peter's threefold denial.[20]

These church fathers were correct in their explanation of the significance of the text. Peter had denied the Lord three times (cf. John 18:15–18, 25–27), and Jesus is officially restoring him to his place of leadership among the Apostles. Leon Morris comments,

> There can be little doubt but that the whole scene is meant to show us Peter as completely restored to his position of leadership. He has three times denied his Lord. Now he has three times affirmed his love for Him, and three times he has been commissioned to care for the flock. This must have had the effect on the others of a demonstration that, whatever had been the mistakes of the past, Jesus was restoring Peter to a place of trust.[21]

---

[18] *Epistle* 2:1.

[19] *Treatise* 1:4. Later interpolations were added to this statement of Cyprian to make it teach Petrine supremacy, but the additions have been definitively proven to be later forgeries.

[20] *Harmony of the Gospels*, III:2:6; *On the Gospel of St. John*, Tractate XLVII:2 (NPNF; vol. VII, p. 260).

[21] Leon Morris, *The Gospel According to John*, NICNT, (Grand Rapids: Wm. B. Eerdmans Publishing Co., 1971), 875.

Protestants do not deny that Peter held a leadership role in the early Church and among the twelve Apostles. What is not found either explicitly or implicitly in this text, however, is the concept of the modern Roman papacy. Peter was restored by Jesus to his place of leadership in the early Church (cf. Acts 1–2). There is nothing in this text concerning a succession of supreme universal monarchical bishops. There is no consciousness that the text meant such in the early Church. Historically speaking, it was only after the later creation of the papacy that anyone began to search out proof texts that could be used to give credence to the idea of a papacy. Even then, only a handful of texts could be found, and not only do they give no direct exegetical support to the concept of the papacy, the interpretation of those texts found in the early fathers is, more often than not, in direct contradiction with the Roman interpretation.

THE JERUSALEM COUNCIL (ACTS 15:6–29)

The account of the Jerusalem Council in Acts 15 is very important for our understanding of the authority of the Church. It also sheds additional light on the role of Peter in the early Church. The context for the Jerusalem Council is found in verse 1 of the chapter:

> And certain men came down from Judea and taught the brethren, "Unless you are circumcised according to the custom of Moses, you cannot be saved."

These Judaizers were upsetting the Gentile believers to such a degree that a council had to meet to settle the issue. When the Apostles arrived in Jerusalem, some of the Pharisees who had become believers arose and echoed the claim that Gentiles must be circumcised and keep the law in order to be saved (v. 5). Then we read,

> So the Apostles and elders came together to consider this matter. And when there had been much dispute, Peter rose up and

said to them: "Men and brethren, you know that a good while ago God chose among us, that by my mouth the Gentiles should hear the word of the gospel and believe. So God, who knows the heart, acknowledged them by giving them the Holy Spirit just as He did to us, and made no distinction between us and them, purifying their hearts by faith. Now therefore, why do you test God by putting a yoke on the neck of the disciples which neither our fathers nor we were able to bear? But we believe that through the grace of the Lord Jesus Christ we shall be saved in the same manner as they."

Peter, as the leader of the Apostles, has the privilege of speaking first. He reminds those present that the matter had actually been settled years earlier when He had gone to Cornelius and the Gentiles and they had received the gift of the Holy Spirit (Acts 10:1–11:18). While some see universal Petrine supremacy implied in verse 7, additional scriptural context reveals such a reading to be unwarranted. It is true that Peter was the first to go to the Gentiles, but it was Paul who was appointed by God to be the Apostle to the Gentiles (Rom. 11:13). This paralleled Peter's appointment as Apostle to the Jews (Gal. 2:7–9). After Peter's speech, we read the following:

Then all the multitude kept silent and listened to Barnabas and Paul declaring how many miracles and wonders God had worked through them among the Gentiles. And after they had become silent, James answered, saying, "Men and brethren, listen to me: Simon has declared how God at first visited the Gentiles to take out of them a people for His name. And with this the words of the prophets agree, just as it is written: 'After this I will return and will rebuild the tabernacle of David which has fallen down. I will rebuild its ruins, and I will set it up, So that the rest of mankind may seek the LORD, even all the Gentiles who are called by My name, says the LORD who does all these things.' Known to God from eternity are all His works. Therefore I judge that we should not trouble those from among the Gentiles who are turning to God, but that we write to them to abstain from things

polluted by idols, from sexual immorality, from things stran-
gled, and from blood. For Moses has had throughout many generations those who preach him in every city, being read in the
synagogues every Sabbath."

Following Peter's initial speech, Barnabas and Paul speak to the
assembly (v. 12). When they are finished, James speaks, summing
up what Peter reminded them and also reminding them of what
was taught in the prophets (vv. 13–18). Interestingly, in verse 19,
he sums up the deliberations with the decisive words, "Therefore
I judge." Contrary to those who attempt to represent Peter as
having the "final word" at this council,[22] the text places the final
word in the mouth of James. In Greek, James' words read, *dio ego
krino.* The first word *dio* simply means "therefore" or "for this reason." *Ego* is the first person personal pronoun, which is translated
"I." The Greek *krino* means "to judge." It is often used in the judicial context of a courtroom. After hearing all of the evidence on
both sides James acts as the final judge and declares the final word
on the matter.[23]

The passage is illustrative of several aspects of apostolic ecclesiology. First, in the case of a serious dispute, it was deemed
necessary to call a council. Some problems were simply too large
for a single church or a single man to handle. If this is true of the
Apostles themselves, how much more true in our case? The decision of the council was sent to the churches via written letter (vv.
22–29) and was received with joy by the Gentiles. A second important point is that the passage strongly implies the absence of
any concept of a universal monarchical bishop in the apostolic
Church. Peter's leadership of the Apostles did not entail a universality of ecclesiastical jurisdiction. He had the first word at the
Jerusalem Council, but he did not have the final word.

---

[22] Ray, op. cit., 54, n. 72.

[23] It cannot be doubted that if these words had been spoken by Peter instead of James
that this text would be used as a primary proof-text for the papacy. Since they are spoken
by James, they are usually ignored or explained away by Roman Catholic apologists.

THE OLIVE TREE AND THE BRANCHES (ROMANS 11:17–22)

Romans 11:17–22 is a significant text because of its implications for the question of infallibility. Paul is discussing the question of the Jews' rejection of Christ and says to his Gentile readers in the Roman church,

> And if some of the branches were broken off, and you, being a wild olive tree, were grafted in among them, and with them became a partaker of the root and fatness of the olive tree, do not boast against the branches. But if you boast, remember that you do not support the root, but the root supports you. You will say then, "Branches were broken off that I might be grafted in." Well said. Because of unbelief they were broken off, and you stand by faith. Do not be haughty, but fear. For if God did not spare the natural branches, He may not spare you either. Therefore consider the goodness and severity of God: on those who fell, severity; but toward you, goodness, if you continue in His goodness. Otherwise you also will be cut off.

Paul teaches a number of great truths in this passage, but the relevant issue for our discussion is the warning he gives to the Roman church about the possibility of being broken off as a branch if they do not continue in faith. Rome today teaches that it is impossible for the Roman church to fall away from the faith because of her understanding of Christ's promise to Peter that the gates of hell would never prevail against His Church.[24]

The Roman Catholic presumption of her inability to be broken off stems from at least three errors. We have already discussed the first major error—the misinterpretation of Matthew 16:18. The promise Christ gave implied the final victory of the entire Church. It promises nothing about perpetual infallibility to any specific local church. Not only does Matthew 16:18 not promise infallibility to any specific local church, it does not promise immediate perfection to any local church or to the Church as a whole. The Church is at war; it has not yet achieved the final consummative victory.

[24] Cf. *Catechism of the Catholic Church*, par. 834.

Rome's second major error is to ignore the teaching of texts like Romans 11:17–22 that explicitly teach the possibility of a particular church, in this case Rome, falling away and being broken off.[25] Romans 11 is particularly important because the Jewish branches who were broken off also believed they had received an unconditional promise. The olive tree is Old Testament Israel. Those ethnic Israelites who did not believe in the Messiah were cut off, leaving the remnant—true Israel. Gentile branches from a wild olive tree were grafted into this already existing olive tree forming the New Covenant church. Now Paul warns the Gentiles about boasting. As Thomas Schreiner observes,

> Ironically, by capitulating to pride Gentile believers were falling into the same problem that plagued the Jews. Paul warns the Jews throughout Romans (esp. chapters 1–4) of the danger of vaunting themselves above Gentiles because of their elect status. Now he admonishes the Gentiles that they are prone to the same deception. . . . It also follows, therefore, that the warnings addressed to the Jews can be applied in principle to believers of today since 11:17–24 indicates that Gentiles (and therefore all people) are liable to the same sin committed by the Jews.[26]

Rome does not believe this warning applies to her, but we must remember that whatever else the promise in Matthew 16:18 means, it does not guarantee the continuation in the faith of every individual local church (cf. Rev. 2:5). In light of the fact that there is no explicit promise to the local church of Rome to the contrary, and in light of the fact that Romans 11:17–22 was originally written specifically to the Roman church, it is nothing short of presumption to claim an exception for the Church of Rome.

The third major error Rome falls into is a failure to take into account the conditional nature of biblical predictions. Even had

---

[25] Cf. Rev. 2:5, where Christ warns the church at Ephesus that unless they repent He will come and remove their lampstand from its place.

[26] Thomas Schreiner, *Romans*, BECNT, (Grand Rapids: Baker Book House, 1998), 606.

there been a prediction that the church at Rome would continue forever, it would be subject to the same implicit conditions inherent in other biblical predictions. Richard Pratt has addressed this highly significant issue.[27] After examining the different types of predictions found in the Old Testament along with their fulfillments, Pratt points out that "the original recipients of Old Testament predictions could rest assured that Yahweh would fulfill all of his covenant promises, but no particular prophecy was completely free from the potential influence of intervening historical contingencies."[28] The paradigmatic Old Testament passage on the conditionality of prophecy is Jeremiah 18:1–12. Pratt asks,

> Did tacit conditions apply only to a small class of unqualified predictions? Or did conditions attach to all of these prophecies?[29]

He continues,

> An answer to this question appears in the eighteenth chapter of Jeremiah, the prophet's experience at the potter's house. This passage stood against the backdrop of false views concerning the inviolability of Jerusalem. Many Jerusalemites opposed Jeremiah because they believed divine protection for Jerusalem was entirely unconditional (e.g., Jer. 7:4). Jeremiah 18:1–12 amounted to a rebuttal of this false security. It stated that *all* unqualified predictions, even those concerning Jerusalem, operated with implied conditions.[30]

The central section of Jeremiah 18 which pertains to this issue is vv. 7–10.

> The instant I speak concerning a nation and concerning a kingdom, to pluck up, to pull down, and to destroy it, if that nation

---

[27] Richard L. Pratt, Jr., "Historical Contingencies and Biblical Predictions," *III M Magazine Online*, Vol. 1, No. 3 (May 24–30, 1999), www.thirdmill.org

[28] Ibid., 22.

[29] Ibid., 13.

[30] Ibid.

against whom I have spoken turns from its evil, I will relent of the disaster that I thought to bring upon it. And the instant I speak concerning a nation and concerning a kingdom, to build and to plant it, if it does evil in My sight so that it does not obey My voice, then I will relent concerning the good with which I said I would benefit it.

The Roman church simply has no grounds to claim that she alone is free from the possibility of having her lampstand removed (cf. Rev. 2:5). First, there is no prediction that she alone would continue forever. Second, if there were such a prediction, it would explicitly or implicitly include the condition of continuing obedience to God. Third, there is a specific passage written to the Roman church by Paul explicitly warning her of the possibility of her disobedience and falling away.

NO OTHER GOSPEL (GALATIANS 1:8–9)

The Epistle to the Galatians was written to a church on the verge of forsaking the gospel of Christ. In this letter Paul includes a warning which contains an important principle. He writes,

> But even if we, or an angel from heaven, preach any other gospel to you than what we have preached to you, let him be accursed. As we have said before, so now I say again, if anyone preaches any other gospel to you than what you have received, let him be accursed.

The principle in this passage to which we must give special attention at this point is the principle of testing. Throughout the Old and New Testaments, believers are warned to test those who claim to speak for God. In the Old Testament, those claiming to be prophets were to be tested (cf. Deut. 13:1–5; 18:21–22); and in the New Testament, those claiming to be Apostles were to be tested (cf. Gal. 1:8–9; Rev. 2:2). There are repeated warnings throughout the New Testament to test all things (cf. Rom. 16:17; 1 Thess. 5:21; 1 John 4:1). The reason that such testing is absolutely necessary is because there will be false apostles and false prophets among the sheep who will seek to destroy them and lead them astray (cf. Matt. 7:15; 24:5, 11, 24; Mark 13:6, 22; Acts 20:29–30; 2 Cor. 11:13–15; 1 Tim. 4:1; 2 Pet. 2:1–2; 1 John 2:19; 4:1; 2 John 7; Jude 4).

The significance of Galatians 1:8–9 is that Paul tells the church that even if he himself should bring another gospel to them, they must reject it. Even if an angel from heaven should bring another gospel to them, they must reject it. Paul tells the Corinthian church that Satan transforms himself into an angel of light and that his ministers are deceitful workers who transform themselves into Apostles of Christ (2 Cor. 11:13–15). If such is the case, and if testing is required, there must of necessity be a fixed public standard by which such testing may be accomplished. If the final authority is simply anyone claiming to be an Apostle, then there is no means of distinguishing between a true apostle of Christ and a false apostle. Paul is a true Apostle and tells the Galatians that even *he* cannot return to them and bring another gospel without falling under the curse of God. This implies that *all* who claim such authority must be subjected to testing.

If the Galatians are to test Paul himself by another standard, what is that standard? He tells them that it is the gospel that they have already received—a gospel that he reiterates throughout this and his other epistles. The important point is that if Satan and his ministers can transform themselves into apostles of Christ, it is no more difficult for them to transform themselves into those claiming to be the successors of the Apostles of Christ. But if the successors themselves are considered inherently infallible, then it is impossible to distinguish between true successors and false successors. The standard of testing, according to Paul, has to be other than the person himself, and it must be something to which the entire Church has access. At the time Paul wrote this epistle, that standard—the apostolic gospel—had been communicated both orally and by letter. The Church today still has the apostolic gospel in these letters, and it remains the standard by which the Church must test all who claim to be teachers of truth.

THE PILLAR AND GROUND OF THE TRUTH (1 TIMOTHY 3:15)

We turn our attention now to a text that sheds more light on the nature of ecclesiastical authority. Contrary to adherents of Tradition 0, the Church is not without any authority. In his first letter to Timothy, Paul writes,

> but if I am delayed, I write so that you may know how you ought to conduct yourself in the house of God, which is the church of the living God, the pillar and ground of the truth.

Paul speaks of the Church as a "pillar" and "ground" of the truth. The words he uses describe a structural foundation. The truth spoken of is the content of the apostolic Christian faith (cf. Gal. 2:5, 14; 5:7; Eph. 4:21; Col. 1:5; 2 Thess. 2:12, 13; 1 Tim. 2:4; 4:3; 6:5; Titus 1:1, 14; 2 Tim. 2:15, 18, 25; 3:7, 8; 4:4). According to Paul, the Church is given the responsibility by God to uphold the truth of Christianity.

It is also important to note that the Church is not identical to the truth. Jesus is the truth (John 14:6), and the Word of God is truth (John 17:17), but the Church is not identical to truth. She is the pillar and ground of truth in the sense that she is called to uphold and proclaim the truth, but she is distinguished from the truth she upholds. This is important because 1 Timothy 3:15 is often used by Roman Catholic apologists to support an ecclesiology which either subordinates Scripture to the Church or else puts the Church on an equal level of authority with the Scripture.[31] The problem with this interpretation is that if it were applied consistently it would also place the Church on an equal or higher level of authority than Christ Himself. Both Christ and the Word of God are explicitly termed "the truth." The Church is explicitly termed the "pillar and ground of the truth." If this terminology puts her on an equal level of authority with the Word of God, it puts her on an equal level of authority with Christ. This is obviously not the case. The Church is the place where the truth may be found, but it is the truth which has the ultimate authority.

[31] Ray, op. cit., 60–61, n. 81.

SUMMARY

This brief examination of some of the most often cited scriptural texts in the debate between Roman Catholics and Protestants has been instructive in several ways. The primary texts used to support the Roman theory of the Church and papacy have far less in the texts themselves than Roman Catholic apologists find there. Scripture simply does not support either the Tradition II or Tradition III concept of authority. Part One showed that Tradition I was the concept of authority held by the Church for the first three centuries of her existence. Part Two showed that Tradition I is the position most consistent with what Scripture itself explicitly says on the subject. There is nothing supporting either Rome's later exaltation of the Church to a place of equal or greater authority than the Word of God or modern evangelicalism's later denigration of the Church to a place of no real authority to interpret the Word of God.

PART THREE:

THE THEOLOGICAL NECESSITY OF SOLA SCRIPTURA

7

A Critique of Roman Catholic and Eastern Orthodox Positions

The previous chapters have surveyed some of the major developments in the history of the Church's understanding of the concept of authority. For the first three centuries of the Church, a general consensus prevailed on the role of Scripture, the Church, and the rule of faith. Tradition was not seen as a second source of revelation but as the apostolic kerygma, and it was coinherent with the content of Scripture. It is this concept of tradition that we, using the terminology of Oberman, have referred to as Tradition I. In the fourth century the first hints of a two-source theory of tradition are seen in the Church. This concept has been termed Tradition II. In the twelfth through fourteenth centuries the two-source theory gained ground among the scholastic theologians and canon lawyers. By the time of the Reformation in the sixteenth century, these two concepts of tradition became part of the larger conflict between the Reformers and Rome. The Reformers advocated the older concept of Tradition I using the terminology of *sola scriptura,* while Rome reacted by clinging to the newer Tradition II theory. This two-source theory was made the official dogma of the Roman Catholic church at the Council of Trent.

At the First Vatican Council (1870), the Roman Catholic church officially dogmatized the doctrine of papal infallibility. This doctrine, together with Cardinal Newman's theory of doctrinal development, gradually led to the adoption of a completely

new theory of tradition in which the magisterium of the Church
is considered the one real source of revelation. This concept,
termed Tradition III by Oberman, co-exists in the Roman Catholic church with the Tradition II concept.

This chapter will lay out some of the major difficulties inherent in both of the positions held within the Roman Catholic communion today, specifically difficulties in the notion of tradition as
a second source of revelation (Tradition II) and problems inherent within the concept of the magisterium and the pope as the
real source of revelation (Tradition III). The following discussion
will also evaluate the Eastern Orthodox concept of tradition,
which did not develop within the same philosophical, theological, and cultural context as Tradition II and Tradition III.

ROMAN CATHOLICISM

The fact that two main but slightly nuanced concepts of tradition exist within the Roman Catholic church today makes clarify-
ing the issue somewhat difficult. Several key issues, however,
undergird each of these concepts. The two-source theory of revelation presupposes a particular understanding of tradition which
is unbiblical, unhistorical, and unworkable. Tradition III specifically presupposes the modern doctrine of the papacy and the
dogma of papal infallibility. Both of these doctrines, in addition to
being historically suspect, can be demonstrated to involve self-
contradictions. The first issue which we must examine is the concept of tradition as a supplementary source of revelation alongside Scripture.

TRADITION

Previous chapters have briefly alluded to some of the problems
inherent in the concept of tradition as a second source of revelation. At this point it is necessary to offer a more detailed critique
of this concept and explain why it cannot be accepted by Christians today. The most obvious problem with Tradition II—its late

origin in the Middle Ages[1]—will not be discussed again. The reader should recall that Rome's claims to be teaching the faith of the apostolic Church notwithstanding, the *oldest* of the two doctrines embraced within her communion is at best no older than the fourth century. In the form Tradition II is taught today, it is no older than the twelfth century. The historical novelty of Tradition II is simply not in debate among patristic and medieval scholars.

In addition to this, the concept of tradition as a second supplementary source of revelation faces other insurmountable problems. A good outline of these problems may be found in Charles Hodge's nineteenth-century magnum opus, his three-volume *Systematic Theology*. In this work he outlines eight major difficulties faced by the Roman Catholic concept of supplementary tradition.

The first major problem with this doctrine is its natural impossibility. Due to the limitations of our human nature combined with the noetic effects of sin, it is simply impossible for us to know with certainty what Paul or Peter may have taught apart from what we find in their writings. Hodge explains,

> Man has not the clearness of perception, the retentiveness of memory, or the power of presentation, to enable him (without supernatural aid) to give a trustworthy account of a discourse once heard, a few years or even months after its delivery. And that this should be done over and over from month to month for thousands of years, is an impossibility. If to this be added the difficulty in the way of this oral transmission, arising from the blindness of men to the things of the Spirit, which prevents their understanding what they hear, and from the disposition to pervert and misrepresent the truth to suit their own prejudices and purposes, it must be acknowledged that tradition cannot be a reliable source of knowledge of religious truth.[2]

---

[1] See Part One for an overview of the late historical origin and development of this concept.

[2] Hodge, op. cit., 1:121.

Of course, Rome claims that this naturally impossible process has been possible because of the supernatural guidance of the Holy Spirit. The tradition, she argues, was not passed on by fallible men but by an infallible Church. Of course, this argument is circular, because it is only on the authority of tradition that the Roman Catholic church can claim infallibility, yet infallibility is required in order to guarantee the truth of the tradition to which Rome appeals.[3]

The second major problem with the supplementary concept of tradition is that there is no promise from God to intervene in the preservation of such a tradition. As Hodge explains,

> Our Lord promised to preserve his Church from fatal apostasy; He promised to send his Spirit to abide with his people, to teach them; He promised that He would be with them to the end of the world. But these promises were not made to any external, visible organization of professing Christians, whether Greek or Latin; nor did they imply that any such Church should be preserved from all error in faith or practice; much less do they imply that instructions not recorded by the dictation of the Spirit, should be preserved and transmitted from generation to generation. There is no such promise in the Word of God, and as such preservation and transmission without divine, supernatural interposition, would be impossible, tradition cannot be a trustworthy informant of what Christ taught.[4]

The intervention of God is simply assumed by Rome without any proof or justification other than the fact that it is necessary to support an already existing concept of tradition. Again it is only on the authority of tradition that this divine intervention is taught, and yet the intervention is necessary in order to trust the tradition which teaches it. Once more Rome finds herself arguing in a vicious logical circle.

---

[3] This dilemma has inadvertently led to the concept termed Tradition III, in which the authority of tradition has become merged with the authority of the Church to the point that the Church has become the only real source of revelation. We shall return to this concept below.

[4] Hodge, op. cit., 1:122.

A third significant difficulty with the Roman concept of supplementary tradition is that it destroys the possibility of having a reliable criterion by which true traditions and false traditions may be distinguished. All admit that false traditions have existed within the Church at different times and in different places, yet if tradition is raised to the status of revelation the false cannot be separated from the true. As Hodge points out, Rome claims to have a criterion in the teaching of Vincent of Lerin.[5] In other words they claim only to accept as true tradition that which has been taught always, everywhere, and by all. The problem with this claim is the historical fact that the doctrines and practices peculiar to Rome have not been taught always, everywhere and by all. Once again, however, we encounter a circular argument. Since Rome considers herself to be infallible, that which the Church *says* has been taught always, everywhere and by all *must* have been taught always, everywhere and by all even if the historical evidence contradicts this claim. As Hodge observes, "The proof that a thing is a matter of common consent, and always has been, is that the Church now believes it."[6] In other words, the criterion for discerning between true and false tradition is the teaching of the present magisterium.

The fourth inherent problem with the supplementary view of tradition as a second standard of faith is the fact that it is inaccessible to God's people. It is nowhere written in any volume to which all can turn. Instead, as Hodge notes, "it is scattered through the ecclesiastical records of eighteen centuries."[7] There is simply no way that most Christians could verify whether a particular tradition was actually taught throughout the entire history of the Church.

A fifth and related problem is the fact that tradition is far more difficult to interpret than Scripture. As Hodge explains,

Romanists argue that such is the obscurity of the Scriptures, that

[5] Ibid., 1:122–23.
[6] Ibid., 1:125.
[7] Ibid., 1:127.

not only the people, but the Church itself needs the aid of tradition in order to their being properly understood. But if the Bible, a comparatively plain book, in one portable volume, needs to be thus explained, what is to explain the hundreds of folios in which these traditions are recorded? Surely a guide to the interpretation of the latter must be far more needed than one for the Scriptures.[8]

Of course, Rome claims that she is that guide. But again the Roman church claims to be that guide only because tradition (and Scripture) as interpreted by them says so.

The sixth problem with this view of tradition is that it necessarily undermines the authority of Scripture. Hodge explains,

Man and his authority take the place of God. As this is the logical consequence of making tradition a rule of faith, so it is an historical fact that the Scriptures have been made of no account wherever the authority of tradition has been admitted. Our Lord said, that the Scribes and Pharisees made the word of God of no effect by their traditions; that they taught for doctrines the commandments of men. This is no less historically true of the Church of Rome. A great mass of doctrines, rites, ordinances, and institutions, of which the Scriptures know nothing has been imposed on the reason, conscience and life of the people.[9]

In some cases Rome hasn't even hesitated to explicitly state that her tradition is not the teaching of the Apostles. In Session V of the Council of Trent, the Roman church made the following dogmatic declaration in the Decree Concerning Original Sin:

This concupiscence, which the Apostle sometimes calls sin, the holy Synod declares that the Catholic Church has never understood it to be called sin, as being truly and properly sin in those born again, but because it is of sin, and inclines to sin. And if anyone is of a contrary sentiment, let him be anathema.

[8] Ibid., 1:128.
[9] Ibid.

This is an astounding statement which is basically an admission that the Roman Catholic church has never understood concupiscence in the way that the Apostle Paul admittedly understood it. Here we see a clear example of tradition undermining the authority of scriptural teaching.

Not only does tradition undermine Scripture, in many cases it also clearly contradicts Scripture. In these cases the choice boils down to following a tradition or following Scripture. Many Roman Catholic traditions concerning Peter, Mary, the Mass, the priesthood, and salvation are not simply difficult to harmonize with Scripture, they are in blatant contradiction with Scripture. One of the clearest modern examples is found in Rome's doctrine of Mary. Scripture teaches that there is one mediator between God and men, the man Jesus Christ (1 Tim. 2:5). Rome teaches that Mary is co-mediatrix.[10] In this and many other ways, Rome holds up as truth traditions that are not supplementary to Scripture but are in opposition to the teaching of Scripture.[11]

The eighth problem with the supplementary concept of tradition is that it is not, as Rome claims, a sufficient ground for our trust in the authority of Scripture. Rome claims that Protestants have to cede authority to supplementary tradition because it is only on the authority of tradition that we know what the canon of Scripture is.[12] In fact, as J.B. Torrance has observed, the formation of the New Testament canon is actually evidence of the supreme authority of Scripture. He explains that the Church must make a distinction between the apostolic tradition and ecclesiastical tradition and that this is what she did when she specified the contents of the canon. "The canon means that the ecclesiastical

---

[10] *Catechism of the Catholic Church*, (par. 969).

[11] In Rome's seemingly never ending quest to elevate Mary far beyond the role God intended for her, she is now toying with the idea of referring to Mary as co-redemptrix. The *Catechism of the Catholic Church* has already included a paragraph declaring that "In a wholly singular way *she cooperated* by her obedience, faith, hope, and burning charity *in the Savior's work of restoring supernatural life to souls*" (par. 968). Emphasis mine.

[12] This important issue shall be dealt with in greater detail in Part Four.

tradition (however important and necessary) is subordinate to and not coordinate with Holy Scripture."[13] In other words, the Church saw it as necessary to gather the divinely inspired books into a single collection. The very act of doing this testified to the supreme authority of these writings.

When we realize that Tradition II was not the teaching of the early Church for centuries and when we take into account all of the additional problems associated with the concept of tradition as a supplementary source of revelation, it is clear that this concept of tradition must be rejected. Ironically, most modern Roman Catholic theologians have conceded the problems with Tradition II and reject the idea of a two-source concept of tradition.[14] Many have instead adopted the concept of tradition we have termed Tradition III, in which the magisterium of the Church is the real source of revelation. It is perhaps inevitable that the problems inherent in Tradition II would have led to Tradition III. Acceptance of Tradition II implicitly elevates the Church to the role of supreme authority. Tradition III does the same, only explicitly.

One of the primary contributing factors to the explicit acceptance of Tradition III was the pronouncement in 1870 at the First Vatican Council of the doctrine of papal infallibility. Because the doctrine of infallibility lies at the foundation of this novel concept of tradition, it must be examined. If the Roman Catholic doctrine of infallibility is false, then Tradition III necessarily falls. It must be shown, therefore, that the doctrine of ecclesiastical and papal infallibility is false.

---

[13] J.B. Torrance, "Authority, Scripture and Tradition," *Evangelical Quarterly*, 59 (1987), 250. According to Torrance, the content of apostolic tradition, unlike ecclesiastical tradition, is coordinate with the content of Holy Scripture.

[14] See Robert Strimple, "Roman Catholic Theology Today," in *Roman Catholicism*, ed. John Armstrong, (Chicago: Moody Press, 1994), 101. The fact that Tradition II has been rejected by virtually every prominent Roman Catholic theologian seems to have escaped many of the more conservative Roman Catholic apologists who still write as if Tradition II remained the consensus within the Roman church.

INFALLIBILITY

Because the Roman Catholic doctrine of infallibility is often misunderstood, we must get clear on what Rome claims. A good concise summary of this doctrine is found in the *Catechism of the Catholic Church* which states,

> In order to preserve the Church in the purity of the faith handed on by the Apostles, Christ who is the Truth willed to confer on her a share in his own infallibility. By a "supernatural sense of faith" the People of God, under the guidance of the Church's living Magisterium, "unfailingly adheres to this faith."
>
> The mission of the Magisterium is linked to the definitive nature of the covenant established by God with his people in Christ. It is this Magisterium's task to preserve God's people from deviations and defections and to guarantee them the objective possibility of professing the true faith without error. Thus, the pastoral duty of the Magisterium is aimed at seeing to it that the People of God abides in the truth that liberates. To fulfill this service, Christ endowed the Church's shepherds with the charism of infallibility in matters of faith and morals. The exercise of this charism takes several forms:
>
> "The Roman Pontiff, head of the college of bishops, enjoys this infallibility in virtue of his office, when, as supreme pastor and teacher of all the faithful—who confirms his brethren in the faith—he proclaims by a definitive act a doctrine pertaining to faith or morals. . . . The infallibility promised to the Church is also present in the body of bishops when, together with Peter's successor, they exercise the supreme Magisterium," above all in an Ecumenical Council. When the Church through its supreme Magisterium proposes a doctrine "for belief as being divinely revealed," and as the teaching of Christ, the definitions "must be adhered to with the obedience of faith." This infallibility extends as far as the deposit of divine Revelation itself.[15]

The *Catholic Encyclopedia* adds some important qualifying explanations by pointing out that infallibility is not to be confused with inspiration or revelation. Whereas God Himself is the author of

---

[15] Par. 889–891.

an inspired utterance, an infallible word remains the word of man although it is preserved from the possibility of error.[16] In addition, infallibility does not mean impeccability. God may give the gift of infallibility to wicked men. The three organs of infallibility that exist according to Rome are the bishops through the world, ecumenical councils under the pope, and the pope himself.[17]

Rome admits that the first of these is practically unworkable and therefore emphasizes the second two.[18] Rome understands ecumenical councils to be organs of infallibility when certain conditions are met. As Leo Donald Davis explains,

> According to the Roman Catholic Code of Canon Law, an ecumenical council is an assembly of bishops and other specified persons, convoked and presided over by the pope, for the purpose of formulating decisions concerning the Christian faith and discipline, which decisions require papal confirmation.[19]

What is obviously problematic with this concept of ecumenical councils is the historical fact that it is inapplicable to many accepted ecumenical councils. Davis explains,

> it is abundantly clear from the history of the first seven ecumenical councils that this neat definition has not always applied. Rather, the first seven ecumenical councils were all called by the emperor, the vote of papal legates not subsequent approval signified papal adherence to conciliar decrees, all five patriarchs had to be present in order that a council be truly ecumenical and councils were sometimes only designated ecumenical by the action of subsequent ecumenical councils.[20]

In other words, Rome's definition of an ecumenical council

---

[16] P. J. Toner, "Infallibility," in *The Catholic Encyclopedia, Volume VII,* Online Edition. www.newadvent.org/cathen/07790a.htm

[17] Ibid.

[18] Ibid.

[19] Leo Donald Davis, *The First Seven Ecumenical Councils (325–787): Their History and Theology,* (Collegeville: The Liturgical Press, 1983), 323.

[20] Ibid.

would rule out the first seven. The pope convoked none of them and could hardly be said to have presided over any of them. Her doctrine of ecumenical councils is simply self-defeating.

A summary of the origin of the concept of papal infallibility appeared earlier.[21] This doctrine, which is peculiar to Rome, originated in the debates between the popes and the Franciscans in the twelfth through fourteenth centuries. There is absolutely no trace of the doctrine in the Scriptures, the early fathers, or most of the Middle Ages. When the doctrine was first suggested to the pope by a group of dissident Franciscans, the pope declared it to be a pernicious novelty.[22]

One of the more interesting problems with papal infallibility is inadvertently raised in the *Catholic Encyclopedia,* which argues that "no *ex cathedra* definition of any pope has ever been shown to be erroneous."[23] The problem with this statement is that although Rome claims that *ex cathedra* statements made by the pope are infallible, she does not even know how many *ex cathedra* statements the pope has made. Rome believes the pope has made infallible *ex cathedra* statements that must be adhered to with the obedience of faith, yet she cannot say with any certainty which of the thousands of papal pronouncements are, in fact, *ex cathedra*. There is no agreement among Roman theologians and apologists on the actual number. Rome has no infallible canon, as it were, of infallible papal statements.[24]

Historically considered, the doctrine of papal infallibility is impossible to maintain. The pope can err because it is a matter of historical fact that the pope has erred.[25] Some of the more well-known examples include the following:

---

[21] See chapter 2.

[22] Tierney, op. cit.

[23] Toner, op. cit.

[24] This is ironic considering the amount of time Roman Catholic apologists spend criticizing Protestants for supposedly having an uncertain canon of infallible Scripture. Rome has *no* canon of infallible papal definitions.

[25] Rome has come up with a number of "explanations" for the examples provided here. In effect they amount to question begging. According to Rome, no one can point to any official papal errors as long as official papal errors are ignored.

Pope Liberius

During the Arian controversy, Pope Liberius was exiled by the emperor for defending Nicene orthodoxy. He was allowed to return to his see when he agreed to sign an Arian confession and excommunicate Athanasius. He later recanted of these views, but his actions demonstrate that it is possible for heresy to infiltrate even the see of Rome.

Pope Zosimus

During the Pelagian controversy, Pope Zosimus reversed the official judgment of a previous pope (Innocent) in an encyclical letter by rebuking Augustine and the North African church for their condemnation of Pelagius. He declared Pelagius to be orthodox. The Council of Carthage met in 418 and specifically condemned Pelagius despite Pope Zosimus' demands to the contrary. After the Council, Pope Zosimus reversed his views on the matter.

Pope Vigilius

During the Second Council of Constantinople (A.D. 553), discussion was centered on the writings of Theodore of Mopsuestia, in particular his *Three Chapters*. The Council condemned Theodore and his writings, including the *Three Chapters*, because of perceived Nestorianism. Pope Vigilius refused to accept this and wrote a treatise entitled the *Constitutum* which condemned certain of Theodore's propositions but not Theodore himself. The *Constitutum* also anathematized those who condemned the *Three Chapters*, in effect anathematizing the bishops and patriarchs at the Second Council of Constantinople. Vigilius later retracted his *Constitutum* and wrote a letter to Patriarch Eutychius repenting of his writing. What we have here is a pope who publicly and officially changes his mind on Christology, a doctrine central to the Christian faith.

Pope Honorius

The heresy of monothelitism was condemned as heresy at the Third Council of Constantinople (A.D. 680). What is interesting is that a pope, Honorius, was also condemned and anathematized by this same council for teaching this heresy. He was anathematized by name in the decrees of the Sixth Council itself. Pope Leo II agreed with the Council and said that he too condemned Honorius for heresy. The Seventh Ecumenical Council (A.D. 787) affirmed the anathema against Honorius by name. And until the eleventh century, all popes took an oath which included an explicit condemnation of the heretic Honorius.

Pope Boniface VIII

In his Bull *Unam Sanctam*, Pope Boniface decreed,

> Indeed we declare, say, pronounce, and define that it is altogether necessary to salvation for every human creature to be subject to the Roman Pontiff.

Vatican II teaches the exact opposite of this declaration. According to the documents of Vatican II, Christians of other denominations may be saved. Non-Christians, specifically Jews and Muslims, may be saved. Pagans may be saved. Even those who do not explicitly know of the existence of God may be saved.[26]

It is logically possible that either *Unam Sanctam* or Vatican II is correct. It is also logically possible that neither *Unam Sanctam* nor Vatican II is correct. It is not logically possible, however, that both *Unam Sanctam* and Vatican II are correct. According to Pope Boniface VIII, "it is altogether *necessary* to salvation for *every* human creature to be subject to the Roman Pontiff." But if non-Roman Catholics, non-Christians, pagans, and atheists may attain to salvation, as Vatican II asserts, then it is *not* altogether *necessary* to salvation for *every* human creature to be subject to the Roman Pontiff. According to Vatican II, some who are not subject to the Roman Pontiff may be saved.

It is sometimes denied that *Unam Sanctam* was an *"ex cathedra"*

---

[26] For specific citations, see Michael Whelton, *Two Paths*, (Salisbury, MA: Regina Orthodox Press, 1998), 148–149.

statement, but if it is not, one rightly wonders what would qualify. It meets all of the explicit criteria set forth to designate an *ex cathedra* statement. It is written in the same form used in the declarations concerning the Assumption of Mary and the Immaculate Conception. It is simply disingenuous to assert that *Unam Sanctam* was not intended by Boniface to be a doctrinal statement written in his presumed capacity as supreme bishop of the Church. And it is manifestly impossible to honestly reconcile his statements with those of the Second Vatican Council.

Pope Sixtus V

Pope Sixtus's notable error consisted of declaring his error-filled 1590 edition of the Vulgate to have plenary authority for all future time. The 1590 edition included a preface by Sixtus which asserted, "By the fulness of apostolic power, we decree and declare that this edition, approved by the authority delivered to us by the Lord, is to be received and held as true, lawful, authentic, and unquestioned, in all public and private discussion, reading, preaching, and explanations." The problem is that his personal involvement and re-editing of the work done by biblical scholars resulted in a Bible version that was so plagued with errors that it had to be corrected and reissued in less than two years. Approximately three thousand errors, including the omission of five verses, had to be corrected in the new edition.

These are simply a few of the many papal errors one encounters when studying the history of the Church. Other errors of fact include the condemnation of Galileo's teaching as heresy and the papal endorsement in the nineteenth century of the cult of St. Philomena. When some relics were found in a Roman catacomb, they were declared to be the remains of a virgin martyr named Philomena. Pope Gregory XVI appointed a feast in her honor and authorized public veneration. Pope Pius IX declared that the cult was not suppressible. Pope Leo XIII granted indulgences to those who visited the sanctuary of her relics. Unfortunately, it turned out that the entire cult of St. Philomena was based upon a mistake. Whoever the remains belonged to, it was certain that they did not belong to a Christian martyr. In 1961, Rome discontinued the feast of St. Philomena and ordered that her name be removed from the calendar.

In regards to moral issues, popes have also erred. Pope Gregory IX (1227–41) allowed for the use of physical torture by the Inquisition. Pope Benedict XIV called for Polish Jews to be ghettoized. The church has changed its mind on moral issues such as slavery, usury, and anti-semitism. It simply cannot be maintained that the pope, or the Roman Catholic church, is infallible without revising or ignoring history. So how has Rome historically handled this situation? As Jaroslav Pelikan observes,

> Because of their doctrine of the church, Roman Catholic theologians. . . were compelled to interpret church history on the basis of a preconceived system and to explain away the many stubborn and embarrassing facts that could not be accommodated to that system. Having absolutized the ecclesiastical organization, they had to go on to absolutize that organization's history by ascribing to it an organizational continuity, ceremonial uniformity, and theological infallibility that had no substantiation from historical evidence.[27]

In other words, church history as seen through the eyes of Rome is fictional. It simply did not happen the way Rome claims it happened.

In addition to the fact that it is contradicted by the facts of church history, the Roman Catholic doctrine of infallibility faces the problem that it necessarily results in an autonomous church. As we have seen, when the Church is declared to be infallible, the inevitable result is that the present teaching of the Magisterium becomes the real source and standard of authority. Scripture and tradition teach whatever the present Magisterium says they teach. Rome becomes a law unto herself.

This is what necessarily happens when the Church denies that Scripture is the final and only infallible norm by which she is to

[27] Pelikan, *Obedient Rebels*, 32.

judge all things. What happens, and what has happened, is that neither Scripture, nor tradition, nor the fathers, nor anything other than the Church's Magisterium—personified in the pope—becomes the final authority and standard of truth. In effect the magisterium of the Roman church becomes autonomous—a law unto itself.

Scripture cannot be appealed to as a higher law because the Church tells us what Scripture is and what it really means. Tradition cannot be appealed to as a higher law because the Church tells us what tradition is and what it really means. The fathers cannot be appealed to as a higher standard because the Church tells us what the fathers really mean. God cannot be appealed to because the Church is said to be the voice of God on earth. And because there is no higher ethical or doctrinal standard to which anyone can appeal, the Church becomes autonomous—a law unto herself.

This, however, is not the scriptural or apostolic model of the Church. Christ is the head of the Church. The Church is to be subject and obedient to Christ her Lord (Eph. 5:24). Scripture is the Word of the living God, and therefore the Church must be obedient to Scripture. But if the Church is to be obedient to Scripture, it necessarily follows that the Scripture (not the submitting Church) is the true final norm or standard. By denying that Scripture is the sole final and infallible norm, and by declaring herself infallible, Rome places herself in the position of sole final and infallible norm. This is autonomy and a rejection of submission to Christ.

The Roman Catholic doctrine of infallibility is nothing more than an erroneous late medieval doctrine which the Roman church would do well to rid herself of once and for all. There is no promise of infallibility in Scripture and numerous assertions to the contrary (e.g., Acts 20:29–30; Rom. 11:17–22; Rev. 2:5). Every biblical warning and prediction of false Christs, false apostles, and apostasy is a denial of the doctrine of infallibility. The Church as a whole is promised final victory, but she is not promised perfection or infallibility.

Not only is the doctrine of infallibility in direct contradiction with the express teaching of Scripture, it is disproven by history. We know that the Church and the popes can err because the Church and the popes have erred often. The Roman church and her popes have taught heresy at times, and she has contradicted her own earlier dogmatic teachings at other times. Rome and her bishop err today and contradict what has been taught "always, everywhere, and by all" by denying the exclusivity of Christ. Infallibility is an unscriptural, ahistorical doctrine that always results in the practical autonomy of the one claiming it for himself.[28]

EASTERN ORTHODOXY

The concept of Scripture, tradition, and the Church in the Eastern Orthodox church does not parallel any of the concepts we have already discussed.[29] It does not fall into the category of Tradition 0, I, II, or III as these have been explained. The isolation of the Eastern church from the Western church led to an entirely different development of this concept. Before proceeding to offer a critique of the claims of the Orthodox church itself, we must briefly examine exactly what the Orthodox church teaches regarding the relationship between Scripture, tradition, and the Church.

INTRODUCTION

First, clearly the Eastern Orthodox concept of Scripture and tradition is not identical to the Roman Catholic concept of Scripture and tradition.[30] According to Orthodoxy, tradition is an all-

---

[28] For a thorough critique of the doctrine of infallibility, which after a century has yet to receive a full response or refutation, see George Salmon, *Infallibility of the Church*, third edition, (London: John Murray, 1899). For an outstanding exhaustive scholarly examination of the origins of the doctrine of papal infallibility, which has also yet to be refuted, see Brian Tierney, *Origins of Papal Infallibility: 1150–1350*, (Leiden: E.J. Brill, 1988).

[29] For a good overview of the Orthodox concept of authority, see Georges Florovsky, *Bible, Church, Tradition: An Eastern Orthodox View,* (Buchervertriebsanstalt, 1987). See also Archimandrite Chrysostomos and Archimandrite Auxentios, *Scripture and Tradition*, (Etna, CA: Center for Traditionalist Orthodox Studies, 1994).

[30] Cf. Florovsky, op. cit.

embracing concept which may be seen as the continuing presence of the Holy Spirit in the Church. While Roman Catholicism and Protestantism tend to distinguish between Scripture and tradition, viewing them as separate concepts, Orthodoxy sees Scripture as part of the larger concept of tradition. Tradition is the life of the Holy Spirit within the Church, yet this mystical view does not mean that there are no outward forms of the tradition. Some of the outward forms are the Bible, the seven ecumenical councils, the fathers, the divine liturgy, the canon law and the icons.[31]

The Orthodox view the Scriptures of the Old and New Testament as God's supreme revelation to man, but the Scriptures are not to be separated from the Church. As Timothy Ware explains, "if Christians are people of the Book, the Bible is the Book of the people; it must not be regarded as something set up *over* the Church, but as something that lives and is understood *within* the Church."[32] In addition, the Orthodox church understands the doctrinal definitions of the seven ecumenical councils to be infallible.[33] These conciliar decrees have an abiding and irrevocable authority in the Church alongside of Scripture. Of all of the decrees composed by the councils, the most important to the Orthodox is the Nicene-Constantinopolitan Creed.

The early church fathers provide the broader context within which the conciliar decisions and decrees must be interpreted. Although the Orthodox do not ascribe infallibility to all of the fathers indiscriminately, the "mind of the fathers" is an important part of the Orthodox concept of authority.[34] According to one Orthodox author, the mind of the fathers is the very "canon" or criterion of Orthodoxy.[35] Of all the fathers revered in the Eastern church, particular emphasis is placed upon Basil the Great, Gregory of Nazianzus, and John Chrysostom.

---

[31] Cf. Timothy Ware, *The Orthodox Church*, New Edition, (London: Penguin Books, 1997), 196–197.

[32] Ibid., 199.

[33] Ibid., 202.

[34] Archimandrite Chrysostomos, op cit., 33–35.

[35] Ibid., 35, cf. p. 77.

In a very real sense it is the Church which embodies the tradition within Orthodoxy. It is the Church from which the Bible draws its authority since the Church decided which books were Scripture and since the Church is believed to be the only source of the true interpretation of Scripture.[36] According to Georges Florovsky, the authority of the Church is a *"charismatic* authority" given to the Church as the pillar and foundation of the truth.[37] Because of this, Orthodoxy considers itself the standard, or criterion, of Christianity.[38]

A PROTESTANT EVALUATION

In contrast to both Protestantism and Roman Catholicism, the concept of tradition in Eastern Orthodoxy is highly mystical. The inherent ambiguity involved in mysticism makes any evaluation difficult. Several important questions about the Orthodox concept of authority need to be raised.

The Canon

One of the first problems we encounter when examining the Eastern Orthodox concept of authority is an inaccurate understanding of the process and relevance of the creation of the canon. As one Orthodox text on the subject says,

> By setting the canon of Scripture, the Church, in turn, established the Scriptures as the canon. In defining the rule of faith, the Church created the rule of faith.[39]

This is simply not true. The Church received the Old Testament from Israel. She received the New Testament from the Apostles of Christ.[40] It is true that there were spurious books being

---

[36] Ware, op. cit., 199.

[37] Florovsky, op. cit., 103.

[38] See Hierodeacon Gregory, *The Church, Tradition, Scripture, Truth, and Christian Life: Some Heresies of Evangelicalism and an Orthodox Response*, (Etna, CA: Center for Traditionalist Orthodox Studies, 1995), 1.

[39] Archimandrite Chrysostomos, op. cit., 18.

[40] For an excellent historical study of the reception of the New Testament books, see Bruce M. Metzger, *The Canon of the New Testament: Its Origin, Development, and Significance.* (Oxford: Clarendon Press, 1987).

circulated at the same time as apostolic books. But the fact that Christ's Church, His sheep, heard His voice amidst the clamoring voices of strangers does not mean that the Church "created" the rule of faith. God created the rule of faith, and the Church heard it, received it and obeys it. Definition does not entail creation. Scientists have defined the God-given laws of physics, but scientists did not create those laws. God created them, and man discovered and defined them.

Ecumenical Councils

A second major problem inherent in the Orthodox concept of tradition involves her understanding of ecumenical councils. As we have noted, the doctrinal definitions of ecumenical councils are considered to be infallible by the Orthodox church. The problem arises when we ask how to recognize an ecumenical council. The Orthodox bishop Timothy Ware asks,

> How then can one be certain that a particular gathering is truly an Ecumenical Council and therefore that its decrees are infallible? Many councils have considered themselves ecumenical and have claimed to speak in the name of the whole Church, and yet the Church has rejected them as heretical: Ephesus in 449, for example, or the Iconoclast Council of Hieria in 754, or Florence in 1438–9. Yet these councils seem in no way different in outward appearance from the Ecumenical Councils. What, then, is the criterion for determining whether a council is ecumenical?[41]

He answers,

> This is a more difficult question to answer than might at first appear, and though it has been much discussed by Orthodox during the past hundred years, it cannot be said that the solutions suggested are entirely satisfactory. All Orthodox know which are the seven councils that their Church accepts as ecumenical, but precisely what it is that makes a council ecumenical is not so clear.[42]

---

[41] Ware, op. cit., 251–252.
[42] Ibid., 252.

This is extremely important because if the Church does not know what it is that makes a council ecumenical, how can the Church say that *any* council is ecumenical? Ware tends to lean toward an answer proposed by Alexis Khomiakov which has become widely accepted within the Orthodox church. According to this theory, "a council cannot be considered ecumenical unless its decrees are accepted by the whole Church."[43] Of course, this answer raises almost as many problems as the original question. Chalcedon was rejected by Syria and Egypt. Does this mean that Chalcedon is not ecumenical? Khomiakov's answer to the problem is circular. An ecumenical council is defined as a council accepted by the whole Church, yet the Church is defined as those who accept the councils. Those who do not accept the council are defined out of the Church in order to maintain the idea that the "whole Church" accepts the council.

In addition, no time frame is mentioned. The whole Church didn't accept Nicea immediately. How long is the whole Church allowed to wrestle over the decisions of a council? The fundamental problem here is that Khomiakov's answer nullifies the whole point of ecumenical councils. The councils were called in order to solve particular pressing problems facing the Church. What the Orthodox concept of ecumenical councils fails to explain is how Nicea could have dealt with the Arian controversy given the current Orthodox understanding of these councils. Alexander Schmemann does not believe this to be a valid objection. He writes,

> But a Western reader should be warned immediately that in the Orthodox church "officialdom" cannot be simply identified with the voice of the church. History is here to remind us that no official pronouncement is of any binding effect unless it is accepted by the whole body of the church, though it is very difficult, if not impossible, to give a clear-cut definition of how such acceptance is to be achieved and expressed.[44]

[43] Ibid.
[44] Alexander Schmemann, "Moment of Truth for Orthodoxy," in *Eastern Orthodox Theology*, ed. by Daniel B. Clendenin, (Grand Rapids: Baker Book House, 1995), 204.

This impossibility results in the added difficulty, if not impossibility, of explaining how Arianism could have been anathematized by a council. Was it unnecessary for the Arian party to accept the council? Or is the "whole Church" only those who agree with the majority decision at the council? Is the majority right? At one point, Athanasius stood virtually alone in the battle against the Arians.

The Orthodox understanding is based on the belief that eventually the truth will prevail. We know Athanasius was orthodox and that the Arians were heretics in retrospect because Athanasius' position ultimately prevailed. Unfortunately, this belief does not help those living at the time of an actual controversy. The only way to determine who is teaching the orthodox position is to check back five hundred or a thousand years later and see which view prevailed. Suppose, however, that you are alive during a time of intense controversy within the Church over a doctrine that all agree is essential to the Christian faith. Suppose you desire with all of your heart, soul, and mind to teach the true doctrine, the apostolic doctrine. How can you know which position is truth and which is damnable heresy if you rely on the Orthodox concept of ecumenical councils? There is no way to know during your lifetime. Suppose an ecumenical council is called. The heretical position might gain the upper hand and carry the council. Do you stand alone against the council in the hope that you are another Athanasius. How do you know if this council is a true ecumenical council or a counterfeit? It is simply pointless to claim that ecumenical councils are infallible and binding if there is no way to identify an ecumenical council.

The Fathers

Another problem we encounter within the Orthodox concept of tradition is its understanding of the fathers. Bishops Chrysostomos and Auxentios explain that "it is in the writings of the Fathers that we find a true source for the *Orthodox position* regarding the authority of Scripture and tradition in the Church."[45] In

---

[45] Archimandrite Chrysostomos, op. cit., 19.

other words, the Orthodox church desires to teach the same concept of Scripture and tradition that the early fathers taught. Yet
the Orthodox church assigns a place to the fathers that the fathers
themselves would reject. Chrysostomos and Auxentios explain
that the "Early Church invoked Tradition as the authentic criterion of scriptural interpretation."[46] Yet elsewhere they add,

> As we have already noted, Orthodox theology draws on the con-
> sistent God-inspired witness of the Fathers in order to formulate
> any theological position. It is the perspective of the Fathers
> which always prevails, and it is to their authority that the Church
> always hearkens.[47]

If the fathers are "inspired" then the patristic understanding these
Orthodox authors desire to maintain is destroyed. Aside from
the fact that the fathers themselves did not claim to be inspired
and in fact often admitted being fallible, it remains that if the patristic writings are God-inspired they are no longer a criterion of
scriptural interpretation, they are *equal* to Holy Scripture.

According to the Orthodox, their theology "in its strictest
sense, proceeds from the Patristic witness, from the 'canon of
theology' found in the *consensus patrum*."[48] But not only is this not
the view of the fathers themselves, it is also quite false. Orthodox
Christian theology, in its strictest sense, proceeds from God who
has revealed Himself. The final revelation was given in and by
Christ. The gospel was committed by Christ to His Apostles who
preached this *kerygma* to the Church. This gospel was written in
the Holy Scriptures which the Church itself refers to as the
"canon" meaning a standard or "rule." This revelation is interpreted and proclaimed by the Church, but the Church is not the
originator or source of the revelation. She is entrusted with the
preservation and proclamation of the revelation given once for all
in Christ and recorded in Scripture.

[46] Ibid., 20.
[47] Ibid., 33.
[48] Ibid., 68.

The fathers of the Church were also interpreters of this revelation, fallible and human interpreters, not sources of revelation
and certainly not God-inspired. Their words are not *theopneustos.*
Their words may *contain* God's words when they accurately interpret God's revelation, but their words cannot be equated with
God's words. To refer to the writings of the fathers as the "canon"
of Orthodox theology contradicts the very fathers whom the Orthodox wish to follow.

Another major problem with the Orthodox understanding of
the "mind of the fathers" is its logical incoherence. Bishops Chrysostomos and Auxentios write, "How do we know that the writings of the Fathers themselves . . . are true and inspired?"[49] Our
criterion for judging the truth of the fathers, they write, is "the
'mind' of the Fathers [which is the 'mind' of the Church]."[50] In
other words, the criterion for judging the mind of the fathers is
the mind of the fathers. This circularity results in the Orthodox
church ultimately declaring itself the criterion of truth since the
ultimate standard of truth—the mind of the fathers—is equated
with the mind of the Church.

The Orthodox on Protestantism

We must briefly mention an Orthodox critique of Protestantism which points out another problem within the Orthodox concept of tradition and Scripture. In their critique of *sola scriptura,*
Chrysostomos and Auxentios assert that "the Protestant notion of
the separability of Scripture and Tradition is unacceptable to the
Orthodox."[51] However, as we have repeatedly demonstrated, this
is *not* the Protestant position. It is an aspect of Tradition 0 which
is *a* Protestant position. The critique does not apply, however, to
Tradition I. Those Protestants who adhere to Tradition I insist on
distinction rather than separation. In the final analysis, Scripture,
the Church, and tradition (understood as the rule of faith) cannot

---

[49] Ibid., 70.
[50] Ibid.
[51] Ibid., 68. Cf. Ware, op. cit., 199.

be separated, but their unique attributes and functions can and must be distinguished. To denigrate distinction as if it necessarily entailed separation would destroy not only a proper concept of authority, it would also destroy the Orthodox concept of God. We distinguish between the persons of the Trinity without separating them, and in the same way we distinguish between Scripture, tradition and the Church without separating them. If it is not proper to distinguish between the unique attributes of each, it is impossible to explain the use of different terms. If we use different terms for these things, we must be able to distinguish the properties of those terms.

Autonomy

The most significant problem with the Orthodox concept of Scripture and tradition is that, like Roman Catholicism, it renders the Church autonomous—a law unto itself. The Orthodox church strongly criticizes the Roman Catholic view of Scripture and tradition believing it to result in the elevation of the pope to a place of virtual final authority in the Church. As Chrysostomos and Auxentios explain,

> The authority of the Church as it is manifested in the infallibility of the pope introduces a perspective on Scripture and Tradition which is uniquely Roman Catholic. The papacy comes to represent the virtual authority of Scripture and Tradition themselves.[52]

Yet the Eastern Orthodox church falls into a similar trap. In the Roman Catholic church, the present church represents the virtual authority of Scripture and tradition, and this authority is personified supremely in the Bishop of Rome—the pope. But in the Eastern Orthodox church, it is the present church which also represents the virtual authority of Scripture and tradition. As Chrysostomos and Auxentios explain, the mind of the fathers is

[52] Ibid., 44.

the final criterion and standard of truth, and the mind of the fathers is the mind of the Church.[53] It is the Church therefore that is the final standard of truth.

In both Roman Catholicism and Eastern Orthodoxy this elevation of the present church to a place of final authority is a necessary result of the doctrine of infallibility. Both Rome and the Orthodox teach the infallibility of the Church. This doctrine necessarily leads to the supremacy and autonomy of the Church regardless of any other professed authorities. If the Church is infallible, then the present Church is *always* going to be the final standard.

Chrysostomos and Auxentios criticize Rome saying that, "A concept of authority which could engender, without careful reservations, a slogan such as 'the Church precedes the Bible,' or envision a personal *magisterium,* is simply too analogous to a legalistic arrangement to commend itself to the Eastern Church."[54] Yet the claims of the Orthodox are equally as incredible. Immediately after criticizing Roman Catholic statements about the Church, the authors say the following about the Orthodox church,

> But true authority, the action of the Holy Spirit as evidenced in the unified revelation of Scripture and Tradition, is wholly mystical. Thus advisedly (since his point can be misunderstood) we can quote Professor Hromadka's contention that: "Not even Christ should be understood and looked upon as an authority to which the Church is subordinated."[55]

Any concept of ecclesiastical authority that can see Hromadka's quote as anything other than cosmic treason is self-evidently false. The quote is blatantly unbiblical (cf. Eph. 5:24). Yet what else can the Orthodox church say when it claims that the final source and standard of truth is the mind of the fathers which is

---

[53] Ibid., 70.
[54] Ibid., 46.
[55] Ibid., 47.

equivalent to the mind of the Church?[56] If the mind of the present Church is the final source and criterion of truth, then either the Church is God or the Church is autonomous.[57] One option is blasphemy of God, and the other option is rebellion against God. Both options must be rejected by any Christian who believes that the Church must be in obedient submission to Christ.

SUMMARY

The concepts of Scripture and tradition as set forth by the Roman Catholic church and the Eastern Orthodox church have both been found wanting. Neither Tradition II nor Tradition III as advocated by Roman Catholic theologians and apologists is historically, biblically, or theologically feasible. The mystical concept of Scripture, Church, and tradition advocated by the Eastern Orthodox church does not fare any better. It results in numerous ambiguities and much circular reasoning. The primary failure of the Roman Catholic and the Eastern Orthodox concepts of tradition is that they both result in an autonomous Church. In both cases the supreme Lordship of Christ the King is compromised as the Church assumes the place of supreme authority. This fact alone necessitates the rejection of the models of authority presented by both Rome and Orthodoxy.

---

[56] Ibid., 77.

[57] Hromadka chooses the first option, explaining that "the Church *is* the Incarnate Christ," p. 81, n. 39.

8

A Critique of the Evangelical
Doctrine of Solo *Scriptura*

In the 1980s and early 1990s, a controversy erupted among dispensationalists which came to be referred to as the Lordship Salvation controversy. On one side of the debate were men such as Zane Hodges[1] and Charles Ryrie[2] who taught a reductionistic doctrine of *sola fide* which absolutized the word "alone" in the phrase "justification by faith alone" and removed it from its overall theological context. Faith was reduced to little more than assent to the truthfulness of certain biblical propositions. Repentance, sanctification, submission to Christ's Lordship, love, and perseverance were all said to be unnecessary for salvation. Advocates of this position claimed that it was the classical Reformation position taught by Martin Luther and John Calvin. On the other side of the debate was John MacArthur who argued that these men were clearly abandoning the Reformed doctrine of justification by faith alone.[3] In addition to the books written by the primary dispensationalist participants, numerous Reformed theologians wrote books and articles criticizing this alteration of the doctrine of *sola fide*.[4] A heated theological controversy began which continues in some circles even to this day.

[1] Zane Hodges, *Absolutely Free!* (Dallas: Redencion Viva, 1989).

[2] Charles Ryrie, *So Great Salvation*, (Wheaton: Victor Books, 1989).

[3] John MacArthur, *The Gospel According to Jesus*, (Grand Rapids: Zondervan, 1988); *Faith Works*, (Dallas: Word Books, 1993).

[4] E.g., Kenneth L. Gentry, Jr., *Lord of the Saved*, (Phillipsburg: P&R Publishing Co., 1992); Michael S. Horton, ed., *Christ the Lord: The Reformation and Lordship Salvation*, (Grand Rapids: Baker Book House, 1992).

Ironically, a similar drastic alteration of the classical Reformation doctrine of *sola scriptura* has occurred over the last 150 years,
yet this has caused hardly a stir among the theological heirs of the
Reformation, who have usually been quick to notice any threat-
ening move against the Reformed doctrine of justification. So
much time and effort has been spent guarding the doctrine of *sola
fide* against any perversion or change that many do not seem to
have noticed that the classical and foundational Reformed doctrine of *sola scriptura* has been so altered that is virtually unrecog-
nizable. In its place Evangelicals have substituted an entirely
different doctrine. Douglas Jones has coined the term solo *scriptura* to refer to this aberrant Evangelical version of *sola scriptura*.[5]

Modern Evangelicalism has done the same thing to *sola scriptura* that Hodges and Ryrie did to *sola fide*. But unfortunately so
little attention is paid to the doctrine of *sola scriptura* today that
even among trained theologians there is confusion and ambiguity
when the topic is raised. Contradictory and insufficient definitions of *sola scriptura* are commonplace not only among broadly
Evangelical authors but among Reformed authors as well. In this
chapter we shall examine this aberrant modern Evangelical concept of solo *scriptura* and explain why it is imperative that the
Evangelical church recognize it to be as dangerous as the distorted concepts of *sola fide* that are prevalent in the Church today.

EVANGELICAL INDIVIDUALISM

The modern Evangelical version of solo *scriptura* is nothing more
than a new version of Tradition 0. Instead of being defined as the
sole *infallible* authority, the Bible is said to be the "sole basis of
authority."[6] Tradition is not allowed in any sense; the ecumenical
creeds are virtually dismissed; and the Church is denied any real
authority. On the surface it would seem that this modern

[5] Douglas Jones, *Putting the Reformation "Solas" in Perspective*, audio tapes, (Moscow, ID:
Canon Press, 1997).

[6] Charles Ryrie, *Basic Theology*, (Wheaton: Victor Books, 1986), 22.

Evangelical doctrine would have nothing in common with the Roman Catholic or Eastern Orthodox doctrines of authority. But despite the very real differences, the modern Evangelical position shares one major flaw with both the Roman Catholic and the Eastern Orthodox positions. Each results in autonomy. Each results in final authority being placed somewhere other than God and His Word. Unlike the Roman Catholic position and the Eastern Orthodox position, however, which invariably result in the autonomy of the Church, the modern Evangelical position inevitably results in the autonomy of the individual believer.

We have already seen that there is a major difference between the concept of Scripture and tradition taught by the classical Reformers and the concept taught by the Anabaptists and their heirs. The Anabaptist concept, here referred to as Tradition 0, attempted to deny the authority of tradition in any real sense. The Scriptures were considered not only the sole final and infallible authority, but the only authority whatsoever. The Enlightenment added the philosophical framework in which to comprehend this individualism. The individual reason was elevated to the position of final authority. Appeals to antiquity and tradition of any kind were ridiculed. In the early years of the United States, democratic populism swept the people along in its fervor.[7] The result is a modern American Evangelicalism which has redefined *sola scriptura* in terms of secular Enlightenment rationalism and rugged democratic individualism.

Perhaps the best way to explain the fundamental problem with the modern Evangelical version of solo *scriptura* would be through the use of an illustration to which many believers may be able to relate. Almost every Christian who has wrestled with theological questions has encountered the problem of competing interpretations of Scripture. If one asks a dispensationalist pastor, for example, why he teaches premillennialism, the answer will be, "Because

---

[7] Cf. Nathan Hatch, *The Democratization of American Christianity*, (New Haven: Yale University Press, 1989). See also Os Guinness, *Fit Bodies Fat Minds*, (Grand Rapids: Baker Book House, 1994), 44–48.

the Bible teaches premillennialism." If one asks the conservative Presbyterian pastor across the street why he teaches amillennialism (or postmillennialism), the answer will likely be, "Because that is what the Bible teaches." Each man will claim that the other is in error, but by what ultimate authority do they typically make such a judgment? Each man will claim that he bases his judgment on the authority of the Bible, but since each man's interpretation is mutually exclusive of the other's, both interpretations cannot be correct. How then do we discern which interpretation is correct?

The typical modern Evangelical solution to this problem is to tell the inquirer to examine the arguments on both sides and decide which of them is closest to the teaching of Scripture. He is told that this is what *sola scriptura* means—to individually evaluate all doctrines according to the only authority, the Scripture. Yet in reality, all that occurs is that one Christian measures the scriptural interpretations of other Christians against the standard of his own scriptural interpretation. Rather than placing the final authority in Scripture as it intends to do, this concept of Scripture places the final authority in the reason and judgment of each individual believer. The result is the relativism, subjectivism, and theological chaos that we see in modern Evangelicalism today.

A fundamental and self-evident truth that seems to be unconsciously overlooked by proponents of the modern Evangelical version of solo *scriptura* is that no one is infallible in his interpretation of Scripture. Each of us comes to the Scripture with different presuppositions, blind spots, ignorance of important facts, and, most importantly, sinfulness. Because of this we each read things into Scripture that are not there and miss things in Scripture that are there. Unfortunately, a large number of modern Evangelicals have followed in the footsteps of Alexander Campbell (1788–1866), founder of the Disciples of Christ, who naively believed he could come to Scripture with absolutely no preconceived notions or biases. We have already mentioned Campbell's naive statement, "I have endeavored to read the Scriptures as though no one had read them before me, and I am as much on my guard against reading them today, through the medium of my own views yesterday, or a week ago, as I am against being influenced by any foreign name, authority, or system whatever."[8]

The same ideas were expressed by Lewis Sperry Chafer, the extremely influential founder and first president of Dallas Theological Seminary. Chafer believed that his lack of any theological training gave him the ability to approach scriptural interpretation without bias. He said, "the very fact that I did not study a prescribed course in theology made it possible for me to approach the subject with an unprejudiced mind and to be concerned only with what the Bible actually teaches."[9] This, however, is simply impossible. Unless one can escape the effects of sin, ignorance, and all previous learning, one cannot read the Scriptures without some bias and blind spots. This is a given of the post-Fall human condition.

This naive belief in the ability to escape one's own noetic and spiritual limitations led Cambell and his modern Evangelical heirs to discount any use of secondary authorities. The Church, the creeds, and the teachings of the early fathers were all considered quaint at best. The discarding of the creeds is a common feature of the modern Evangelical notion of solo *scriptura*. It is so pervasive that one may find it even in the writings of prominent Reformed theologians. For example, in a recently published and well-received Reformed systematic theology text, Robert Reymond laments the fact that most Reformed Christians adhere to the Trinitarian orthodoxy expressed in the Niceno-Constantinopolitan Creed.[10] He openly calls for an abandonment of the Nicene Trinitarian concept in favor of a different Trinitarian concept. One cannot help but wonder how this is any different than the Unitarians rejection of creedal orthodoxy. They call for the rejection of one aspect of Nicene Trinitarianism while Reymond calls for the rejection of another. Why is one consid-

[8] Hatch, op. cit., 179.

[9] Lewis Sperry Chafer, *Systematic Theology*, 8 vols. (Dallas: Dallas Seminary Press, 1948), 8:5–6.

[10] Robert L. Reymond, *A New Systematic Theology of the Christian Faith*, (Nashville: Thomas Nelson Publishers, 1998), xxi.

ered heretical and the other published by a major Evangelical publishing house?

An important point that must be kept in mind is observed by the great nineteenth-century Princeton theologian Samuel Miller. He noted that the most zealous opponents of creeds "have been those who held corrupt opinions."[11] This is still the case today. The one common feature found in many published defenses of heretical doctrines aimed at Evangelical readers is the staunch advocacy of the modern Evangelical notion of solo *scriptura* with its concomitant rejection of the subordinate authority of the ecumenical creeds. The first goal of these authors is to convince the reader that *sola scriptura* means solo *scriptura*. In other words, their first goal is to convince readers that there are no binding doctrinal boundaries within Christianity.

In his defense of annihilationism, for example, Edward Fudge states that Scripture "is the only unquestionable or binding source of doctrine on this or any subject."[12] He adds that the individual should weigh the scriptural interpretations of other uninspired and fallible Christians against Scripture.[13] He does not explain how the Christian is to escape his own uninspired fallibility. The doctrinal boundaries of Christian orthodoxy are cast aside as being historically conditioned and relative.[14] Of course, Fudge fails to note that his interpretation is as historically conditioned and relative as any that he criticizes.[15]

Another heresy that has been widely promoted with the assistance of the modern Evangelical version of solo *scriptura* is hyperpreterism or pantelism.[16] While there are numerous internal

[11] Samuel Miller, *The Utility and Importance of Creeds and Confessions*, (Greenville, SC: A Press, 1991 [1839]), 16.

[12] Edward William Fudge, *The Fire that Consumes*, Rev. ed. (Carlisle: The Paternoster Press, 1994), 2.

[13] Ibid., 3.

[14] Ibid., 4.

[15] For a good scriptural critique of annihilationism, see Robert A. Peterson, *Hell on Trial*, (Phillipsburg: P&R Publishing Company, 1995).

[16] For an introduction and scriptural critique of this new heresy, see C. Jonathin Seraiah, *The End of All Things*, (Moscow, ID: Canon Press, 1999).

squabbles over details, in general advocates of this doctrine insist that Jesus Christ returned in A.D. 70 at the destruction of Jerusalem and that at that time sin and death were destroyed, the Adamic curse was lifted, Satan was cast into the lake of fire, the rapture and general resurrection occurred, the final judgment occurred, mourning and crying and pain were done away with, and the eternal state began. The proponents of pantelism are even more vocal in their rejection of orthodox Christian doctrinal boundaries than Fudge. Ed Stevens, for example, writes,

> Even if the creeds were to clearly and definitively stand against the preterist view (which they don't), it would not be an overwhelming problem since *they have no real authority anyway*. They are no more authoritative than our best opinions today, but they are valued because of their antiquity.[17]

This is a hallmark of the doctrine of solo *scriptura,* and it is a position that the classical Reformers adamantly rejected. Stevens continues elsewhere,

> We must not take the creeds any more seriously than we do the writings and opinions of men like Luther, Zwingli, Calvin, the Westminster Assembly, Campbell, Rushdoony, or C.S. Lewis.[18]

Here we see the clear rejection of scripturally based structures of authority. The authority of those who rule in the Church is rejected by placing the decisions of an ecumenical council of ministers on the same level as the words of any individual. This is certainly the democratic way of doing things, and it is as American as apple pie, but it is not Christian. If what Mr. Stevens writes is true, then Christians should not take the Nicene doctrine of the Trinity any more seriously than we take some idiosyncratic doctrine of Alexander Campbell or C.S. Lewis. If this doctrine of

---

[17] Ed Stevens, "Creeds and Preterist Orthodoxy," Unpublished Paper. Emphasis mine.

[18] Ibid.

solo *scriptura* and all that it entails is true, then the Church has no more right or authority to declare Arianism a heresy than Cornelius Van Til would have to authoritatively declare classical apologetics a heresy. Orthodoxy and heresy would necessarily be an individualistic and subjective determination.

Another pantelist, John Noe, claims that this rejection of the authority of the ecumenical creeds "is what the doctrine of *sola scriptura* is all about."[19] As we have demonstrated, this is manifestly untrue of the classical Reformed doctrine of *sola scriptura*. The doctrine of Scripture being espoused by these men is a doctrine of Scripture that is based upon anabaptistic individualism, Enlightenment rationalism, and democratic populism. It is a doctrine of Scripture divorced from its Christian context. It is no different than the doctrine of Scripture and tradition advocated by the Jehovah's Witnesses in numerous publications such as *Should You Believe in the Trinity?* in which individuals are urged to reject the ecumenical Christian creeds in favor of a new hermeneutical context.[20] Yet the false idea that this doctrine is the Reformation doctrine pervades the thinking of the modern American Evangelical church. Unfortunately the widespread ignorance of the true Reformation doctrine makes it that much easier for purveyors of false doctrine to sway those who have been either unable or unwilling to check the historical facts.

CRITIQUE

The modern Evangelical doctrine of Scripture, or solo *scriptura*, is untenable for a number of reasons.[21] Aside from the fact that it is a novel position based upon rationalistic secular philosophy, and aside from the fact that it is dishonestly presented as if it were the Reformation position, it is also unbiblical, illogical, and

---

[19] John Noe, *Beyond the End Times*, (Bradford, PA: Preterist Resources, 1999), 213.

[20] No author, (Watchtower Bible and Tract Society, 2000).

[21] In one sense this section has already been covered by virtually every published Roman Catholic and Eastern Orthodox critique of what they term *sola scriptura*. These published critiques tend to focus only upon Tradition 0 or solo *scriptura*.

unworkable. At this point we must examine carefully some of the many reasons why solo *scriptura* fails.

SCRIPTURAL PROBLEMS

Scripture itself indicates that the Scriptures are the possession of the Church and that the interpretation of the Scripture belongs to the Church as a whole, as a community. In particular it has been entrusted to specially gifted men. This has already been examined in some detail in the previous discussion of the Bereans and the Jerusalem Council. The Apostles did not tell every individual believer to take their Bibles and decide by themselves and for themselves whether the Judaizers were correct. On the contrary, they gathered in a council as a body and discerned the truth of the matter. Their decision then was given to the various churches. The fundamental point is that Christ established His Church with a structure of authority that is to be obeyed (Heb. 13:7). Even in the first years of the Church, there were those who were specially appointed to the ministry of the Word (Acts 6:2–4). In his letters to Timothy and Titus, Paul indicates that a special teaching ministry was to continue after his death (cf. 1 Tim. 3:1–7; 2 Tim. 4:2; Titus 1:5–9). The modern Evangelical doctrine of Scripture essentially destroys the real authority of ministers of the Word and the Church as a whole.

Adherents of the Evangelical position also ignore the positive scriptural references to tradition. The Gospel was preached for at least 15–20 years prior to the writing of the first book of the New Testament, and that preached gospel was authoritative and binding. This apostolic tradition was the faith of the churches who received the first books of the New Testament, and it was the context within which these books and the books of the Old Testament were to be interpreted. This is the tradition to which the churches were commanded to adhere (e.g., 2 Thess. 3:6). We have already discussed the manner in which this apostolic *kerygma* was taught to every catechumen and recited from memory at baptism. It is important for our purposes here simply to note that this hermeneutical context of Scripture was not abrogated once

Scripture was completed. The Scriptures were written to *already existing* churches, and this means that these churches had the Gospel before they had the completed Scriptures.

HERMENEUTICAL PROBLEMS

An extremely significant problem with solo *scriptura* is the subjectivity into which it casts all hermeneutical endeavors. Ultimately the interpretation of Scripture becomes individualistic with no possibility for the resolution of differences. This occurs because adherents of solo *scriptura* rip the Scripture out of its ecclesiastical and traditional hermeneutical context, leaving it in a relativistic vacuum. The problem is that there are differing interpretations of Scripture, and Christians are told that these can be resolved by a simple appeal to Scripture. But is it possible to resolve the problem of differing interpretations of Scripture by an appeal to another interpretation of Scripture? The problem that adherents of solo *scriptura* haven't noticed is that any appeal to Scripture is an appeal to *an interpretation* of Scripture. The only question is: *whose* interpretation? When we are faced with conflicting interpretations of Scripture, we cannot set a Bible on a table and ask it to resolve our difference of opinion as if it were a Ouija board. In order for Scripture to serve as an authority at all, it must be read, exegeted, and interpreted by somebody. In order for the Holy Spirit to speak through Scripture, some human agency must be involved, even if that human agent is simply one individual reading the text of Scripture.

The adherents of solo *scriptura* dismiss all of this claiming that the reason and conscience of the individual believer is the supreme interpreter. Yet this results in nothing more than hermeneutical solipsism. It renders the universal and objective truth of Scripture virtually useless because instead of the Church proclaiming with one voice to the world what the Scripture teaches, every individual interprets Scripture as seems right in his own eyes. The unbelieving world is left hearing a cacophony of conflicting voices rather than the Word of the living God.

The doctrine of solo *scriptura,* despite its claims to uniquely preserve the authority of the Word of God, destroys that authority by making the meaning of Scripture dependent upon the judgment of each individual. Rather than the Word of God being the one final court of appeal, the court of appeal becomes the multiplied minds of each believer. One is persuaded that Calvinism is more biblical. The other is persuaded that dispensationalism is more biblical. And by what standard does each decide? The standard is each individual's opinion of what is biblical. The standard is necessarily individualistic, and therefore the standard is necessarily relativistic.

HISTORICAL PROBLEMS

It should go without saying that solo *scriptura* was not the doctrine of the early Church or of the medieval Church. However, most proponents of solo *scriptura* would not be bothered in the least by this fact because they are not concerned to maintain any continuity with the teaching of the early Church. On the other hand, some are concerned to claim that their teaching is the doctrine of the classical Reformers. As we have demonstrated already, this is simply false. The classical Reformers did not adhere to Tradition 0 which is essentially all that solo *scriptura* is. Any claim by adherents of solo *scriptura* to be carrying on the teaching of the Reformers is incorrect. It is said either out of ignorance or deceit. The roots of solo *scriptura* lie not in the Apostles, not in the early Church, and not in the Reformers, but instead in the individualism of the Radical Reformation, the rationalism of the Enlightenment, and the democratic populism of early America.

The doctrine of solo *scriptura* also faces serious problems when we consider what rule of faith the Church used in the years between Christ's death and the widespread availability of the entire Scripture. If solo *scriptura* is true, then much of the Church was left without any standard of truth for centuries. In the early centuries of the Church it was not possible to go to a local Christian book store and buy a copy of the Bible. Manuscripts of the Bible had to be hand-copied and were therefore not found in every believer's home. The letters of the New Testament were written over a period of decades. Some churches had some portions, while other churches had others. Only gradually was the New Testament as we know it gathered and distributed as a whole.[22] Additionally, large segments of the Church were illiterate for centuries. If the lone individual Christian is to evaluate everything by himself and for himself according to his Bible, as solo *scriptura* maintains, how would it have worked in the first centuries of the Church for those with no access to a Bible? How would it work for those who could not read a Bible even if they had access to one? Again, the doctrine of solo *scriptura* is observed to be something tailor made by and for modern literate Christians. For many Christians throughout much of the Church's history, it wouldn't even have been possible. The doctrine of solo *scriptura* requires an anachronistic reading of modern conditions back into periods of history when those conditions did not exist.

THEOLOGICAL PROBLEMS

Solo *scriptura* is beset with numerous theological problems, the most significant being the problem of the canon. The canon is the list of books which are inspired by God. According to adherents of solo *scriptura,* the Bible is the only authority because its books are inspired, but the Bible nowhere includes an inspired list of inspired books. What this means is that solo *scriptura* can assert that Scripture is the only authority, but it cannot define with any absolute certainty what Scripture is. When adherents do attempt to define and defend a particular canon, they cannot do so using the Bible as their only authority. In order for solo *scriptura* to be true, the Bible would have to include not only all of the inspired books of the Bible, but also an inspired table of contents telling us which books were really inspired. However, even this would not be enough, for we would not know that the table of contents was inspired apart from an extra-scriptural divine inter-

---

[22] For an outstanding study on the canonization of the New Testament, see Bruce Metzger, *The Canon of the New Testament: Its Origin, Development, and Significance,* (Oxford: Clarendon Press, 1987).

vention or another inspired document telling us that the original list was inspired. Of course then we would just move the problem back another step, and so on into infinity.

Most proponents of solo *scriptura* simply ignore the problem of the canon as if the Bibles they hold in their hands dropped whole and complete from heaven. Yet this is not what happened in actual history. The individual books of Scripture were written over a period of one thousand years. Even the New Testament books were written over a period of decades and only gradually found their way to all of the churches. Numerous apocryphal gospels and epistles were written, some of which were considered authoritative in certain churches. It took time for the New Testament canon of twenty-seven books that we have today to be universally recognized. The doctrine of solo *scriptura* presupposes a complete and closed canon that it cannot account for or defend on its own principles. This fundamental self-contradiction is one of its most obvious flaws.

The doctrine of solo *scriptura* also reduces the essential doctrines of the Christian faith to no more than opinion by denying any real authority to the ecumenical creeds of the Church. We must note that if the ecumenical creeds are no more authoritative than the opinions of any individual Christian, as adherents of solo *scriptura* must say if they are to remain consistent, then the Nicene doctrine of the Trinity and the Chalcedonian doctrine of Christ are no more authoritative than the doctrinal ideas of any opinionated Christian. The doctrine of the Trinity and deity of Christ become as open to debate as the doctrine of exclusive psalmody in worship.

It is extremely important to understand the importance of this point. If the adherents of solo *scriptura* are correct, then there are no real objective doctrinal boundaries within Christianity. Each individual Christian is responsible to search the Scripture (even though he can't be told with any certainty what books constitute Scripture) and judge for himself and by himself what is and is not scriptural doctrine. In other words, each individual is responsible for establishing his or her own doctrinal boundaries—his or her own creed.

If the ecumenical creeds have no real authority, then it cannot be of any major consequence if a person decides to reject some or all of the doctrines of these creeds—including the Trinity and the deity of Christ. If the individual judges the Trinity to be an unbiblical doctrine, then for him it is false. No other authority exists to correct him outside of his own interpretation of Scripture. This is precisely why solo *scriptura* inevitably results in radical relativism and subjectivity. Each man decides for himself what the essential doctrines of Christianity are, each man creates his own creed from scratch, and concepts such as orthodoxy and heresy become completely obsolete. The concept of Christianity itself becomes obsolete because it no longer has any meaningful objective definition. Since solo *scriptura* has no means by which Scripture's propositional doctrinal content may be authoritatively defined (such definition necessarily entails the unacceptable creation of an authoritative ecumenical creed), its propositional content can only be subjectively defined by each individual. One individual may consider the Trinity essential, another may consider it a pagan idea imported into Christianity. Without an authoritatively defined statement of Christianity's propositional doctrinal content, neither individual can definitively and finally be declared wrong. Solo *scriptura* destroys this possibility, and thereby destroys the possibility of Christianity being a meaningful concept. Instead, by reducing Christianity to relativism and subjectivity, it reduces Christianity to irrationalism and ultimately nonsense.

PRACTICAL PROBLEMS

The problems listed above all reveal practical problems inherent in the doctrine of solo *scriptura*. It is simply unworkable in either theory or in practice. We have already discussed the practical hermeneutical problems that arise from solo *scriptura*. At this point we must discuss how solo *scriptura* necessarily leads to schism and factionalism, and how it undermines real ecclesiastical authority.

The Christian Church today is split into literally tens of thousands of denominations with hundreds of new divisions arising daily. Much of the responsibility for this divisiveness rests with the doctrine of solo *scriptura*. When each individual's conscience becomes the final authority for that individual, differences of opinion will occur. When men feel strongly enough about their individual interpretations, they separate from those they believe to be in error. In the world today, we have millions of believers and churches convinced of thousands of mutually contradictory doctrines, and all of them claim to base their beliefs on the authority of Scripture alone.

Not only has solo *scriptura* contributed heavily to this division and sectarianism, it can offer no possible solution. Solo *scriptura* is the ecclesiastical equivalent of a nation with a constitution but no court of law to interpret that constitution. Both can lead to chaos. At best solo *scriptura* can offer an abstract doctrinal statement to the effect that "Scripture" is the sole authority. But using Scripture alone, it cannot tell us what "Scripture" is or what it means. It simply cannot resolve differences of interpretation, and the result is more and more division and schism. The resolution of theological differences requires the possibility of authoritatively defining the propositional doctrinal content of Christianity, and it requires the possibility of an authoritative ecclesiastical "Supreme Court." Since neither of these possibilities are allowed within the framework of solo *scriptura,* there can be no possibility of resolution.

Solo *scriptura* also undermines the legitimate ecclesiastical authority established by Christ. It negates the duty to submit to those who rule over you, because it removes the possibility of an authoritative teaching office in the Church. To place any kind of real hermeneutical authority in an elder or teacher undermines the doctrine of solo *scriptura*. Those adherents of solo *scriptura* who do have pastors and teachers to whom they look for leadership do so under the stipulation that the individual is to evaluate the leader's teaching by Scripture first. What this means in practice is that the individual is to measure his teacher's interpretation of Scripture against his own interpretation of Scripture. The playing field is leveled when neither the ecumenical creeds nor the

Church has any more authority than the individual believer, but Christ did not establish a level playing field. He did not establish a democracy. He established a Church in which men and women are given different gifts, some of which involve a special gift of teaching and leading. These elders have responsibility for the flock and a certain authority over it. Scripture would not call us to submit to those who had no real authority over us (Heb. 13:17; Acts 20:28).

AUTONOMY

Ultimately, the fundamental problem with solo *scriptura* is the same problem that exists within the Roman Catholic and Eastern Orthodox concepts of Scripture and tradition. All of these concepts result in autonomy. All result in final authority being placed somewhere other than God and His Word. The Roman Catholic and Eastern Orthodox doctrines result in the autonomy of the Church. Solo *scriptura* results in the autonomy of the individual believer who becomes a law unto himself. Scripture is interpreted according to the conscience and reason of the individual. Everything is evaluated according to the final standard of the individual's opinion of what is and is not scriptural. The individual, not Scripture, is the real final authority according to solo *scriptura*. This is rebellious autonomy, and it is a usurpation of the prerogatives of God.

Adherents of solo *scriptura* have not understood that "Scripture alone" doesn't mean "me alone." The Bible nowhere gives any hint of wanting every individual believer to decide for himself and by himself what is and is not the true meaning of Scripture. The classical Reformed doctrine of *sola scriptura* meant that Scripture is the sole final and infallible authority. It does not mean that the lone individual is the one to determine what that Scripture means. Scripture was given to the Church within a certain pre-existing doctrinal context that had been preached by the Apostles for decades. Solo *scriptura* denies the necessity of that context, and it denies the necessity of that Church. In doing so it denies Christ who established that Church and who taught that doctrine to His disciples. It is rebellion in the name of God against the authority of God for the sake of preserving the authority of man.

SUMMARY

Proponents of solo *scriptura* have deceived themselves into thinking that they honor the unique authority of Scripture. But unfortunately, by divorcing the Spirit-inspired Word of God from the Spirit-indwelt people of God, they have made it into a plaything and the source of endless speculation. If a proponent of solo *scriptura* is honest, he recognizes that it is not the infallible Scripture to which he ultimately appeals. His appeal is *always* to his own fallible interpretation of that Scripture. With solo *scriptura* it cannot be any other way, and this necessary relativistic autonomy is the fatal flaw of solo *scriptura* that proves it to be an un-Christian tradition of men.

9

The Doctrine of *Sola Scriptura*

In this survey of the history of the Church's thinking on the subject of Scripture and tradition, we have seen that the focus of the modern debate is often misplaced. The debate today is too often framed in terms of Scripture vs. tradition, when the real question is Scripture and *which* concept of tradition. The teaching of the classical Reformers maintained continuity with the teaching of the early Church and included a proper concept of tradition. Ironically both Roman Catholicism and much of modern Evangelicalism have departed from the teachings which they claim to maintain. Roman Catholicism has radically departed from the teaching of the early Church on this subject, and much of modern Evangelicalism has radically departed from the teaching of the classical Reformers.

Having examined the doctrines of Roman Catholicism, Eastern Orthodoxy, and modern Evangelicalism, it is evident how these faulty concepts of Scripture and tradition result in one form of autonomy or another. The doctrine of Roman Catholicism and Eastern Orthodoxy eventually results in the autonomy of the Church, and the doctrine of modern Evangelicalism eventually results in the autonomy of the individual. In addition to resulting in autonomy, the doctrines of Rome, Orthodoxy and modern Evangelicalism are beset with major scriptural, historical, and practical problems.

Although framed in the polemical language of *sola scriptura,* the position of the magisterial Reformers was essentially that which was held in the early Church and throughout most of the medieval Church—that Scripture was the sole source of revelation; that it was the final authoritative norm of doctrine and practice; that it was to be interpreted in and by the Church; and that it was to be interpreted according to the *regula fidei*. But what does this doctrine mean, and why is it essential for the well-being of the Church?[1]

SCRIPTURE IS THE SOLE SOURCE OF REVELATION

One of the consistent teachings of the early Church of the first three centuries was that the Scripture was the sole source of normative revelation in the post-apostolic era. There was no hint of a dual source theory of revelation until at least the fourth century. The classical Reformers echoed this ancient teaching, insisting that today we have only one source of apostolic revelation—holy Scripture. There are two theological elements of this important doctrine. To say that the Holy Scripture is the sole source of normative apostolic revelation today is to say that the Holy Scripture has the qualities of perfection and sufficiency. Each of these closely related qualities requires further explanation because both have been the source of unnecessary confusion.

PERFECTION

When we speak of the perfection of Scripture in this particular context, we are referring essentially to the question of its completeness as a source of revelation.[2] Because it is God's Word we know it is perfect in the sense of being inspired and inerrant. Proponents of a two-source theory would also grant that sense of perfection. They would deny, however, that it is perfect in the

---

[1] Part Four shall examine some of the objections that are raised against the concept of *sola scriptura* and some of the major difficult issues that must be dealt with by proponents of this doctrine—including the identity of the Church, the canon of Scripture, the role and authority of creeds, and practical issues of interpretation.

[2] In various systematic theology texts, this doctrine is explained under various headings including perfection, completeness, and sufficiency. Because of the confusion surrounding the issue, the question of sufficiency will be addressed separately although it is often virtually indistinguishable from the doctrine of the perfection of Scripture.

sense of being a perfectly complete and adequate source of revelation.

Wayne Grudem has provided a helpful definition of this characteristic of Scripture. It means that Scripture "contained all the words of God he intended his people to have at each stage of redemptive history, and that it now contains everything we need God to tell us for salvation, for trusting him perfectly, and for obeying him perfectly."[3] This teaching is evident in many places in Scripture. In Deuteronomy 29:29, for example, Moses says that "the secret things belong to the LORD our God, but those things which are revealed belong to us and to our children forever, that we may do all the words of this law." The implication here is that all revelation necessary for obedience to the Law at this point in redemptive history was revealed not only to a select few but to all of the people.

The same point is made by Jesus in the parable of the rich man and Lazarus. As the rich man suffers in torment, he begs Abraham to send Lazarus to his brothers with a special revelation to warn them of the fate that awaits them if they do not repent. Abraham tells the rich man, "They have Moses and the Prophets; let them hear them" (Luke 16:29). The clear implication in this text is that everything necessary for the salvation of the rich man's brothers may be found in Scripture. No secret revelation is needed. No extra-scriptural sources of revelation are needed.

The Apostle Paul teaches this doctrine as well when he tells Timothy that the Scriptures "are able to make you wise for salvation through faith which is in Jesus Christ" (2 Tim. 3:15). Again, we are able to find all the revelation we need for salvation in the Holy Scripture. The Holy Scripture is a perfect and complete source of revelation for the Christian faith and life.

We must notice, however, that there is a difference between saying that Scripture is the only source of revelation needed for the Christian faith and life and saying that Scripture is the only

[3] Wayne Grudem, *Systematic Theology*, (Grand Rapids: Zondervan Publishing House, 1994), 127.

thing needed for the Christian faith and life. There are a number of different things needed for the Christian life. Scripture is one of these and it has a unique role in that it is our source of divine revelation. The Church is also needed, but it has a different role. Scripture is the truth; the Church is the pillar and ground of truth. The two must be distinguished, but they cannot be separated without destroying the Christian faith. It is very important that we keep this distinction in mind as we proceed because many times when classical Protestants say that Scripture is the only source of revelation necessary for the Christian faith, others assume that they are saying Scripture is the only thing necessary for the Christian faith. Such a misunderstanding is not an accurate view of the classical Protestant position.

SUFFICIENCY

Although the sufficiency of Scripture and the perfection of Scripture are to an extent synonymous, we shall deal separately with the question of sufficiency simply because it has become the focus of much debate today. In many cases the doctrine of *sola scriptura* is reduced to and virtually identified with the doctrine of the sufficiency of Scripture. The Protestant pastor and teacher Dr. John F. MacArthur, Jr., for example, asserts, *"Sola Scriptura simply means that all truth necessary for our salvation and spiritual life is taught either explicitly or implicitly in Scripture."*[4] Although this is an adequate definition of the sufficiency of Scripture, it is an incomplete definition of *sola scriptura.* The sufficiency of Scripture is not the totality of the doctrine of *sola scriptura,* and to define *sola scriptura* in this way seriously undermines the entire doctrine.

Some Evangelicals may deny that the classical Protestant doctrine, or Tradition I, can really be couched in the language of *sola scriptura* because it insists that the Church and the *regula fidei* are also necessary. An illustration of why this charge is false may

---

[4] John F. MacArthur, Jr., "The Sufficiency of the Written Word" in *Sola Scriptura: The Protestant Position on the Bible*, edited by Don Kistler, (Morgan, PA: Soli Deo Gloria), 165. Emphasis his.

prove helpful. When discussing the doctrine of *sola fide,* or justification by faith alone, classical Protestants have always maintained that justification is by faith alone, but not by a faith that is alone.[5] This is maintained in order to guard the doctrine against simplistic misunderstandings of *sola fide.* Yes, we are justified by faith alone, but a faith that does not produce good works and spiritual fruit is a dead faith that does not result in justification.

In the same way we may say that our final authority is Scripture alone, but not a Scripture that is alone. Scripture alone is the source of revelation. Scripture alone is inspired and inherently infallible. Scripture alone is the supreme normative standard. But Scripture does not exist in a vacuum. It was and is given to the Church within the doctrinal context of the apostolic gospel. Scripture alone is the only final standard, but it is a final standard that must be utilized, interpreted and preached by the Church within its Christian context. If Scripture is not interpreted correctly within its proper context, it ceases to *function* properly as a standard.[6] In other words, when Scripture is defined as sufficient, it is important to recognize how the term "sufficiency" is being used.

Tradition I recognizes that Scripture is sufficient as the one-source of divine revelation, as the one final supreme and infallible norm for the Church. But no one asserts that a Bible can enter a pulpit and preach itself. No one asserts that a Bible can read itself. Scripture cannot be interpreted or preached apart from the involvement of some human agency, even if that human agency is simply one individual reading the Scripture. But this obvious truth does not invalidate the supreme authority of Scripture. Scripture remains objectively what it is whether anyone reads it, preaches it or hears it. It remains the objective and infallible Word of God always. In order for it to function as a standard, however, some person or persons must take the Scripture, open

---

[5] E.g., John H. Gerstner, "The Nature of Justifying Faith" in *Sola Scriptura: The Protestant Position on the Bible*, edited by Don Kistler, (Morgan, PA: Soli Deo Gloria), 113.

[6] Note that it does not cease to *be* the standard; it ceases to *function* usefully as one.

it, read it, interpret it, and use it as a standard from which the gospel is preached and against which all doctrines are measured. This is a logically undeniable fact that all participants in the debate have to grant unless they desire to maintain that the Bible is an entity that can preach itself. But the admission of this fact is no more a denial of *sola scriptura* properly understood than an insistence on living faith is a denial of *sola fide.*

SCRIPTURE IS THE FINAL AUTHORITATIVE NORM

Of significant importance to the doctrine of *sola scriptura* is the insistence that Scripture is the one final and authoritative norm of doctrine and practice. It is important to notice that *sola scriptura*, properly understood, is not a claim that Scripture is the only authority altogether. That is the claim of Tradition 0 or solo *scriptura.* There are other real authorities which are subordinate and derivative in nature. Scripture, however, is the only inspired and inherently infallible norm, and therefore Scripture is the only final authoritative norm.   ·

INSPIRATION

We have already discussed 2 Timothy 3:16 in which Paul tells Timothy that "all Scripture is given by inspiration of God." We have noted that the Greek word used here is *theopneustos,* which literally means "God-breathed." The words of Scripture are the very words of God. Charles Hodge explains the theological definition of "inspiration":

> On this subject the common doctrine of the Church is, and ever has been, that inspiration was an influence of the Holy Spirit on the minds of certain select men, which rendered them the organs of God for the infallible communication of his mind and will. They were in such a sense the organs of God, that what they said God said.[7]

---

[7] Hodge, op. cit., I:154.

Inspiration was necessary in order to guard the revelation of God against the inherent propensity of fallen man to err. The prophets and Apostles were not inherently infallible men (e.g., Gal. 2:11–13), but when God used them to communicate His revelation they "spoke as they were moved by the Holy Spirit" (2 Pet. 1:21). The important point we must observe is that *all* Scripture is inspired (2 Tim. 3:16). Traditionally the Church has held that every part of the entire Scripture was given by inspiration of God, so that the whole of Scripture is the very Word of God.[8]

Throughout history, some have claimed divine inspiration for supposed second sources of revelation—typically tradition, the fathers, or the Church. This claim, however, is inaccurate. Inspiration is a unique characteristic of Scripture; it is that which defines canonical Scripture. The very fact that the Church recognized the canon of Scripture and referred to it as the "canon" (or rule), testifies to this unique attribute of Scripture.

Suppose, just for the sake of argument, the possibility of other inspired revelation in tradition, the fathers, or the Church. We must note that, unlike Scripture, no one claims that everything found in the tradition is inspired, or that every writing of every church father is inspired, or that every official utterance of the Church is inspired. Even Rome does not claim infallibility for every utterance of either the pope or the magisterium. So if there were inspired traditions, inspired patristic writings or inspired Church decrees, all would have to admit that these inspired revelations are mixed with fallible uninspired human dross. The voluminous writings of the Church cannot claim and do not claim complete verbal and plenary inspiration. This is a claim rightly reserved for Scripture alone. In other words, the traditions, the fathers, and the Church are all inherently fallible standards.

What this means is that these fallible traditions, these fallible fathers, and this fallible Church must be measured against the one infallible perfect standard. It is impossible to detect the errors

---

[8] Louis Berkhof, *Introduction to Systematic Theology*, (Grand Rapids: Baker Book House, 1979 [1932]), 144–145.

within the tradition if one is measuring the tradition against itself. It is impossible to detect the errors within the fathers if one declares the fathers to be inspired and then measures the fathers against the fathers. It is impossible to discern the true teachings within the Church from the false if the Church is declared to be the infallible standard of truth itself. Standards that are not always and everywhere inspired and infallible cannot be the final infallible standards of truth. Such is a contradiction in terms.

Within the reciprocal nexus of Scripture, Church and the rule of faith then, Scripture occupies an absolutely unique place and role. It alone is verbally and completely inspired by God from its first word to its last. It alone is always and everywhere the very Word of the living God. Scripture alone, therefore, can function as the "canon," the rule, the final authoritative standard of truth against which all else is measured. Yes, it is the Church which does the measuring, and yes the rule of faith provides basic parameters of measurement, but it is Scripture and Scripture alone that *is* that standard norm.

INFALLIBILITY

Because Scripture is inspired, because it is God-breathed, and because it is the very Word of God Himself, Scripture is inherently infallible. Infallibility simply means the inability to err, or the impossibility of error. Infallibility entails inerrancy—the actual absence of any error. Again we must observe that it is only for Scripture that any plausible claim can be made for plenary inspiration, and therefore it is only for Scripture that any logical claim can be made for plenary infallibility and thus inerrancy.

Catholicism and Orthodoxy both claim in different ways an infallibility for the Church, and Rome adds the additional doctrine of papal infallibility. However, neither claims plenary or full infallibility for the Church, and Rome does not claim plenary infallibility for the pope. One may open Scripture randomly and will always know that he is reading the inspired and infallible Word of God. But even if one grants the theological systems of Roman Catholicism or Eastern Orthodoxy, one cannot simply open the canons and decrees of any Church council at random or read any papal bull or decree and be assured that he is reading an infallible statement. Neither Catholicism nor Orthodoxy has an infallible list of all supposedly infallible Church decrees, and Roman Catholicism has no authoritative and infallible list of infallible papal decrees.

Even if the Roman Catholic church or the Eastern Orthodox church had a *charism* of infallibility, it would be of no practical use since neither can say with any real degree of certainty exactly when and where it has been used in every case. Rome, for example, teaches that the pope is infallible in certain cases, but she has not ever provided an infallible and definitive list of every one of those cases. Her theologians continue to argue to this day about which papal statements were made *ex cathedra* and which were not. Some say only two were infallible. Some say more, but no one can say with certainty. The point is simply this: a standard that is not always and everywhere infallible is not an infallible standard and cannot function as an infallible standard.

Infallibility demands inerrancy, and the presence of even one error negates any possible claim to infallibility. It is universally admitted that one can find factual and doctrinal errors in the writings of the Church and in the writings of the popes. Logically therefore, it is impossible to claim an inherent unconditional infallibility for either the Church or the pope. But Rome will argue that she does not claim inherent unconditional infallibility for the pope or for the Church. It is only under particular circumstances that Rome claims infallibility for either. The pope, for example, as we have noted, is only said to be infallible when he speaks *ex cathedra,* in the act of defining a doctrine of faith or morals with the intention of binding the whole Church to that doctrine. In other words, the pope is not *always* infallible. He operates, according to Rome, with a conditional and limited infallibility.

The same is true of the Church herself. Since the Church is composed of redeemed sinners still struggling with the presence and power of sin, the Church is not perfect and is not inherently infallible. The Church is still being conformed to the image of

Christ; she is still being sanctified. She has not achieved absolute sinless perfection yet. We have already noted how often Scripture itself teaches the fallibility of the Church by warning of apostasy and backsliding. Individual churches, including Rome, are warned of the possibility of being severely disciplined and even removed for disobedience. Because of the Church's propensity to wander from the true path, she needs a standard of truth that remains constant and sure, and that standard cannot be herself. It can only be the inspired and infallible Scripture.

Finally, we must always be mindful that claims to infallibility by the Church or any member of the Church inevitably lead to autonomy on the part of the one or ones claiming such infallibility. Even such qualified infallibility as that which is claimed by Rome has led to virtual autonomy. The Roman church has become a law unto herself. Against what higher standard can an infallible Church be measured? None. The only standard against which Rome allows herself to be measured is Rome. However, God alone can rightfully claim infallibility, and since Scripture is simply His inspired Word, it can rightfully claim His infallibility as well.

AUTHORITY

It is because the Scripture alone is God's inspired and infallible Word that Scripture carries unique authority—the binding final authority of God Himself.[9] Rome claims that the authority of the Church is logically and temporally prior to that of Scripture and therefore denies the self-attesting nature of scriptural authority. Scripture, according to Rome, owes its very existence to the decisions of the Church, and therefore the Church's authority is in a very real sense prior to that of Scripture.

Classical Protestantism has historically denied this claim, arguing instead that Scripture's nature as the inspired Word of God

---

[9] See John H. Armstrong, "The Authority of Scripture" in *Sola Scriptura: The Protestant Position on the Bible*, edited by Don Kistler, (Morgan, PA: Soli Deo Gloria), 96–150, for a helpful discussion of scriptural authority.

gives it inherent divine authority. Rome has made the mistake of confusing the recognition of authority with the conferral of authority. John the Baptist was chosen to prepare the way for Jesus the Messiah (Matt. 3:3). And John the Baptist recognized the Messiah, saying, "Behold! The Lamb of God who takes away the sin of the world!" (John 1:29). But the fact that John recognizes Jesus does not imply that John is greater in authority than Jesus. Neither does the fact that the Church recognized the divine inspiration of Scripture imply that the Church has greater authority than Scripture. The sheep hear and know the voice of their Shepherd (John 10:4), but this does not place the sheep on a level of authority equal to or greater than the Shepherd.

The unique authority of Scripture should be self-evident to any confessing Christian, yet centuries of controversy have clouded a rather simple truth. It must be continually repeated and affirmed for each generation of Christians. God has within Himself, by virtue of Who He is, an absolutely unique and sovereign authority. It is the height of arrogance and rebellion for any man or church to claim to have equal authority with Almighty God. It is a mark of the man of sin to make such a claim (2 Thess. 2:4). The simple fact to be observed here is that man is not God, and man does not have the authority of God. Because it is inspired, or God-breathed, Scripture is the very Word of the uniquely sovereign and authoritative God. Because of inspiration, we can say that what Scripture says, God says. And as the voice of Almighty God, Scripture carries all of the authority of God Himself. That being the case, it is self-evident that no man or church shares this unique authority. It is very difficult to find an individual or church within conservative Christendom who will claim to have an authority equal to that of almighty God. The blasphemy of such an assertion is simply too self-evident. But ironically there are large segments of Christendom which have no problem asserting equal or greater authority than Scripture—which is God's Word, even though such an assertion is essentially identical to asserting an authority equal to or greater than God Himself. If Scripture truly is God's Word, as virtually all of the churches involved in the present debate insist, then the issue of final and normative authority is actually settled.

Classical Protestantism affirms that the Church is the pillar and ground of the truth (1 Tim. 3:15), but like Jesus (John 14:6), Scripture claims to be the truth itself (John 17:17). There is a qualitative difference between the truth itself and a pillar of truth. The Church's role as the pillar and ground of truth does not mean that the Church has the same or greater authority than Scripture any more than it means the Church has the same or greater authority than Jesus Himself. Scripture has unique final authority because God has unique final authority, and Scripture alone is completely the Word of God.

SUPREME NORMATIVITY

Scripture's unique, infallible and final authority means that it stands as the Church's supreme norm. This was a primary element of early classical Protestant formulations of the doctrine of *sola scriptura*.[10] To Scripture alone can we ascribe the term *norma absoluta*—"absolute norm"—because it is Scripture alone that is God-breathed. The supreme normativity of Scripture is the logical corollary of its inspiration, infallibility, and unique authority. If Scripture truly is the divinely inspired Word of the living God; if it is therefore completely, absolutely, and unconditionally infallible; if it does carry the very authority of God Himself, then it is self-evident that Scripture is our supreme norm or standard.

No other proposed norm can claim these qualities for itself. The writings of the fathers are not God-breathed. The canons and decrees of the Councils are not God-breathed. The Church does not speak with the inherent self-authority of God. The Church is the Bride of Christ. She is the Body of Christ with Christ as her head. She has been promised that the gates of hell would not prevail against her, but she has not been promised perfection or infallibility this side of the consummation, and it is presumption to claim such perfection and infallibility. God-breathed

---

[10] Cf. Richard Muller, *Dictionary of Latin and Greek Theological Terms*, (Grand Rapids: Baker Book House, 1985), 284.

Scripture is the supreme norm to which the Church is to submit and to which her creeds are to conform.

SCRIPTURE IS TO BE INTERPRETED IN AND BY THE CHURCH

The third element in the definition of scriptural authority has to do with the role and authority of the Church. This aspect of the doctrine of authority is often ignored or dramatically downplayed in Protestant writings on the subject, but it remains an integral part of the apostolic and Reformed faith. Scripture is truth, and the Church is the pillar and ground of truth. There is a reciprocal relationship between the Spirit-inspired Word of God and the Spirit-indwelt people of God. Unfortunately modern Evangelical Christianity has abandoned the older covenantal understanding of the Church which could and did incorporate a proper understanding of ecclesiastical authority in favor of an egalitarian notion of Christianity in which the individual is sovereign. In order for us to have a proper understanding of the authority of Scripture, we must also have a proper understanding of the authority of the Church.

ECCLESIASTICAL AUTHORITY

To assert that the Bible is the sole infallible authority, and that the Bible is the final and supreme norm, in no way rules out the necessity or reality of other secondary and penultimate authorities. The Church is one such subordinate authority recognized by the early Church and by the Reformers.[11] The Church was established by Jesus Christ Himself and given authority by Him. Jesus gives the Church an authority of "binding and loosing" that is not given to every member of the Church as individuals (Matt. 18:18). He gives the Church the authority to teach and disciple the nations (Matt. 28:18–20). The Church is Christ's body (Eph. 1:22–23). The Church is Christ's bride (Eph. 5:32;

---

[11] Cf. Richard Muller, *Post-Reformation Reformed Dogmatics*, (Grand Rapids: Baker Book House, 1993), 2:358.

cf. Rev. 21:9). The Church is the instrument through which God makes the truth of His Word known (Eph. 3:10).

It is only within the Church that we find Scripture interpreted rightly, and it is only within the Church that we find the gospel. As Martin Luther observed, "outside the Christian church (that is, where the gospel is not) there is no forgiveness."[12] John Calvin spoke in similar language in his Catechism:

> *Minister:* Why do you subjoin the forgiveness of sins to the Church?
> *Child:* Because no one obtains it, unless he has previously been united with the people of God, cultivates this unity with the body of Christ up to the end, and thus testifies that he is a true member of the Church.
> *Minister:* You conclude from this that outside the Church there is no salvation but only damnation and ruin?
> *Child:* Certainly. Those who disrupt from the body of Christ and split its unity into schisms, are quite excluded from the hope of salvation, so long as they remain in dissidence of this kind.[13]

Unlike modern Evangelicalism, the classical Protestant Reformers held to a high view of the Church. When the Reformers confessed *extra ecclesiam nulla salus,* which means "there is no salvation outside the Church," they were not referring to the invisible Church of all the elect. Such a statement would be tantamount to saying that outside of salvation there is no salvation. It would be a truism. The Reformers were referring to the visible Church, and this confession of the necessity of the visible Church was incorporated into the great Reformed confessions of faith.[14]

It is not only the necessity of the visible Church that is confessed by the classical Protestant Reformers; her authority is also confessed. The Reformers even use the traditional language of the fathers when they refer to the Church as our "mother." John Calvin, for example, wrote,

---

[12] Cited from Luther's Larger Catechism by John R. Muether, "A Sixth Sola?" *Modern Reformation*, Vol. 7, No. 4 (July/August 98), 24.

[13] Cited by Muether, op. cit., 25.

[14] E.g., *The Westminster Confession of Faith*, XXV:2

[L]et us learn even from the simple title "mother" how useful, indeed how necessary, it is that we should know [the church]. For there is no other way to enter life unless this mother conceive us in her womb, give us birth, nourish us at her breast, and lastly, unless she keep us under her care and guidance until, putting off mortal flesh, we become like the angels. Our weakness does not allow us to be dismissed from her school until we have been pupils all our lives. Furthermore, away from her bosom one cannot hope for any forgiveness of sins or any salvation.[15]

The authority of the Church is real, but it is not to be confused with the authority of God's Word in Scripture. The Church is the pillar and ground, the interpreter, teacher, and proclaimer of God's Word. But it is only the scriptural Word she proclaims that carries supreme authority. Apart from the Word, the Church is mute.

It must be emphasized that the fallibility of the Church does not render her authority invalid. Like any human mother, she need not be perfect to carry real authority. And when this fallible Church does err, it is her responsibility to correct herself according to the final and perfect standard of Scripture. As Douglas Jones notes, "After all, to her alone, not the state, not the family, not Dad, not the parachurch, did Christ give promises of truth and eternal perseverance."[16] The Church has authority because Christ gave the Church authority. The Christian who rejects the authority of the Church rejects the authority of the One who sent her (Luke 10:16).

The authority of the Church is important for our discussion because of the fact that the Church is given the authority by Christ to teach and preach the gospel. The Church is the body with the ability and authority to speak. The Scripture contains the content of what she is to speak. Scripture does not and cannot preach itself. And a Church without the Scripture has nothing to say. It is to the Church as a visible body that we must turn to find

15 Cited by Muether, op. cit., 26.
16 Douglas Wilson and Douglas Jones, *Angels in the Architecture: A Protestant Vision for Middle Earth*, (Moscow, ID: Canon Press, 1998), 94.

the true interpretation and preaching of the good news of Christ. It is therefore to the Church that we must turn for the true interpretation of the Scripture, for it is in the Scripture that the gospel is found.[17]

As Francis Turretin explains, there are essentially three aspects to the authority of the Church: "the first dogmatic or its power respecting articles of faith; the second ordaining (*diataktiken*) or the power to make (*diataxeis*) constitutions and canons conducting to good order (*eutaxian*); the third judicial (*kritiken*), which regards the exercise of discipline."[18] It must be immediately noted that the Church's doctrinal authority does not consist in any authority over the Word or in any supposed infallibility. This authority consists in the fact that the Church has been entrusted with the Scriptures (Rom. 3:2); in the fact that she is the proclaimer and defender of Scripture (1 Tim. 3:15); and in the fact that she must make doctrinal judgments for the sake of the communion (Acts 15:6–35).[19] These judgments usually find their public expression in the creeds and confessions of the Church. But these authoritative judgments are not to be confused with the final authority of Scripture. Their authority derives from and depends upon their conformity with the inherently authoritative Word of God. The Church may be likened to a *court* of law, but she is not to be confused with the *source* of law.[20]

PRIVATE AND CORPORATE JUDGMENT

The fact of the Church's authority in doctrinal matters raises an important question about the conscience and judgment of the private individual as it relates to the judgment of the Church. Unfortunately an enormous amount of unnecessary confusion arises

---

[17] Because of its importance, we shall address the significant issue of the identity of the visible Church in Part Four.

[18] Francis Turretin, *Institutes of Elenctic Theology*, Trans. George Musgrave Giger; Ed. James T. Dennison, Jr., (Phillipsburg: P&R Publishing, 1997), 3:281.

[19] Cf. Ibid., 3:282.

[20] Cf. David C. Steinmetz, "Luther and Calvin on Church and Tradition," *Michigan Germanic Studies*, 10.1–2 (1984), 109.

when we speak of the true authority of the Church. Because of the widespread influence of radical individualistic thinking (as opposed to biblical covenantal thinking), it is often automatically assumed that the recognition of the Church's doctrinal authority must automatically result in tyranny over the consciences of individuals. This is not the case. There are several important distinctions that must be remembered.

First, we must observe that there is an enormous difference between the role the individual conscience plays *in the individual* and the role it plays *in the Church.* The individual believer is not to be confused with the corporate Church. If he is a Christian he is a member of the body, but he is not the whole body. Although individuals can and must read and study Scripture in order that their conscience may ultimately be bound by the Word of God, final *ecclesiastical* authority does not and cannot rest in the judgment of each individual member of the Church.

The individual Christian can and must read and study the Scripture because he is responsible before God for His faithfulness and obedience to Christ. We observe throughout Scripture that God's Word is repeatedly addressed to the people and not only to the leaders of the Church (cf. Deut. 6:4; Rom. 1:7; 1 Cor. 1:2; 2 Cor. 1:1; Gal. 1:2; Eph. 1:1; Phil. 1:1; Col. 1:1; 1 Thess. 1:1; 2 Thess. 1:1; Rev. 1:4). However, we must also observe that the individual should not study Scripture in isolation from the Church. Obviously this does not mean that the Christian cannot study Scripture *alone.* It means that he should not study Scripture *individualistically,* in isolation from the communion of saints— past and present.

Individual private judgment, however, does not replace the corporate judgment of the covenant community. The creeds of the Church are the authoritative confessions of the communion of saints as the covenantal body of Christ. Excommunication is an authoritative judgment of the communion of saints as the covenantal body of Christ. And teaching the Word is the authoritative duty of the communion of saints as the covenantal body of Christ. Modern American Evangelicalism in particular has completely lost sight of the covenantal doctrine of the communion of saints, viewing the Church instead as simply a voluntary collection of individuals with only as much authority as those individuals decide to grant it.

The corporate judgment of the Church normally operates through those who have been especially gifted by the Holy Spirit with leadership and teaching gifts (cf. Matt. 18:17; Acts 15:6–35; 1 Cor. 12:28; Eph. 4:11–13). We have to remember that even though the Word of God is addressed to the people and not only to the leaders of the Church, there still *are* leaders in the Church to whom we owe obedience and submission (Heb. 13:17). Is their authority unconditional and infallible? Certainly not, but neither is the real authority of our earthly fathers or the civil magistrates to whom we also owe respectful submission and obedience. And when the Church does err, God will discipline her and raise up Elijahs to call her to repentance. God does not call His people to be schismatics, rending the Church apart on account of every issue of private judgment.

As Turretin explains, although the corporate doctrinal judgment of the Church is not infallible and does not have an authority equal to that of Scripture, it does have true authority over those who are members of the visible communion of the Church. What then is the relationship between private judgment and this corporate judgment? What is an individual Christian to do if he believes the corporate judgment found in the creeds and confessions to be in error? Turretin explains,

> Hence if they think they observe anything in them worthy of correction, they ought to undertake nothing rashly or disorderly (*atakos*) and unseasonably, so as to violently rend the body of their mother (which schismatics do), but to refer the difficulties they feel to their church and either to prefer her public opinion to their own private judgment or to secede from her communion, if the conscience cannot acquiesce in her judgment. Thus they cannot bind in the inner court of conscience, except inasmuch as they are found to agree with the word of God (which alone has the power to bind the conscience).[21]

---

[21] Turretin, op. cit., 3:284.

THE DOCTRINE OF SOLA SCRIPTURA 273

There is a difference then between the external ecclesiastical court and the internal court of conscience. The inward court of the individual conscience cannot be ultimately bound by anything other than the Word of God, but the Church does have doctrinal authority in the external ecclesiastical court. This authority is given to preserve unity in the Church's faith and to reject the errors of heretics.

As Turretin observes, it is this authority to establish normative doctrinal boundaries that has become the source of many attacks upon the true authority of the Church's creeds. He explains, "Unorthodox persons and heretics are such who, seeing that they are checked by such formulas as by a bridle that they may not scatter their errors to the winds, endeavor in every way, either openly, or secretly and by cunning, to destroy their authority."[22] As noted earlier, the great nineteenth-century Reformed theologian Samuel Miller observed the same phenomenon in his own day when he wrote, "A further argument in favour of Creeds and Confessions, may be drawn from the remarkable fact, that their most zealous opposers have generally been latitudinarians and heretics."[23]

SCRIPTURE IS TO BE INTERPRETED ACCORDING TO THE RULE OF FAITH

The doctrinal authority of the Church is intimately connected with the question of the creeds and the *regula fidei* or rule of faith. As already observed, the *regula fidei* was a summary of the apostolic doctrine preserved by the Church, taught to the catechumens, and gradually inscripturated in complete form in the canonical books by the Apostles. This *regula fidei* functioned as a hermeneutical context for the Church in the centuries following the death of the Apostles. The Church recognized heretics in this formative era because they did not interpret Scripture according

---

[22] Ibid., 3:284–285.
[23] Samuel Miller, *The Utility and Importance of Creeds and Confessions*, (Greenville, SC: A Press, 1991 [1839]), 15.

to the rule of faith. There are several related issues that must be addressed if we are to grasp the importance and necessity of this aspect of the doctrine of scriptural authority.

HERMENEUTICAL CHAOS

One of the most obvious facts facing any intelligent person who has been a Christian for more than a few days is the reality of multitudes of conflicting interpretations of Scripture. The Christian is inevitably faced with numerous questions. How do we interpret the creation account? How do we interpret the role of the law in the life of the Christian? How do we interpret the Old Testament prophets? How do we interpret the sacraments? How do we interpret the Book of Revelation? These and thousands of other hermeneutical questions have been asked and answered by generations of Christians. And often disagreements about the answers have led to conflict and even schism. For almost five hundred years Rome has pointed to the divisions within Protestantism and argued that these divisions are the inevitable result of the Protestant doctrine of Scripture since it allows for no infallible teaching magisterium to interpret Scripture.

Although Rome's claim to have the infallible teaching magisterium is specious, this does not completely resolve the problem. If Rome is not the answer, what is the answer? Is there any way to ever resolve the hermeneutical chaos and anarchy that exists within the Protestant church largely as a result of its adoption of radical individualism? Most Protestants do not seem to have taken this question seriously enough if they have considered it at all. If we proclaim to the unbelieving world that we have the one true and final revelation from God, why should they listen to us if we cannot agree about what that revelation actually says? Jesus prayed for the disciples that they would be one (John 17:21a). And why did He pray for this unity? He tells us the reason, "that the world may believe that You sent me" (17:21b). The world is supposed to be hearing the Church preach the gospel of Christ, but the world is instead hearing an endless cacophany of conflicting and contradictory assertions by those who claim to be the

Church of Christ. This is the heart of the hermeneutical problem we face in the Church today.

Aside from the use of the Church's common confessional rule of faith, there is no possible way to even begin resolving the multitudes of hermeneutical conflicts. The apostolic gospel that served as the hermeneutical context and rule of faith for scriptural interpretation during the early centuries of the Church when she was under attack from numerous heresies must regain its place in our hermeneutics today. Without it, the task of hermeneutics is essentially an exercise in subjectivism and a denial of absolute truth. This hermeneutical context which is so ably and concisely set forth in the Nicene Creed and in the Chalcedonian Definition cannot be abandoned in the name of some modernistic appeal to the sovereignty of the individual or the so-called irrelevance of the past.

THE RULE OF FAITH AS TRADITION

In the conception of the early Church, we have seen that the idea of tradition was not incompatible with an understanding of Scripture as the sole source of divine revelation. Tradition was simply the body of doctrine committed to the Church by Christ and His Apostles whether through written or oral revelation. The content of the revelation was identical regardless of the mode of revelation. Paul did not preach one gospel orally and another gospel when he wrote his epistles. The apostolic tradition was gradually written down over time in the canonical Scriptures. There were no secret, gnostic revelations given by Christ to a select few. Revelation was given to the Church as a whole in Scripture. The revelation of the gospel was public. The early Church was therefore able to view Scripture and tradition as coinherent concepts. There was no conflict because the content was essentially the same.

We have seen that this concept of tradition, which has been termed Tradition I, is not only the doctrine of the early Church, but also the doctrine of the classical Reformers. We have seen that the concepts of tradition currently advocated by Rome

(Tradition II and Tradition III) and modern Evangelicalism (Tradition 0) are not only concepts unknown in the early Church, they are concepts that are inherently self-destructive. Each of these newer concepts of tradition confuses the locus of final authority, ultimately placing it in either the mind of the Church or the mind of the individual. This always results in autonomy and rebellion against the authority of God and His Word.

The Church today must regain the understanding of tradition held by the early Church and by the best of the Reformers. The fact that the Reformers did not use the exact terminology the early Church used to express this doctrine must not deter us from incorporating this necessary concept into our thinking. The Reformers used the language of *sola scriptura* because they were battling a concept of tradition (Tradition II) within Roman Catholicism that was not the doctrine of tradition found in the early Church. The newer Roman Catholic doctrine of tradition destroyed the final authority and normativity of inspired Scripture which was part of Tradition I.

Unfortunately many of the heirs of the Reformation rejected Tradition I as well, and in doing so they unwittingly rejected *sola scriptura*. In an extreme reaction against the abuses of ecclesiastical authority found in Rome, these men rejected all ecclesiastical authority. Their doctrine (Tradition 0) rejected the authority of the Church, of creeds and of tradition of any kind. This doctrine of solo *scriptura* has become the predominant doctrine within Evangelical Protestantism, but it has caused as many if not more problems than it sought to correct. By denying the authority of the corporate judgment of the Church, solo *scriptura* has exalted the individual judgment of the individual to the place of final authority. It is the individual who decides what Scripture means. It is the individual who judges between doctrines on the basis of his individual interpretation of Scripture. It is the individual who is sovereign.

If the Church is to regain a credible witness in the world, she must reject Tradition 0 as strenuously as she rejects Tradition II and III. She must regain the doctrine of the Apostles and of the early Church. She must regain this doctrine which the classical Reformers attempted to re-introduce into the Church. The traditional apostolic rule of faith is the foundational hermeneutical context of Scripture. To reject this rule of faith on the basis of an appeal to Scripture is to immediately read Scripture outside of its Christian context. For too long, the concept of tradition has been misused and abused in the Christian Church. It has been both unduly exalted and unnecessarily reviled. Neither of these attitudes is Christian.

Tradition, properly understood, plays an important part in the Christian concept of scriptural authority. It helps the Church to guard against passing theological fads and trends. It guards against a myopic parochialism which cannot see outside the boundaries of one's own denomination. And it also guards against the error of theological over-emphasis on particular doctrines.[24] In other words it guards the Church from those individuals and groups who wrench Scripture out of its context, twist its meaning to fit their own notions about what Christianity is or should be, and falsely propagate those notions under the banner of Christianity.

CREEDS AND CONFESSIONS

If the rule of faith is necessary, how is it expressed in the Church today? It is important to grasp the relationship between the rule of faith and the creeds of the Church. As we discovered in our historical survey, the Church's early creed was essentially a continuation of the *regula fidei,* expressing the same truths in a fuller way. Although many Evangelicals have an aversion to creeds, they are inescapable. The term "creed" comes from the Latin *credo,* which simply means "I believe." The question is not whether one will have a creed or not have a creed. The only question is what creed one will have.

Creeds and confessions are necessary to a proper understanding of scriptural authority. Without the use of creeds, it is impossible to establish objective doctrinal boundaries within the

---

24 Cf. Jaroslav Pelikan, *Obedient Rebels,* (London: SCM Press, Ltd., 1964), 184–187.

Church. The modern Evangelical denial of creedal authority necessarily results in the impossibility of authoritatively and objectively defining the propositional content of Scripture. The very act of authoritatively defining the propositional doctrinal content of Scripture would be the creation of a creed—that which is deemed unacceptable within the framework of solo *scriptura*. This leaves the responsibility for defining Scripture's doctrinal content to each individual. In other words, the modern Evangelical denial of genuine creedal authority reduces the doctrinal content of Christianity to mere subjectivism. Solo *Scriptura* destroys any possibility of Christianity being a meaningful objective revelation from God.

The modern Evangelical church must come to the realization that if the ecumenical creeds have *no* authority, then there are *no* essential or necessary doctrines of the Christian faith. There would be only subjective individual opinions of what the "essential truths" of the Christian faith are. In our modern relativistic age, this may not even be perceived as a problem. As long as we all claim to believe the Bible, all is well. But as Samuel Miller notes, all is not well.

> It is not enough for attaining this object, that all who are admitted profess to agree in receiving the Bible; for many who call themselves Christians, and profess to take the Bible for their guide, hold opinions, and speak a language as foreign, nay, as opposite, to the opinions and language of many others, who equally claim to be Christian, and equally profess to receive the Bible, as the east is to the west.[25]

Miller explains, "In short, there are multitudes who, professing to believe the Bible, and to take it for their guide, reject every fundamental doctrine which it contains."[26]

If the rule of faith as outlined in the Ecumenical Creeds is rejected, we reject the possibility of defining Christianity's essential

---

[25] Miller, op. cit., 4–5.
[26] Ibid., 5.

and authoritative doctrinal content. The Trinity becomes simply another doctrinal opinion that the individual Christian is free to accept or reject depending upon how it measures up to his interpretation of Scripture. The deity of Christ becomes one of many interpretations the individual is free to accept or reject depending upon how it measures up to his individual interpretation. Every doctrine of the faith becomes a matter of individual determination. While this may appeal to modernistic liberals and modernistic Evangelicals, it destroys the possibility of a coherent Christianity.

THE PERSPICUITY OF SCRIPTURE AND THE CREEDS

It is interesting to observe that the authority of these ecumenical creeds necessarily follows from one of the fundamental qualities of Scripture itself—its perspicuity. Scripture itself indicates it's essential perspicuity or clarity on basic and essential matters. Charles Hodge has brilliantly explained the relationship between the perspicuity of Scripture and the authority of the ecumenical doctrines:

> If the Scriptures be a plain book, and the Spirit performs the functions of a teacher to all the children of God, it follows inevitably that they must agree in all essential matters in their interpretation of the Bible. And from that fact it follows that for an individual Christian to dissent from the faith of the universal Church (i.e., the body of true believers), is tantamount to dissenting from the Scriptures themselves. [27]

The point is quite simple although it has escaped the attention of much of Evangelicalism. If we confess the perspicuity of Scripture, then a confession of the ecumenical creeds inevitably follows. The ecumenical creeds are simply the written form of the confession of the faith of the universal Church. They are a confession of what the Church as a whole has read in the Scriptures.

[27] Hodge, op. cit., I: 184.

The ecumenical creeds represent the hermeneutical consensus already reached by the Church. They declare the basic essential truths which have been confessed by all Christians from the first days of the Church until today. They represent that which the entire Church has seen in Scripture. As Hodge points out, a denial of this consensus of faith is not only a denial of the perspicuity of Scripture, it is in effect a denial of Scripture itself. Why? If the essential teachings of Scripture are clear (perspicuous); if the Holy Spirit has been promised to guide the Church into the knowledge of the truth of Scripture; if the entire Church for thousands of years confesses to being taught by the Spirit the same essential truths in Scripture, then it follows that those truths are what Scripture says.[28]

Ironically, many modern Evangelical advocates of solo *scriptura,* who claim to believe in the perspicuity of Scripture, deny that perspicuity by their rejection of the ecumenical creeds—the common consensual faith of the Church. They reject the perspicuity of Scripture not only by questioning or denying outright various elements of the ecumenical creeds but also by interpreting Scripture in ways unheard of for millennia. How can we proclaim the perspicuity of Scripture and at the same time promote doctrines that no one in the Church ever taught for eighteen or nineteen centuries? Evangelicals criticize Roman Catholics for the creation of new dogmas unheard of in previous centuries, yet Evangelicalism has created far more novel doctrines than Roman Catholicism.

Does this mean that there cannot be new insights into the Scripture? Certainly not, but those insights must be consistent with the Christian rule of faith as expressed in the ecumenical creeds. Many times new language and terms are needed to explain old truths in the face of modern denials of those truths. But Evangelicals have confused explanation and insight with distortion and denial. It is Evangelicals who are at the forefront of many of the modern denials of the common faith of the Church.

[28] Ibid., I:114.

Evangelicals are some of the primary movers behind such modern denials or reinterpretations of the Christian faith as the Openness of God theology, Pantelism (hyper-preterism), and Religious Inclusivism. Many of these modern denials of the creedal faith of the Church are couched in the lofty language of a return to the clear and perspicuous Scripture alone. Such language is simple deception, however, because these new doctrines deny what the entire communion of saints led and taught by the Holy Spirit for two millennia, has confessed as the common scriptural faith of the Church. By denying the common confessional faith of the Church, these heretics deny the very foundation upon which they wish to stand—the clear teaching of Scripture.

SUMMARY

The only historical concept of scriptural authority that does not reduce to either autonomy or absurdity is the concept that the Church universally held for the first three centuries of her existence, which the majority of the Church held for the bulk of the Middle Ages, and which was re-emphasized under the banner of *sola scriptura* by the magisterial Reformers during the sixteenth century. Accordingly, Scripture must be confessed as the sole source of revelation; it must be confessed as the only infallible, final and authoritative norm of doctrine and practice; it is to be interpreted in and by the Church; and it is to be interpreted according to the *regula fidei*.

PART FOUR:

OBJECTIONS AND ISSUES

10

Answering Objections

The doctrine of *sola scriptura* is facing more intense criticism at this point in history than it has faced at any time since the sixteenth century. Unfortunately most Evangelicals remain completely unaware of the number and persuasiveness of the objections that are being voiced, especially by those who have left Protestantism for either Roman Catholicism or Eastern Orthodoxy.[1] While Evangelicals bicker among themselves over every doctrine imaginable, the very foundation that allows for the possibility of any theology at all is being repeatedly attacked by critics.[2] And while Evangelicals continually argue over unessential matters, a steadily increasing number of converts are being convinced that the criticisms of *sola scriptura* are valid.

This study has attempted to provide brief answers to a number of potential objections to the Reformation doctrine of scriptural authority. At this point, however, we must examine some of the common objections to this doctrine more thoroughly and

---

[1] E.g., Patrick Madrid, ed., *Surprised by Truth*, (San Diego: Basilica Press, 1994); Scott and Kimberly Hahn, *Rome Sweet Home*, (San Francisco: Ignatius Press, 1993); David, Currie, *Born Fundamentalist, Born Again Catholic*, (San Francisco: Ignatius Press, 1996); Peter Gillquist, ed., *Coming Home: Why Protestant Clergy are Becoming Orthodox*, (Ben Lomond, CA: Conciliar Press, 1992); Frank Schaeffer, *Dancing Alone*, (Brookline: Holy Cross Orthodox Press, 1994).

[2] E.g., Robert A. Sungenis, *Not by Scripture Alone: A Catholic Critique of the Protestant Doctrine of Sola Scriptura*, (Santa Barbara: Queenship Publishing Co., 1997); Mark Shea, *By What Authority?* (Huntington, IN: Our Sunday Visitor, 1996); Clark Carlton, *The Way: What Every Protestant Should Know About the Orthodox Church*, (Salisbury, MA: Regina Orthodox Press, 1997).

systematically. The criticisms raised by Roman Catholic and Eastern Orthodox apologists are significant and cannot be lightly dismissed. This chapter shall attempt to answer common objections raised not only by Roman Catholics and Eastern Orthodox apologists but also some objections raised by modern Evangelicals.

Before proceeding, it should be noted that a large percentage of the objections raised by critics of *sola scriptura* are due to a failure to distinguish between Tradition I and Tradition 0, between *sola scriptura* and solo *scriptura*. Part of this failure is the fault of Protestants who have confused the two themselves. And part of this is the fault of the critics who have either failed to carefully distinguish the two or found it easier to demolish a straw man. The point is that many of the criticisms raised by the Roman Catholic and Eastern Orthodox apologists are absolutely true, but they are only true of solo *scriptura*. They have effectively demonstrated the impossibility of solo *scriptura* (Tradition 0), and for that classical Protestants should be thankful. These apologists are mistaken, however, in thinking that a criticism of solo *scriptura* is necessarily a criticism of *sola scriptura*.[3] The two are entirely different doctrines with entirely different origins.

ROMAN CATHOLIC OBJECTIONS

ANY DEFINITION OF SOLA SCRIPTURA IS MEANINGLESS

One of the more unusual objections to surface in the recent critiques of *sola scriptura* is the claim that any definition of *sola scriptura* is meaningless. Robert Sungenis makes this statement a number of times in his book *Not By Scripture Alone*.[4] He asserts,

> First, any proposed definition of *sola scriptura* is by its very nature meaningless, except, perhaps as a starting point to debate its existence or nonexistence. The definition is strictly a product of its

---

[3] This explains the necessity of the lengthy and detailed historical chapters in Part One.

[4] E.g., Sungenis, op. cit., 211,220.

adherent, who, wishing to promote the teaching, formulates his definition to encompass what he desires *sola scriptura* to be. Since no statement in Scripture defines *sola scriptura,* any proposed definition is in reality begging the question and is subject to the biases and misconceptions of its proponent.[5]

The point that Sungenis is attempting to make is that if one says Scripture is the sole source of authority, and if he denies any doctrinal defining authority to the Church, then his doctrinal definitions (including his doctrinal definitions of Scripture itself) are necessarily subjective and arbitrary.

The problem with this argument is that, if it is applicable at all, it would only address a problem with solo *scriptura*—the Tradition 0 position. It does not apply to *sola scriptura*—the Tradition I position, and it is possible that it does not even apply to solo *scriptura.* Sungenis's criticism makes it difficult to see how any axiomatic or presuppositional statement could ever be made by anyone —including himself. In any case this criticism illustrates why it is crucial to distinguish between the two positions. The position of the early Church and that of the classical Reformers that Sungenis criticizes from the later Medieval perspective of Tradition II does not necessitate such utter subjectivity.

SOLA SCRIPTURA IS UNBIBLICAL

Many Evangelicals are taken by surprise when they hear Roman Catholic apologists criticize *sola scriptura* as an unbiblical doctrine. What could be more biblical than to say that Scripture is our only authority? Patrick Madrid refers to this, however, as *sola scriptura's* "fatal flaw."[6] It is asserted that adherents of *sola scriptura* cannot point to any passage of Scripture that explicitly says Scripture is the only abiding authority for the Church. Once again, however, the criticism applies to solo *scriptura* and not to the classical Reformation view of *sola scriptura* or Tradition I.

[5] Ibid., 211.
[6] Patrick Madrid, "*Sola Scriptura*: A Blueprint for Anarchy" in Sungenis, op. cit., 19.

Adherents of Tradition I do not deny the authority of the Church to make doctrinal definitions in accordance with and submission to divine revelation as found in the inspired Scripture. The entirety of this book is a defense of the proposition that *sola scriptura,* properly understood, is not only biblical, but historical and necessary.[7]

Part of the difficulty involved in this discussion centers on the difference between the material sufficiency of Scripture and the formal sufficiency of Scripture. Robert Sungenis explains the definitions of these terms in his critique of Protestantism,

> "Formal" sufficiency requires that doctrine be formulated only from explicit statements in Scripture, whereas "material" sufficiency requires only that Scripture contain implicit statements. Catholic theologians, by and large, do not have much of a problem with material sufficiency, but they will always deny formal sufficiency, and, in fact, claim that Scripture is *formally insufficient.*[8]

There are several problems in this statement. We have already noted that an acceptance of material sufficiency was not, however much modern Catholic apologists would like to deny it, the position of the Council of Trent nor of Roman Catholic theologians for the three hundred years following Trent. Sungenis's statement is an example of reading Rome's current teaching back into her past teaching.

Additionally, classical Protestantism's doctrine of *sola scriptura* never claimed that "doctrine be formulated only from explicit statements in Scripture." In The Westminster Confession of Faith, for example, we find the following statement:

> The whole counsel of God concerning all things necessary for His own glory, man's salvation, faith and life, is *either* expressly

---

[7] For this reason I direct readers to all of the previous chapters of this book for a response to this specific objection.

[8] Sungenis, op. cit., 221.

set down in Scripture, *or by good and necessary consequence may be deduced from Scripture:* unto which nothing at any time is to be added, whether by new revelations of the Spirit or traditions of men.[9]

Here, in one of the great confessions of the Reformation tradition, we find a clear rejection of the idea that doctrine must be formulated only from explicit statements of Scripture. On what basis, therefore, can adherents of the doctrine of *sola scriptura* be criticized for adhering to a particular position which they explicitly reject?

SOLA SCRIPTURA IS UNWORKABLE

One of the most frequent objections to *sola scriptura* found in Roman Catholic and Eastern Orthodox apologetic works is the assertion that *sola scriptura* is unworkable. Patrick Madrid writes, for example,

> We have reached that point at which the "rubber" of *sola scriptura* meets the "road" of everyday life. The final question we should ask the Protestant is this: "Can you show where in history *sola scriptura* has worked?" In other words, where, throughout Protestantism's relatively brief life-span, can we find examples (just one will do) of *sola scriptura* actually working, functioning in such a way that it brings about doctrinal certitude and unity of doctrine among Christians? The answer: *nowhere.*[10]

In response to Madrid's question we must first determine whether he is really referring to Tradition 0—solo *scriptura* or Tradition I—*sola scriptura.* If he is asking about Tradition 0, the response he has provided is absolutely correct—"*nowhere.*" Solo *scriptura* has never been able to work in practice, and it will never be able to work in practice.[11]

---

[9] WCF 1:6; emphasis mine.
[10] Madrid, op. cit., 26.
[11] See chapter 8.

If Madrid is asking about Tradition I, which was framed by the classical Reformers in terms of *sola scriptura,* then the response to his request for "just one" example of when it has worked would be the first three to four hundred years of the Church. This was a time prior to the existence of either of the positions Rome has advocated for the last five hundred years, and Tradition I worked fine. What about its workability during Protestantism's "relatively brief life-span"? We cannot point to the same kind of practical success of Tradition I over the last five centuries for several reasons. First, the Reformation occurred long after the Church had initially split, and this initial split created problems which the Reformation could not possibly solve immediately. Second, the rather rapid substitution of solo *scriptura* for *sola scriptura* within Protestant circles led to the rapid fragmentation of Protestantism. Third, the radical individualism of the Enlightenment in Western Europe contributed to the weakening of virtually every branch of Christendom.[12] In any case, there has been at least one lengthy period of Church history when Tradition I worked—the early Church. It worked without a universal bishop, and it worked without any claims to ecclesiastical infallibility.

SOLA SCRIPTURA IS LOGICALLY INCONSISTENT

According to Roman Catholic apologist Philip Blosser, the doctrine of *sola scriptura* is logically inconsistent in two different ways. He argues that it is "self-referentially inconsistent" and that "it involves a tacit violation of the principle of sufficient reason."[13] Concerning the first inconsistency he quotes Peter Kreeft,

> First, as Kreeft notes, "it is self-contradictory, for it says we should believe only Scripture, but Scripture never says this! If we believe only what Scripture teaches, we will not believe *sola scriptura,* for Scripture does not teach *sola scriptura.* . . ."[14]

---

[12] The questions of practical ecclesiology will be explored more fully in chapter 11.

[13] Philip Blosser, "What are the Philosophical and Practical Problems with *Sola Scriptura?*" in Sungenis, op. cit., 49.

[14] Ibid., 50.

He continues, listing three more ways in which *sola scriptura* is self-referentially inconsistent.

> Second, it assumes that the "essential" teachings of Scripture are sufficiently clear to be understood by anyone, but is not itself sufficiently clear even to be considered a scriptural teaching by all. In fact, *sola scriptura* represents a minority position among Bible-believing Christians; and historically it is a relative novelty, entertained by nobody explicitly prior to Wycliff in the fourteenth century.
>
> Third, it claims that the Bible is the ultimate authority, but in fact subordinates the Bible to the extrabiblical (traditions of) interpretation of this or that individual, or group, about what the Bible says. This means, practically speaking, that *sola scriptura* leads to hermeneutical subjectivism. The claim that Scripture is "self-interpreting" is self-serving and sophistical at this point, because conflicting and even contradictory interpretations of Scripture are held by those asserting this claim. Recourse to what the Church (or "historic Christianity") has traditionally taught would be a catholic option, but not consistent with *sola scriptura*. . . .
>
> Fourth, *sola scriptura* is self-referentially inconsistent because the Bible contains no inspired index of its own contents and cannot even be identified as a divine revelation except on extrabiblical grounds of tradition—but in violation of the *sola scriptura* principle.[15]

Regarding the second type of logical inconsistency Blosser again quotes Kreeft,

> As Kreeft notes, "it [the doctrine of *sola scriptura*] violates the principle of causality: that an effect cannot be greater than its cause. The Church (the apostles) wrote Scripture; and the successors of the apostles, i.e., the bishops of the Church, decided on the canon, the list of books to be declared scriptural and infallible. If Scripture is infallible, then its cause, the Church, must be infallible."[16]

[15] Ibid., 50–51.
[16] Ibid., 60

We noted above Robert Sungenis's claim that any definition of *sola scriptura* "is strictly a product of its adherent, who, wishing to promote the teaching, formulates his definition to encompass what he desires *sola scriptura* to be." We observed that this objection is probably not applicable to anyone except possible adherents of solo *scriptura*. Roman Catholic apologists should note that it may also apply to themselves. Quite often it seems that the Roman Catholic definitions of *sola scriptura* are strictly a product of its opponent, who, wishing to criticize the teaching, formulates his definition to encompass what he desires *sola scriptura* to be. The objections offered by Blosser are a case in point. There is a complete and total confusion and blending of solo *scriptura* and *sola scriptura*.

We shall respond to the objections in the order that they have been raised. Blosser's first criticism is essentially nothing more than the claim that *sola scriptura* is unbiblical, a claim to which we have already responded in this chapter and elsewhere. Unfortunately, it is essentially a criticism of solo *scriptura*, and it has no bearing whatsoever on the doctrine of *sola scriptura*.

In response to Blosser's second criticism concerning the sufficient clarity of essential scriptural doctrine and *sola scriptura's* fourteenth-century origin, we simply observe once more that Tradition I was the universal teaching of the entire Church for the first several centuries of the Church. *Sola scriptura,* insofar as it maintains continuity and essential identity with Tradition I, is not a historical novelty. Tradition II and Tradition III, the two doctrines to be found within the Roman communion, on the other hand, are historical novelties. One originated no earlier than the fourth century while the other has only originated in the last century and a half.

Blosser's third criticism is an excellent observation concerning solo *scriptura*. In fact, in many cases solo *scriptura* has gone beyond hermeneutical subjectivism into the realm of hermeneutical solipsism. Blosser's only real error in this brief paragraph is his claim that recourse to the Church or to historical Christianity is inconsistent with *sola scriptura*. As we have attempted to demonstrate throughout this work, that claim is false. It applies only if *sola scriptura* is wrongly defined in terms of Tradition 0.

The fourth objection mentioned concerns the canon of Scripture. Because of its importance, this objection will be addressed in the following chapter. At this point we shall simply observe that within a framework of Tradition I, the issue of canonicity does not present an insurmountable problem. However logically inconsistent it may be with solo *scriptura,* it is not inconsistent with *sola scriptura.*

In response to Blosser's final objection—that *sola scriptura* violates the principle of sufficient reason—we must make several observations. First, the ultimate cause, or author, of Scripture was not the Church: it was the Holy Spirit (2 Tim. 3:16). Yes, human beings were involved, but God was the ultimate cause. There is no violation of the principle of sufficient reason here. Second, Kreeft writes and Blosser quotes the following sentence: "The Church (the apostles) wrote Scripture; and the successors of the apostles, i.e., the bishops of the Church, decided on the canon, the list of books to be declared scriptural and infallible." This is an incredibly misleading sentence. It gives the reader the false impression that the Apostles wrote the books, then the bishops drew up a canon and presented it to the Church as an infallible list of biblical books. Nothing of the sort happened. The canon was first addressed in local synods in Hippo (A.D. 393) and Carthage (A.D. 397 and 419). The See of Rome did not offer an official opinion on the subject of the canon until 1439 at the Council of Florence, and it was not until 1546, at the Council of Trent, that the question of the canon was made an absolute article of faith by Rome.[17]

Finally, in Blosser's final sentence, after asserting that the "Church (the apostles) wrote Scripture," he writes, "If Scripture is infallible, then its cause, the Church, must be infallible." Based on his understanding of the principle of sufficient reason, Blosser

[17] For further historical information, see Bruce Metzger, *The Canon of the New Testament,* (Oxford: Clarendon Press, 1987), esp. pp. 229–247.

asserts that an infallible New Testament requires an infallible Church. But if that is the case, then an infallible Old Testament requires an infallible Israel. The same logic applies. Israel (the prophets) wrote Scripture (Rom. 3:1–2). If Scripture is infallible, then its cause, Israel, must be infallible. Interestingly, however, Rome does not assert the infallibility of the Jews, of Israel—the Old Testament "Church."[18] It is readily admitted that Israel was not infallible. But if an infallible Old Testament does not require an infallible Israel, then an infallible New Testament does not require an infallible Church. The infallibility of both Testaments is due to the inspiration of the infallible Holy Spirit.

SOLA SCRIPTURA IS HISTORICALLY IMPROBABLE

One of the common attacks upon the doctrine of *sola scriptura* is an attack upon its historicity. It is claimed that the doctrine cannot be true because it is a historical novelty. Philip Blosser objects that *sola scriptura* is unhistorical and explains,

> The doctrine that Scripture *alone* is sufficient to function as the *regula fidei*—the infallible rule for the ongoing faith and life of the Church—is of highly improbable orthodoxy since. . . it had no defender for the first thirteen centuries of the Church. It does not belong to historic Christianity. . . . It wasn't until the theologians of the Protestant Reformation elevated the notion into a principle in the sixteenth century that it became widespread.[19]

Several observations are in order. First, it cannot be emphasized often enough that the definition Blosser provides is the definition of solo *scriptura* not *sola scriptura*. Tradition 0 is simply not the same thing as Tradition I.[20]

---

[18] Protestant apologists often use the fallibility of the Old Testament "church" as an illustration of the general truth of the Church's fallibility. Rome does not deny Israel's fallibility because she cannot. Israel, as a covenantal people, rejected their Messiah. There is no greater error that they could have made. Israel's fallibility destroys the validity of Blosser's objection to *sola scriptura*.

[19] Blosser, op. cit., 66.

[20] I have already granted that much of this confusion is due in large part to Protestants

Second, while it is true that one will not find any historical defenders of Tradition 0 until the Radical Reformation, the same cannot be said of Tradition I. It is the universal position of the early Church, and the fact that many of the classical Reformers framed it in the polemical language of *"sola scriptura"* does not change its essential content. The medieval debate was primarily between adherents of Tradition I and Tradition II. Many of the early Protestants opted for the more ancient position (Tradition I) while Rome opted for and dogmatized a later position (Tradition II).[21] If historical novelty means a position has improbable orthodoxy, then Rome is in a precarious position because one of the positions she espouses (Tradition II) is no older than the fourth century, and the other position she espouses (Tradition III) is no older then the nineteenth century. Neither position currently found within her communion is the position of the first three centuries of Church history.

SOLA SCRIPTURA IS INCONSISTENT WITH THE PRACTICE OF THE NEW TESTAMENT CHURCH

Another argument we find leveled at the doctrine of *sola scriptura* is that it is inconsistent with the practice of the New Testament Church.[22] It is argued that since the New Testament Church did not have a universally available copy of the entire New Testament for several centuries, the New Testament Church could not have functioned under the notion of *sola scriptura*. This, however, is simply another case of blurring the distinctions between Tradition 0 and Tradition I. It is certainly true that Tradition 0 (solo *scriptura*) could not have functioned in these first

---

who have not carefully stated the difference, but the Roman Catholic apologists also bear some of the responsibility for perpetuating this confusion. The works of Oberman, McGrath and others on this subject have been in print for decades. Oberman's important essay, *"Quo Vadis, Petre?* Tradition from Irenaeus to *Humani Generis"* is even cited in the bibliography of Sungenis's massive work *Not By Scripture Alone* in which Blosser's chapter may be found. Yet in the entirety of this 629 page book, there does not appear to be any interaction whatsoever with Oberman's argument.

21 See Part One for a more detailed overview of the history of this debate.

22 Blosser, op. cit., 67–69.

years of the Church. But it is also certainly true that the Church *did* function with the concept of Tradition I. It is precisely the teaching of the early fathers that the essential *kerygmatic* content of the apostolic tradition and the content of the New Testament documents were "coinherent." The Church was the locus of authoritative interpretation and reception of this teaching, but that is not inconsistent with Tradition I. It is only inconsistent with the notion of solo *scriptura*—a notion that cannot be equated with *sola scriptura*.[23]

SOLA SCRIPTURA OVERLOOKS EXTRABIBLICAL INFLUENCES ON ITS ADHERENTS

An interesting objection is raised by Blosser, when he asserts, "A certain disdain for history and lack of historical consciousness fostered by *sola scriptura* can make its adherents particularly vulnerable to extrabiblical historical influences on their own thinking."[24] What Blosser is pointing out is something that many Evangelical authors have pointed out in recent years. Much of modern Evangelicalism is antihistorical and functions as if the Church exists within a historical vacuum. By doing so, Evangelicals read their philosophical assumptions into Scripture.

Blosser is in error when he attributes this problem to *sola scriptura.* Part of the problem within the Evangelical church is certainly due to the adoption of the more anabaptistic notion of solo *scriptura,* but other factors have contributed to the problem as well. In any case, the primary point that Blosser makes should be heard. All Christians must realize the fallacy of assuming they come to Scripture as absolutely neutral observers. We all come to Scripture with certain assumptions, biases, worldviews, and philosophies. Evangelicals tend to come to Scripture with radically individualistic presuppositions. Roman Catholics come to Scripture with the presupposition that Rome's interpretation of

---

[23] See Part One for a more in-depth treatment of the way in which Scripture, the Church, and the *regula fidei* functioned within the New Testament Church.

[24] Blosser, op. cit., 70.

Scripture is ultimately infallible. The question we all have to ask is whether the presuppositions we bring to Scripture are the presuppositions that Christ and the Apostles intended us to bring to Scripture. This is one of the most important reasons why Christians cannot remain ahistorical or antihistorical.

SOLA SCRIPTURA OVERLOOKS EXTRABIBLICAL HISTORICAL INFLUENCES ON ITSELF

Blosser continues his historical objections to *sola scriptura* by arguing that the doctrine overlooks extrabiblical historical influences that led to its development. Blosser asks,

> What were the historical influences that contributed to the rise of *sola scriptura?* Doubtless there were many factors, some of them political and economic (like the desire for independence from Rome's hegemony and the need to theologically justify defying her authority), and some of them social and cultural (like the invention of printing, which not only made Bibles widely available, but reinforced the individualism of the act of reading, as opposed to hearing, Scripture). Still other factors were intellectual and spiritual. . . . My own hunch is that the most significant influences on *sola scriptura* stemmed from a profound shift in intellectual and spiritual climate during the late middle ages, associated with the rising influence of nominalism.[25]

Blosser concludes that "the extrabiblical influence of late medieval nominalism, together with various practical exigencies involved in trying to justify revolt against the Church and the whole ecclesiastical tradition, combined to facilitate the development of *sola scriptura* and to make each Protestant, in principle, his own pope."[26]

Several points must be made in response to Blosser's assertions. First, if the evidence of the early Church is relevant at all, the primary historical influence that led to the rise of Tradition I,

[25] Ibid., 72.
[26] Ibid., 74.

or *sola scriptura* as its sixteenth-century adherents preferred to term it, was apparently the fact that it was taught by the Apostles. Blosser's criticism at this point is a perfect example of his failure to observe the warning of his previous objection. His criticism is only meaningful if we share his presupposition that Rome is the Church Christ founded. If his presupposition is not true, the bulk of his criticism is simply a claim that he personally disagrees with *sola scriptura*—not a meaningful objection to the doctrine itself.

We have already discussed the historical aspects of this debate at some length, so it would be unnecessary to repeat everything that has already been said.[27] It should be observed, however, that Blosser's objection does not take into account the most relevant point of all. Until the fourth century at the earliest, there was one view on the relationship between Scripture, the Church, and tradition—Tradition I. During the Middle Ages a second view began to gain a hearing in the Church—Tradition II. The language *sola scriptura* arose within the context of the late medieval debate between these two concepts. *Sola scriptura* was an appeal to the older position which Rome had abandoned. As the Protestants became more firm in this insistence, Rome became more firm in advocating Tradition II. It is one of the fundamental ironies of this historical debate that Roman Catholics criticize Protestants for adhering to a doctrine that cannot be traced to the apostolic Church when both of Rome's predominant positions on the subject can be traced back no further than the fourth century (in the case of Tradition II) or the nineteenth century (in the case of Tradition III). Rome, of course, will always deny that her current doctrine is not the doctrine of the Apostles and the early Church. She is forced to deny this because of her belief in her own infallibility. But such a denial of novelty is not a proof; it is merely an assertion.

---

[27] See Part One.

SOLA SCRIPTURA ASSUMES THE BIBLE CAN BE UNDERSTOOD APART FROM TRADITION

A further objection to *sola scriptura* presented by Roman Catholic apologists is the claim that the doctrine assumes the Bible can be understood apart from tradition. Blosser states the objection in this manner: *"Sola scriptura* assumes no ultimate need for the larger context of the Church's tradition and teaching."[28] Let us observe again the basic definition of Tradition I, which is accepted by adherents of *sola scriptura,* and discover whether this Roman Catholic objection is valid.

Tradition I asserts that Scripture is the sole source of revelation; that it is the only infallible, final and authoritative norm of doctrine and practice; that it is to be interpreted in and by the Church; and that it is to be interpreted according to the *regula fidei*. Having already noted many of the implications of this doctrine, the point to observe here is that Blosser's objection does not apply to it in any relevant way. His objection, like many of the others, only applies to solo *scriptura,* a doctrine which classical Protestantism also rejects.

If "tradition" is understood as the *regula fidei,* then *sola scriptura* does not assume the Bible can be understood apart from "tradition." Adherents of *sola scriptura* only reject "tradition" when "tradition" is re-defined according to the later concepts of Tradition II or Tradition III. *Sola scriptura* does reject tradition understood as a second source of revelation as did the Church of the first four centuries. *Sola scriptura* also rejects the modernistic Roman Catholic doctrine which tends to see in the Roman Magisterium the one true source of revelation. *Sola scriptura* does not reject Tradition I and is, in fact, a call to return to that earliest position. Rome has always rejected this call because a return to the Church's earliest concept of tradition would necessarily entail a rejection of Roman Catholicism.

[28] Blosser, op. cit., 74.

SOLA SCRIPTURA LEADS TO THE
MISINTERPRETATION OF THE CHURCH FATHERS

Blosser argues that Protestant adherents of *sola scriptura* misinterpret the church fathers because, while they are able to find fathers who affirm the unique inspiration of Scripture, they cannot find "a Church Father who affirms that the whole content of God's revelation for the ongoing instruction of His Church was committed wholly to Scripture without residue, so that it serves in that capacity as a text, *apart* from the larger sacred tradition and ongoing community of memory of which it is a part."[29]

There are a couple of problems with this objection. First it is assumption disguised as argument. The entire objection presupposes that Rome's interpretation of the fathers is correct. That, however, is the very heart of the disagreement. For a Roman Catholic to argue that Protestants misinterpret the fathers because they do not interpret the fathers in the same way that Rome interprets the fathers begs the question. This is simply another case of Rome's autonomy in which all things are measured against herself as the final standard of truth.

Second, adherents of *sola scriptura* would not attempt to find fathers who teach that Scripture operates *apart* from the Church or the context of the *regula fidei*. Adherents of solo *scriptura* may attempt to do so, and we would agree with Blosser that such an attempt is futile. The fathers did not adhere to Tradition 0. But, and this is the important point, there is absolutely no evidence that they held to either Tradition II or Tradition III either. In other words the earliest fathers did not teach what Rome teaches concerning Scripture and tradition.[30]

SOLA SCRIPTURA LEADS TO UNHISTORICAL
UNDERSTANDING AND DISTORTION OF FACT

Blosser concludes his historical objections with the argument that *sola scriptura* leads to unhistorical understandings and

---

[29] Ibid., 78.
[30] See Chapter One for an introduction to this issue.

distortions of fact. He lists such problems as the failure to distinguish matters of dogma from matters of discipline, failure to understand the principle of doctrinal development, failure to distinguish official teaching from private opinion, failure to reckon with history, and failure to translate Scripture accurately.[31]

Once more we are faced with an objection that is based upon the unproven assumption that Roman Catholicism has a proper historical understanding and an accurate grasp of the "facts." However, as more and more historical study is done, and as more and more documents come to light, we discover that if anything leads to unhistorical understanding and distortion of fact it is Roman Catholicism. The Roman Catholic doctrine of infallibility combined with Cardinal Newman's nineteenth-century concept of development has led to more blatant historical revisionism and distortion of fact than Protestantism could ever achieve. Infallibility demands that whatever Rome teaches today *must* be the apostolic tradition, and Newman's development theory provides a handy catch-all explanation for the numerous times when the historical evidence indicates that it isn't.

Neither of Rome's concepts of tradition (Tradition II or Tradition III) can be found in the earliest centuries of the Church, but because Rome teaches them now, it is *asserted*—not proved—that they were there then. The same is true of numerous other important Roman dogmas. Papal infallibility, for example, is a doctrine utterly unknown in the Church until the late Middle Ages.[32] But once it is declared to be the teaching of the Church, it becomes the responsibility of the theologians and apologists of Rome to read it back into the evidence. There is an ever widening gap between competent historical research and dogmatic Roman

---

[31] Blosser, op. cit., 81–90.

[32] See Tierney, *Origins of Papal Infallibility*, op. cit. It is interesting to note the typical Roman Catholic responses to the exhaustive historical research of men such as Tierney into the origin of this and other doctrines. Rather than refute the historical evidence, the authors are simply written off as "liberals" or "anti-Catholics." In other words, the only real response given to this research is *ad hominem* arguments.

Catholic historical claims. Rome's scientific errors eventually collapsed under the weight of the evidence. Only time will tell how long it will take for Rome's numerous historical errors to also collapse under the evidence. Roman Catholic historiography at present is nothing more than an exercise in fideism.

Blosser argues that *sola scriptura* leads to a failure to distinguish matters of dogma from matters of discipline. While it may very well be true that Protestants can and do misunderstand Roman Catholic distinctions such as that between dogma and discipline, it can hardly be argued that *sola scriptura* leads to this failure. It could be argued that a lack of study or confusion on the part of a Protestant leads to this misunderstanding, but there is no logical connection between *sola scriptura* and such misunderstandings. If such were the case, it could be argued that Blosser's Roman Catholicism leads to his failure to understand the difference between *sola scriptura* and solo *scriptura*.

Blosser continues, saying that *sola scriptura* leads to a failure to understand the principle of doctrinal development. This too is a *non sequitur.* Many adherents of *sola scriptura* reject Cardinal Newman's particular *theory* of doctrinal development, but most reject it precisely because they do understand it. In addition many Eastern Orthodox reject Cardinal Newman's theory of doctrinal development, but since the Eastern Orthodox do not adhere to *sola scriptura,* that doctrine cannot be considered the cause of this rejection. Protestant adherents of *sola scriptura* accept the principle of doctrinal development, but they reject a theory which allows contradiction to be termed "development." Blosser's argument here is another case of presupposing the correctness of the Roman Catholic concept of development.

Blosser argues that *sola scriptura* leads to a failure to distinguish official teaching from private opinion. Like Blosser's objection concerning the misunderstanding of the distinction between dogma and discipline, this type of misunderstanding cannot be attributed to *sola scriptura.* What Blosser is concerned to avoid here is anyone attempting to prove that the Church can and has erred by pointing to actual errors she has made. One of the common

Roman tactics used to excuse actual errors Rome has made is to attribute many of them to "private opinion." Protestant adherents of *sola scriptura* understand this distinction. Many simply consider it to be special pleading. Rome is said to be infallible as long as we ignore the many instances of Roman error. The doctrine of Roman infallibility simply dies the death of a thousand qualifications.

Blosser claims that *sola scriptura* leads to a failure to reckon with history. The Protestant doctrine of Scripture, he asserts, leads to historical ignorance which in turn leads to absurd argumentation. Once again we note that historical ignorance cannot be logically attributed to the doctrine of *sola scriptura*. Many Roman Catholics and Eastern Orthodox are equally as ignorant of history as the typical American Evangelical. Historical ignorance is a problem that must be dealt with on its own terms regardless of where it is found. Those who advocate Tradition I are calling the entire Church to reject historical ignorance as well as historical revisionism.[33]

Blosser's final objection regarding unhistorical understandings and distortions of fact is his objection that *sola scriptura* leads to a failure to translate Scripture accurately. While it is manifestly true that there are bad translations of Scripture, this cannot be attributed to the doctrine of *sola scriptura*. All translation involves interpretation, so all translations are going to suffer from the unconscious biases of their translators. This, however, is not an exclusively Protestant phenomenon. If one reads the New American Standard Bible, he will detect the influence of conservative Protestantism. If one reads the Revised Standard Version, he will detect more liberal tendencies. But if one reads the Jerusalem Bible, he will also detect Roman Catholic biases.

In addition, the *absence* of *sola scriptura* has not preserved the Church from translating Scripture inaccurately. One is

---

[33] As already pointed out, Roman Catholicism bears much more responsibility for failing to deal with history than those she accuses of this error. As more historians take note of this fact and publish the results of their research, this truth will become too overwhelming for Rome to deny.

immediately reminded of Pope Sixtus V's 1590 version of the
Vulgate. This version of Scripture was filled with thousands of errors, so many in fact that it had to be completely corrected within
two years despite the fact that Pope Sixtus declared the plenary
authority of the 1590 edition "for all future time" (*hac nostra per-
petuo valitura constitutione*). Sixtus declared,

> By the fulness of apostolic power, we decree and declare that this
> edition, approved by the authority delivered to us by the Lord, is
> to be received and held as true, lawful, authentic, and unques-
> tioned, in all public and private discussion, reading, preaching,
> and explanations. [34]

Sixtus forbid any alteration to be made to the 1590 version.
Those who violated this prohibition would incur the wrath of
God and His Apostles, Peter and Paul. Yet two years later, Sixtus's successor was forced, because of the sheer number of obvious errors in the 1590 edition, to alter it. Obviously the absence
of *sola scriptura* did not preserve the Church from this major
translational error. And it is not *sola scriptura* that causes an ob-
server to notice that Sixtus's declarations are not stated in the
form of private opinion.

SOLA SCRIPTURA RESULTS IN HERMENEUTICAL ANARCHY

In addition to logical and historical objections, Blosser raises
some important practical objections to the doctrine of *sola scriptura*. The first, and perhaps the most significant, is the claim that
sola scriptura results in heremeneutical anarchy. Blosser explains
the point of this objection,

> The fact that hundreds of denominations, each professing to de-
> rive its teaching by means of the Holy Spirit's guidance from

---

[34] Cited in Salmon, op. cit., 226.

"Scripture alone," cannot even agree on the fundamentals of that faith, such as the meaning of baptism or the Lord's Supper or even the means of salvation, constitutes a powerful *prima facie* case against it. The principle itself becomes impracticable and self-undermining—a recipe for anarchy.[35]

There is no doubt that heremeneutical anarchy reigns in much of Protestantism. The question is whether this anarchy is the result of *sola scriptura* or solo *scriptura* or a combination of factors. The Evangelical doctrine of solo *scriptura* can do nothing but lead to heremeneutical individualism because it *is* heremeneutical individualism. Proponents of this doctrine have always taken the old phrase *sola scriptura* and misinterpreted the point of the word *sola*. The fact that Scripture is the sole source of revelation today, and the fact that Scripture is the only inherently infallible and authoritative norm or standard does not imply that this standard is to be taken out of its ecclesiastical and historical context. *Sola scriptura* means "Scripture alone," not "me alone." Additionally, the meaning of the word "*sola*" in relation to "*scriptura*" is not absolute. It points to those characteristics that are unique to Scripture. It does not mean that Scripture is to be taken in isolation from the Church and the rule of faith.

Sola scriptura (Tradition I) did not cause the hermeneutical anarchy that exists today, but a proper grasp of the doctrine would go a long way towards correcting it. There are numerous problems within the Church that have resulted not only from radical individualism, but from rationalism, modernism, paganism, consumerism, liberalism, populism, and a host of other influences. It will likely take centuries of patient prayer and diligent work to overcome these problems. It will also take abandoning the self-destructive notion of solo *scriptura* and regaining a proper perspective on the relationship between the roles of Scripture, the Church, and the rule of faith.

[35] Blosser, op. cit., 91.

SOLA SCRIPTURA RESULTS IN
DENOMINATIONAL FACTIONALISM

Intimately tied to the question of hermeneutical anarchy is the question of denominational factionalism. Blosser argues,

> As a result of its hermeneutical anarchy, *sola scriptura* has splintered into denominational factionalism. It has spawned thousands of denominations, and sects and conventicles.[36]

Again the objection is that *sola scriptura* simply cannot work in practice. Again we would have to respond that in the last five hundred years *sola scriptura,* or Tradition I, has really not been presented with much of a chance to work.[37] To begin with, the Church had already split long before the sixteenth century. Surely Roman Catholic and Eastern Orthodox apologists cannot lay this first and most significant fragmentation at the feet of the Protestant Reformers. And it matters little that this split resulted in two branches rather than three, four, or a hundred. In either case, the "Church" is no longer presenting a unified front to the world.

In the second place, the call for a return to Tradition I did not last long. Solo *scriptura,* as we have observed, quickly became the predominant view within much of Protestantism with devastating results. While keeping the phrase *sola scriptura,* adherents of the more anabaptistic notion imported an entirely different meaning into it. And as long as solo *scriptura* is held by the majority of Protestants, whether under the guise of liberalism or fundamentalism, Protestantism will continue to divide and create the kind of public scandal that Blosser points out. A complete overhaul of the way Evangelicals think about the Bible, the

---

[36] Ibid., 93.

[37] The question of how Tradition I could possibly work in the present ecclesiastical context will be addressed in Chapter 11.

Church, and history will be necessary before anything resembling practical progress can occur. The predominant Evangelical theory of authority is an incoherent mass of theological self-contradictions. It is not surprising then that the Evangelical practice is an incoherent mass of denominational self-contradictions. Ideas have consequences, and bad ideas have bad consequences.

SOLA SCRIPTURA RESULTS IN THE UNDERMINING OF PASTORAL AUTHORITY AND DISCIPLINE

Blosser's final practical objection is that *sola scriptura* results in the undermining of pastoral authority and discipline. He explains,

> What does it mean for *him* to "submit" to his spiritual leaders? Clearly the Bible enjoins him to do so. But to which leaders? And what does it mean for him to *submit,* if his spiritual leaders are to gain his submission only in so far as their leadership and teaching agree with (his own interpretation of) Scripture?[38]

The problem, he points out, is logical circularity. We have already attempted to point out this same problem in our discussion of the problems with solo *scriptura.* Blosser has done a fine job of rephrasing the objection in different terms. He is mistaken in assuming that he is referring to *sola scriptura,* but so are most Evangelicals who are involved in this dilemma. Tradition I did not lead to any such dilemma for four centuries when the Church was young. Therefore it is not logically necessary that it do so now. The problem that exists now, and which has existed at least since the Church first split into two branches, is an ecclesiastical problem, not a problem with Tradition I.[39]

---

[38] Blosser, op. cit., 102.
[39] This problem will be addressed in the following chapter.

EASTERN ORTHODOX OBJECTIONS

The objections to *sola scriptura* raised by Eastern Orthodox apologists are virtually identical to those raised by Roman Catholic apologists. The overlapping arguments will not be repeated here. We must first note that the same problem which plagues Roman Catholic apologists is also found within Orthodox apologetic works. Both consistently confuse *sola scriptura* with solo *scriptura.* Clark Carlton, despite recognizing that there have been different doctrines affirmed using the phrase *sola scriptura,* describes the essential feature of *sola scriptura* as follows: "In the final analysis, *sola Scriptura* is not so much an affirmation about the Bible as it is a denial of tradition."[40] As we have seen, however, this is an overly simplistic argument. The statement is either true or false depending on what definition of tradition is being used. Tradition has been understood in a number of ways historically, and *sola scriptura* only rejects some of them. Carlton doesn't define "tradition" in this particular context, and therefore his definition of *sola scriptura* can be very misleading.

Carlton also argues, "No Father or council of the early church ever asserted that the Scriptures, in and of themselves, without any reference to the Church, are the self-sufficient rule of faith."[41] But the inclusion of the phrase "without any reference to the Church" into this statement destroys its effectiveness as an argument against *sola scriptura.* We have repeatedly pointed out that Tradition I, even when framed in terms of *sola scriptura,* does not assert that the Scriptures function apart from any reference to the Church. This objection is not relevant to the discussion of *sola scriptura.*

SCRIPTURE DOES NOT INTERPRET SCRIPTURE

One of the specific objections Carlton raises against the doctrine of *sola scriptura* is the argument that Scripture does not interpret Scripture. He writes,

---

[40] Clark Carlton, *The Way: What Every Protestant Should Know About the Orthodox Church,* (Salisbury, MA: Regina Orthodox Press, 1997), 90.
[41] Ibid., 91.

The idea that the Scriptures are self-interpreting is patently absurd. It assumes a degree of absolute objectivity that would make the most ardent positivist cringe with embarrassment. . . . Texts do not exist in the abstract. Yet, this is exactly what the doctrine of *sola Scriptura* assumes: a bare text that somehow imposes its meaning on the reader.[42]

Carlton, as well as many others who raise this objection, have badly misunderstood the meaning of the phrase "Scripture interprets Scripture." The claim must be understood in its historical context. The Reformers made this claim at a time when Scripture was buried in scholastic commentaries and glosses. One of the main points they were attempting to make was that these glosses were obscuring the text of Scripture.

A second observation is that when Protestants (at least classical Protestants) say "Scripture interprets Scripture," they are not claiming that the Bible is some kind of personal entity that climbs into a pulpit apart from any human interaction and preaches itself. There are some Evangelicals who speak and act as if this were possible, but it is not the meaning of the phrase. It is simply a call to interpret Scripture within its own context. This does not demand radical individualism. The Church is to interpret Scripture within its own context. If a text of Scripture appears to have a meaning that is in contradiction with the meaning of another text, then the problem is with the interpretation of one or both of those texts—not with the inspired Word of God. This is the fundamental point of the phrase "Scripture interprets Scripture," despite its misuse by numerous Evangelicals.

WHO DISTINGUISHES CLEAR TEXTS FROM LESS CLEAR TEXTS?

Carlton's second objection concerns the claim made by many Evangelicals to the effect that unclear passages of Scripture should be interpreted in light of the clear.[43] But is it always obvious which are the clear texts and which are the unclear texts?

42 Ibid., 100.
43 Ibid., 103.

This is the heart of Carlton's objection. Who determines which are the clear texts and which are the obscure texts? If one adheres to solo *scriptura,* it is difficult to see how one would respond to this objection without resorting to complete arbitrariness. The "clear" texts would be those that each particular individual believed were the "clear" texts.

This is another of the reasons why Tradition I or *sola scriptura* is necessary. Rather than depending on the witness of the Holy Spirit to the individual, there is a dependence on the corporate witness of the Holy Spirit to the entire communion of saints. Understood in this way, the Church should interpret disputed passages in light of undisputed passages. She should move from the known of the *regula fidei* to the unknown of disputed doctrines.

EVANGELICAL OBJECTIONS

IS TRADITION I REALLY SOLA SCRIPTURA?

There are likely many adherents of solo *scriptura* who will object that what has been described in this book is not *sola scriptura*.[44] They will deny that Tradition I, which emphasizes the necessity of the Church and the rule of faith, can possibly be considered *sola scriptura.* This objection, however, is one which simply assumes that the doctrine being presented as *sola scriptura* today is the same doctrine taught by the Reformers.[45] As we have labored to demonstrate, this is simply not true. It is the modern Evangelical doctrine of solo *scriptura* that is not the Reformation doctrine.

As already pointed out, many Evangelicals have done exactly the same thing to *sola scriptura* that was done to *sola fide* during the

---

[44] The Evangelical objections dealt with in this section are anticipated objections. Aside from heretical authors who realize the danger a true understanding of *sola scriptura* poses to their teaching, very few Evangelical authors have consciously addressed the difference between solo *scriptura* and *sola scriptura.*

[45] See Part One for an historical study of this question.

so-called "Lordship Salvation Controversy." The slogan was taken by Evangelicals and redefined in an entirely novel way. Just as *sola fide* was redefined to exclude any mention of repentance, the Lordship of Christ, and the necessity of faith being a living, fruit-bearing faith, in the same way *sola scriptura* has been redefined to exclude any mention of the Church or the rule of faith. In both cases, the Evangelical versions of these doctrines bear very little resemblance to the Reformation doctrines which used those same slogans.

The doctrine of *sola scriptura* was part of an ongoing medieval debate between adherents of Tradition I and Tradition II. It was the slogan used by the Reformers in an attempt to call the Church back to the doctrine held in her first centuries. It was a call to return to Tradition I. Rome rejected *sola scriptura* because it challenged her growing autonomy. Evangelicals have rejected it because it challenges their individual autonomy. The question Evangelicals should ask themselves is not whether Tradition I is really *sola scriptura,* but whether solo *scriptura* is really *sola scriptura.* The clear answer to that question is: No. To the extent that Evangelicalism has adopted solo *scriptura,* it has abandoned the Reformation and its call for a return to apostolic faith. Solo *scriptura* is simply a turning to the individual self as the ultimate authority by which all things (including Scripture) are to be interpreted. This is inconsistent with the actual doctrine of the Reformation, it is inconsistent with logic, and most importantly, it is inconsistent with Christianity.

DOES TRADITION I PLACE US UNDER ROME?

Some Evangelicals may object that the definition of scriptural authority provided within these pages necessarily places believers in submission to Rome. This objection, however, is based upon the assumption that the Church can be equated with Rome. Obviously Rome claims that this assumption is a true assumption, but her only evidence is her own claim. The Holy Spirit has certainly not witnessed to the truth of this claim in the whole of the communion of saints. Rome can only argue that the Spirit has done this by arbitrarily limiting the communion of saints to Rome, and then saying that the Spirit has witnessed to this truth in the entire communion of saints (i.e., Rome). The argument is viciously circular.

Christians are to be in submission to the Church, but the Church is not identical to Rome. The difficulty today is that the Church has been fragmented into many pieces making identification of the "Church" a significant problem. The correction of this problem is not something that can be accomplished overnight. There are no twelve-step programs for this kind of situation. The correction of this problem will require generations of prayer, patience, and humility. It has taken the Church over a thousand years to get herself into this current situation. We do not know how long it will take for the problem to be corrected. We can rest assured that no progress will be made unless the problem is acknowledged.[46]

SUMMARY

Numerous objections to the doctrine of *sola scriptura* have been raised in recent years, especially by Roman Catholic apologists. As we have seen, a large percentage of these objections do not actually address *sola scriptura*. Many address solo *scriptura,* and a few address figments of the critic's imagination. Unfortunately, the lack of careful distinction on the part of the critics as well as a lack of careful study on the part of readers has led large numbers of Christians to conclude that these objections have disproved the possibility of *sola scriptura* when, in fact, the most they have been able to do is disprove the Evangelical counterfeit version of *sola scriptura.* There are no substantial objections to *sola scriptura* that are not also objections to apostolic Christianity.

---

[46] This issue will be dealt with at greater length in chapter 11.

11

The Canon, the Church,
and the Creeds

Throughout this discussion of the history of the debate over Scripture, several crucial questions have surfaced. Many of these have been addressed, but there are a handful of issues which require special attention because of their particular significance. To begin with, we must see how the doctrine of *sola scriptura* is not only theoretically compatible with the existence of an authoritative canon, but historically compatible with the actual process of canon formation. In addition, the extremely important question regarding the nature and identity of the Church must be addressed. Is it possible for *sola scriptura* to function within the fragmented Church that exists today? Finally, we must also consider the meaning and significance of the creeds of Christianity, and how they relate to the authority of Scripture.

SOLA SCRIPTURA AND THE CANON OF SCRIPTURE

Probably the most common objection one finds in literature critical of *sola scriptura* is the objection that the Protestant doctrine of Scripture cannot account for the canon of Scripture. Patrick Madrid concisely states the heart of the objection:

> Another problem for sola scriptura is the canon of the New Testament. There is no "inspired table of contents" in Scripture that tells us which books belong and which ones do not. That

information comes to us from outside Scripture. Moreover the knowledge of which books comprise the canon of the New Testament must be infallible; if not, there is no way to know for certain if the books we regard as inspired really are inspired. Further, this knowledge must be binding; otherwise men would be free to create their own customized canon containing those books they value and lacking the ones they devalue. This knowledge must also be part of divine revelation; if not, it is merely a *tradition of men,* and if that were so, Protestants would be forced into the intolerable position of championing a canon of purely human origin.[1]

Many evangelicals have not realized the force of this criticism, and it is a devastating criticism for adherents of solo *scriptura.* Adherents of this position cannot point to an inspired verse of Scripture that lists the table of contents. As Douglas Wilson rightly observes, "before we come to the Word of God at Genesis 1:1, we come to the word of the Church at the Table of Contents."[2] Based upon their own stated thesis that only that which is stated by Scripture is authoritative, adherents of solo *scriptura* have no reason to accept the authoritative nature of the table of contents.[3] This leaves adherents of solo *scriptura* in a quandary. They can say that only Scripture is authoritative, but they can't say with any authority exactly what Scripture is. Any attempt to authoritatively define a canon, or table of contents, is automatically a denial of solo *scriptura.*

Despite the fact that Madrid has raised a legitimate problem for adherents of solo *scriptura,* he has not raised an objection against Tradition I or *sola scriptura.* The issue of the canon is

---

[1] Patrick Madrid, *"Sola Scriptura*: A Blueprint for Anarchy" in Sungenis, op. cit., 22.

[2] Douglas Wilson, "A Severed Branch," *Credenda Agenda,* Vol. 12, no. 1, p. 4.

[3] There are some who are self-consciously consistent with solo *scriptura* and reject the authoritative nature of the table of contents. I have even been told in personal correspondence with one rather vocal adherent of solo *scriptura* that it is the responsibility and duty of each individual Christian to determine the canonicity of each book of the Bible for himself. This, of course, is the absurd result to which adherents of solo *scriptura* are driven if they remain consistent with their principles. It also demonstrates once again that with solo *scriptura,* the individual, not Scripture, is the sole final authority.

admittedly and obviously an impossible dilemma for Tradition 0, but it is not an impossible problem within the context of Tradition I, in which the Church does have genuine authority. This does not mean that the issue of the canon is a simple question. Even a cursory perusal of works discussing the origin and development of the canon will quickly reveal that the issue is a highly complex one. Several points, however, must be made in response to this objection.

First, it is extremely important for the purposes of this discussion to grasp the distinction between the concepts of infallibility and inerrancy. Infallibility means the inability to err. Inerrancy means the actual absence of error. Infallibility necessarily entails inerrancy. But it is important to note that fallibility does not necessarily entail errancy. In other words, although it is impossible for something or someone who is infallible to make an error, it is not impossible for someone or something who is fallible to make a statement that is inerrant (i.e., without error). If I say, "2 + 2 = 4," I have made an inerrant statement. I am even able to make an inerrant theological statement if I say, "Jesus is Lord." Does this mean that I am infallible? Certainly not. It is logically and theologically possible for any fallible individual or church to make an inerrant statement. The point is this: the fallibility of the Church does not mean she *must* always err, it only means she can err.

Second, Madrid's theory of what "must" be the case in order for the Church to have a functionally authoritative and inerrant canon is simply not consistent with facts that both Roman Catholics and Protestants claim to agree upon. It is important to examine these facts because they shed light upon this extremely difficult issue. First of all, God entrusted the Old Testament oracles to the Jews. This is the express declaration of the Apostle Paul in Romans 3:1–2. It was to the Jews that God entrusted the books of the Old Testament. This is not a disputable fact. The Old Testament books were not entrusted to the pagans, and the New Testament Church did not come into existence until the advent of Christ, several hundred years after the writing of the last

Old Testament book, so there cannot be much serious argument about the truthfulness of this assertion Paul makes.[4]

The next fact that is commonly agreed upon is that the Old Testament Jewish "Church" was fallible. In fact when Protestant apologists point out the fallibility of the Old Testament "Church" as an illustration of the fallibility of the Church in general, Rome always responds that the obvious fallibility of the Old Testament "Church" does not apply to the New Testament Church. The point is that we at least agree the Old Testament Jewish "Church" was fallible. Rome does not teach the infallibility of the Old Testament "Church." Her repeated idolatry, apostasy, exile, and ultimate rejection of Christ all point to the obvious fact of her fallibility.

Yet despite the fallibility of the Old Testament Jews, they managed to preserve the canon of Old Testament Scripture. Jesus used the Scriptures the Jews had preserved. The Apostles used the Scriptures that the Jews had preserved. There is no mention in the New Testament that would indicate the Jews did not accomplish this task for which God had chosen them.[5] Yet they did this without a *charism* of infallibility, without an infallible "Church" council to delineate the canon, without any of the things that critics of Protestantism claim is absolutely necessary

---

[4] The assertion of Paul that the Jews were entrusted with the oracles of God (the Old Testament) would largely resolve the question of the so-called "Apocryphal" books were it not for Rome's insistence on her own autonomy and infallibility. When dealing with that which was entrusted to the New Testament Church, even Trent agrees with all of God's people. Rome erred, however, in usurping an authority which had never been granted her—the power of determining the Old Testament canon. The canon of the Old Testament had been entrusted to God's Old Covenant people—the Jews—and was essentially settled before Christ was born [See F. F. Bruce, *The Canon of Scripture*, (Downers Grove: InterVarsity Press, 1988), 27–42]. Rome's sixteenth-century addition to the Old Testament canon was unlawful and has caused unnecessary division in the Church.

[5] Obviously this line of argumentation assumes the present New Testament canon. But we are arguing that if we assume what Roman Catholics (as well as Protestants) adhere to, then there is no basis for the claims of Roman Catholicism concerning the *grounds* of our faith in the New Testament canon. In other words, regarding the canon, Rome's own assumptions are internally self-contradictory. If Rome's New Testament canon is correct, and if her claims about Israel's fallibility are correct, then her claims about the necessity of her own infallibility to preserve the New Testament canon are incorrect.

to have an authoritative canon. The Jews lived for fifteen hundred years without an infallible or inspired "Church" declaration concerning the parameters of the Old Testament canon. But they did not have to wait until the coming of Christ and His endorsement of their canon before they could know they had the inspired Word of God.

The point is that the fallible Jewish "Church" was entrusted with the Old Testament books for around fifteen hundred years and through His providential guidance managed to preserve an inerrant canon, so there is no *prima facie* reason why we cannot believe that God could entrust the New Testament books to a fallible New Testament Church and that they would also be able, under His providential guidance, to preserve an inerrant and authoritative canon.

How does this happen apart from an infallible decree from an infallible Church telling the people of God which books are truly the Word of God? Jesus said His sheep hear His voice and do not hear the voice of strangers (John 10:4–5). God's people in the Old Testament era heard His voice, and God's people in the present era hear His voice. Apart from such supernatural providential intervention, there is no way to explain the extent of unanimity that gradually arose concerning the twenty-seven canonical books of the New Testament.

The criticisms of Protestantism on the issue of the canon do not even fit the actual historical process by which the New Testament canon came into existence. Madrid and many other apologists claim that unless we have an infallible Church infallibly declare what books are canonical and what books are not, we cannot have an authoritative Scripture. But what actually happened in history? If such an infallible decree is necessary, why do we not find Rome, the pope, or a council "infallibly" telling the Church what the canon is for centuries? There are local synods in Hippo in A.D. 393, and in Carthage in A.D. 397 and in A.D. 419 that deal with the question. But Rome did not authoritatively define the canon at these councils. As we have already observed, there were still scattered questions about particular books for the next thousand years. The Book of Laodiceans, for example, is found in early medieval editions of the Vulgate and in different translations into the fifteenth century.[6] Where is the dogmatic declaration of Rome that is said to be necessary for the Church?

The Roman See did not express its opinion on the question of the canon until the Council of Florence (1439–1443) when efforts were made to re-unify the Western and Eastern churches. But the first time in the history of the Church that Rome dogmatically and officially defined the content of the canon as an article of faith was 1546 at the Council of Trent.[7] This was over fifteen hundred years after the death of Christ. Rome's criticisms of Protestantism are self-destructive because the Western Church existed for fifteen hundred years before Rome actually did what Rome claims is absolutely necessary to have a certain scriptural authority in the Church.

The actual historical outworking of the canon points to something other than dogmatic ecclesiastical decrees as our basis of assurance in the New Testament canon. As Dr. Roger Nicole has pointed out in a perceptive article on the issue, the best way to describe the way in which we know the canon is "the witness of the Holy Spirit given corporately to God's people and made manifest by a nearly unanimous acceptance of the NT canon in Christian churches."[8] The unanimity is not due to coincidence, and it is not due to centuries of conciliar decrees; it is due to the action of the Holy Spirit enabling God's people to hear His voice.

Sola scriptura, when understood within the classical Protestant context of Tradition I, is not affected by Rome's self-defeating criticism because it does not assert that Scripture is the only authority. It asserts that Scripture is the only inherently infallible authority. But although the Church is a fallible authority, Tradition I does not assert that this fallible Church cannot make

---

[6] Bruce Metzger, *The Canon of the New Testament,* (Oxford: Clarendon Press, 1987), 239–240.

[7] Ibid., 246.

[8] Roger Nicole, "The Canon of the New Testament," *Journal of the Evangelical Theological Society,* Vol. 40, no. 2 (June 1997), 204.

inerrant judgments and statements. In fact, in the case of the canon of the New Testament, adherents of Tradition I would confess that the fallible Church has made an inerrant judgment. But do we believe this because a particular Church tells us so? No, we believe this because of the witness of the Holy Spirit, which was given corporately to all of God's people and has been made manifest by a virtually unanimous receiving of the same New Testament canon in all of the Christian Churches. This is not an appeal to subjectivism because it is an appeal to the corporate witness of the Spirit to the whole communion of saints. The Holy Spirit is the final authority, not the Church through which He bears witness and to which He bears witness.

SOLA SCRIPTURA AND PRACTICAL ECCLESIOLOGY

According to *sola scriptura,* as framed in terms of Tradition I, the true interpretation of Scripture is found only in the Church. Yet the true Church is identified largely by its adherence to the true interpretation of Scripture. How then do we identify the Church when there are numerous communions claiming to be the Church? Is it possible to answer the question without falling into radical subjectivism or logical circularity? If there were only one claimant to the title "Church," the dilemma would be lessened. The sad fact, however, is that there are multitudes of divided communions each claiming to be the "Church." So how does one even begin to proceed when the criteria for discerning the true Church and the criteria for determining the true interpretation of Scripture are largely reciprocal? In order to address this question, it is necessary to explore several different but related issues.

BRANCH THEORY

The first observation we must make is that if *sola scriptura* is true then some form of a "branch theory" of the visible Church is a necessary corollary—not as an expression of the ideal, but as a description of the reality. But why is a "branch theory" of some kind necessary? First, we must remember that, according to *sola scriptura,* the Church is the true interpreter of Scripture. But where is this Church? With the existence of numerous visibly fragmented communions claiming to be true churches, we essentially have two choices. A person could assert that only one branch is the true visible Church. This is the answer of Rome, Orthodoxy, and some Protestant communions. But on what basis can one make that claim?

One could argue that his branch is the one true branch because it is closest to the teaching of Scripture (a Protestant denomination), or to the fathers (Rome and Orthodoxy). But according to *whose* interpretation of the Scripture or the fathers is this one branch closest to the teaching of Scripture or the fathers? A person could say it is according to his own interpretation of the Scripture or the fathers, but then he is once again trapped in radical subjectivity. The person would have to say that Rome is the true branch (or Orthodoxy, or a Protestant denomination) because it comes closest to *his* interpretation of what the Scriptures (or the fathers) teach.

Instead of appealing to his own individual interpretation, a person could say that according to the interpretation of one branch (Rome, Orthodoxy, or a Protestant denomination), only that one branch is the true visible Church. But then he is caught in an untenable circular argument. Rome would be the one true Church because Rome adheres to the teaching of Scripture and/ or tradition, as those are interpreted by Rome. Orthodoxy would be the one true Church because Orthodoxy adheres to Scripture and/or tradition, as those are interpreted by Orthodoxy. One Protestant denomination or another would be the one true Church because that denomination adheres to the teaching of Scripture, as it is interpreted by that denomination. The question-begging circularity of the argument is vicious.

If we cannot assert that only one branch is the only true visible Church without falling into one form of arbitrariness or another, what is our other choice? The remaining choice is to assert that the one invisible Church is found scattered throughout numerous visible "fragments" or "branches." This would allow an appeal to the corporate witness of the Holy Spirit because the Holy Spirit bears a remarkably unanimous witness to the common confession of faith that has been handed down over the centuries. If we are not to fall into relativistic subjectivity or viciously circular arguments we must examine the idea of the corporate witness of the Spirit as it relates to the identification of the true branches of the Church.

CORPORATE WITNESS OF THE HOLY SPIRIT

In a sense the issue we are addressing is similar to the question of the canon of Scripture. With the New Testament canon believers were faced with the existence of genuine apostolic books mingled with noninspired books and forgeries. In our day believers are faced with the existence of fragments of the true visible Church mingled with non-Christian sects. The same criterion is applicable to both situations in a similar, not identical, way.

In the case of the canon, we observed that the criterion was the witness of the Holy Spirit given corporately to God's people and made manifest by a nearly unanimous acceptance of the New Testament canon in Christian churches. But this criterion assumes that we know what the "Christian churches" are. One way in which we identify the Christian churches is their adherence to the apostolic *regula fidei*. But what does this mean? It means that we can identify the fragments of the true visible Church by their acceptance of the common testimony of the Holy Spirit in the rule of faith, especially as expressed in written form in the ecumenical creeds of Nicea and Chalcedon. The Holy Spirit has born a miraculously unanimous witness to the same twenty-seven books of the New Testament throughout a confessing Christendom, and the Holy Spirit has born a miraculously unanimous witness to a common fundamental creed throughout this same Christendom. This means that ultimately the Holy Spirit is the criterion of truth. But His testimony is made manifest through the corporate witness He bears in the hearts and minds of Christ's people. The Holy Spirit bears witness corporately to the canon; He also bears witness corporately to the essential truths of

Christianity—the rule of faith. Christ's sheep hear their Shepherd's voice in the true books of Scripture, and they hear His voice when His truth is confessed in the churches.

What this means practically speaking is that believers may immediately rule out such communions as the Jehovah's Witnesses and the Mormons, which reject the Holy Spirit's corporate testimony to Christ's sheep throughout history. These groups verbally and vocally condemn and reject the common Christian creed. These groups fall well outside the boundaries of the visible Church and are wolves in sheep's clothing. This also means that believers may immediately recognize the counterfeit nature of liberal churches and teachers who use the words of the Christian creed but deliberately change their meaning. As J. Gresham Machen observed early in the twentieth century, liberalism is not a version of Christianity, it is a different religion altogether.[9] Believers may also identify as false churches those professing conservative churches which reject or alter these fundamental doctrines of Christianity. Only those communions which honestly adhere to and teach the common confession of Christianity, to which the Holy Spirit has born consistent witness, are part of the true visible Church.

EXTRA ECCLESIAM NULLA SALUS

One problem that we immediately encounter is the fact that several of the communions which share the ancient common confession reject the idea that the other communions are part of the true visible Church. Rome officially declares communion with herself to be the criterion of a true church. The Eastern Orthodox church also declares herself to be the one true visible Church. Numerous fundamentalist Protestants immediately consign to eternal perdition any who do not belong to their particular denomination or who do not hold to their particular biblical interpretations.

---

[9] J. Gresham Machen, *Christianity and Liberalism*, (Grand Rapids: Wm. B. Eerdman's Publishing Co., 1992 [1923]).

While it is true that most confessional Churches adhere to the ancient maxim: *extra ecclesiam nulla salus* ("outside the Church there is no salvation"), it is also true that most confessional churches, at least theoretically, grant the possibility of salvation in communions outside of their own. Once that possibility is granted, however, it is logically impossible to strictly and exclusively identify one's own communion with the totality of the Church. If salvation is possible within a particular communion, then that communion is necessarily part of the true visible Church in some sense. The communion in question may be a sick branch, a diseased branch, even a partially broken branch, but if salvation is possible within it, it must be a branch (John 15:1–7).

Roman Catholicism and Eastern Orthodoxy are forced by their respective theologies to assert self-contradictory notions in respect to these doctrines. Each of these communions asserts that salvation is not possible outside the Church. Each also asserts that the Church is to be identified strictly and exclusively with their communion. Yet each allows for the possibility of salvation outside of their respective communions.[10] But if the first two propositions are true, then the third is an impossibility. If the third proposition is true, at least one of the first two is false. If salvation is possible within the bounds of any communion, that communion must be in some way a part of the true Church of Jesus Christ. Roman Catholicism and Eastern Orthodoxy are caught in a fundamental self-contradiction at this point.

Those fundamentalist Protestant churches and denominations which identify themselves as the one true Church apart from which there is no salvation are usually more self-consistent than Rome or Eastern Orthodoxy. They would assert that there is no salvation outside the true Church, and they would identify their church or denomination as the one true Church. And

---

[10] For an example of the Orthodox statement of these propositions, see Timothy Ware, *The Orthodox Church*, second edition, (London: Penguin Books, 1997), 246–247. For an example of the Roman Catholic statement of these propositions, see the *Catechism of the Catholic Church*, paragraphs 816–818; 834–843; 846–848.

consistently with those two propositions they would deny the possibility of salvation outside of their church or denomination. But although the propositions themselves are self-consistent, the foundation upon which the second proposition rests is either pure subjectivism or logical circularity. As we have already observed, the identification of their church or denomination as the one true branch can only rest upon their own individual judgment and interpretation or the question-begging interpretation of their church or denomination.

IDEAL VS. ACTUAL

Some communions, such as Rome and Orthodoxy, would argue that to speak of the visible Church as "fragmented" is a denial of the promises of Christ. This, however, is not true. The Church is promised ultimate and final victory by her Lord Jesus Christ (Matt. 16:18). But Christ does not promise that her victory will be instantaneous. The Church's "progressive sanctification" throughout the present age will be a spiritual war, and like all wars it will include setbacks and advances (2 Cor. 10:3–6). The point is that we are nowhere required to assume that the visible Church at present is in an ideal or perfect state. The fact of the matter is that she is not. Since there is only one Lord, one faith, one baptism, and one body of Christ, the Church *ideally* should be visibly one in the same way it is invisibly one (cf. Eph. 4:5; 1 Cor. 12:12–13). This is the necessary implication of Jesus' prayer in John 17:20–21. Jesus prays here that His people may be one "that the world may believe." The world cannot see an invisible Church unity. Since the unity Christ speaks of is to serve an evidential purpose for the watching world, it must include visible unity.

Sadly the one body of Christ has been visibly fragmented. This fragmentation and rending of the body of Christ is the responsibility of the entire confessing Church. It began prior to the Reformation and continued with fervor after the Reformation. This fragmentation has had numerous tragic results. One such result is that it presents a cacophonous witness to the world exactly contrary to that which Christ explicitly says He desires. Its second tragic result is the dilemma that is placed before every believer who desires to know where the visible Church is. The fragmentation in the visible Church has led many Christians to the belief that they must find the answers to all of their questions by themselves, apart from the communion of saints, because they do not know for sure where to find the true communion of saints. Because the Church does not clearly speak with one voice, the voice of the Shepherd to His Church and to the world becomes unnecessarily difficult to discern.

The Church at the present time is in a temporary state analogous to that of Israel when she sinned against God. The Church is in something of an "exile." Individual Christians at this point in history are in a situation analogous to that of Daniel in exile. This Christian *"diaspora"* is not permanent, however. Christ's prayer will be answered, and there will be visible unity in the Church again. This unity will be the work of God. It will be a visible unity based in Christian truth, not a Roman uniformity based on late medieval papal theories or an ecumenical unity based on compromising the essentials of the faith. It will be a biblical and ecclesiastical unity under one Lord, confessing one faith, and administering one baptism. The one visible Church will once again recognize and confess the rightful role of Scripture and her proper relationship with it.[11]

Although God will accomplish His promised victory in and through the Church, we are still left with millions of present day Daniels living in ecclesiastical exile. What are they to do right now? There is a very real sense in which we have to do exactly what Daniel did. We all have to live in the situation in which God has providentially placed us, trusting in His sovereignty, faithfulness and mercy. We have to pray to God to forgive us of our many sins and restore us as a unified communion of saints with a unified biblical witness to the world. We have to pray that God will make

[11] Keith Mathison, *Postmillennialism: An Eschatology of Hope*, (Phillipsburg: P&R Publishing Co., 1999).

the invisible Church visible and work toward this goal in our respective communions.

Those who are part of different "fragments" will have slightly
different problems to face because each "fragment" has a different
history, a different context, and different sins to overcome. Some
of the branches of the Church will face decisions that will result
either in a strengthening of faith and obedience or a complete
falling away from the truth.[12] Some individual believers will face
difficult decisions concerning their relation to the visible Church.
The most difficult problems facing each of the "branches" will be
their interaction with other "branches."

IS ROME A PART OF THE VISIBLE CHURCH?

The issues we have addressed raise another serious question.
Many Protestants do not deny the possibility of salvation outside
of their particular communions. Most would readily grant that at
least some different denominations are part of the true visible
Church. For many confessing Protestants the only serious question would be whether Rome and Orthodoxy are to be considered in *any* sense whatsoever branches of the visible Church. The
difficulty stems from the breach that occurred in the sixteenth
century over the doctrine of justification. Since the differences
over this doctrine have historically been considered crucial by
both sides, the question must be faced squarely and without
glossing over real problems.[13]

If Tradition I is correct and if the corporate witness of the Holy

---

[12] It is beyond the scope of this book to examine the different problems and difficulties
facing each particular branch of the visible Church. It will be up to Christians within those
particular communions to prayerfully seek God for the wisdom they will need to begin
addressing some of these questions. One of the first questions that many of these communions will have to face is the question raised in this book—the question of authority.

[13] Recent attempts to deal with this question, such as *Evangelicals & Catholics Together*,
have been complete failures largely because they have closed their eyes to the very real
differences that exist in these communions, deciding instead to offer vague documents
that can be interpreted in so many different ways that they become useless. We do no
favors to Protestants or to Roman Catholics by pretending there are really no differences
between us.

Spirit to the common confession of faith in the *regula fidei* is the fundamental criterion of a visible Church, then it seems that Rome would have to be considered a part of the visible Church in some sense. We have already observed that a lone individual or a lone branch of the Church cannot identify that one branch as the only true visible Church without immediately falling into subjectivism or circular argumentation. We have also seen how Rome and Orthodoxy both fall into self-contradiction when they attempt to assert that they alone are the one true visible Church while simultaneously allowing for the possibility of salvation outside of their communions. It is even more difficult for Protestants to assert that they alone are the one true visible Church because, in addition to the other logical problems involved, Protestantism doesn't have the claim of infallibility to fall back upon. Because of the serious and controversial nature of this question, it is necessary that we discuss the issues in some detail.

Charles Hodge, the great Reformed Princeton theologian, addressed the question of Rome's status in the middle of the nineteenth century, and it was as controversial then as it is now.[14] His essay is instructive for us as we examine this issue. Hodge takes the position that Rome must be considered a part of the visible Church in some sense. He begins by pointing out the importance of distinguishing between that which is a description of a perfect ideal and that which is an enumeration of essential attributes. Just as there is a difference between the definition of an ideal Christian and a description of that which is essential for a man to be treated as a Christian, there is a difference "between an enumeration of what belongs to a pure church, and what is necessary to the being of a church."[15] If we confuse the two, he observes, it would be virtually impossible to consider any individual a true Christian or any

----

[14] Charles Hodge, *Essays & Reviews*, (New York: Robert Carter & Brothers, 1857). Although Hodge does not explicitly address the question of the Eastern Orthodox church, many of the arguments would apply to that communion as well. The relevant chapter of this book is titled "Is the Church of Rome a Part of the Visible Church?" This chapter is available in HTML format at www.markers.com/ink/chrome.htm

[15] Ibid., 225.

professing church a real church. No individual believer perfectly meets the standards of a Christian in this life, and no communion perfectly meets the standards of a visible Church prior to the consummation. All individuals and all communions are fallible.

Hodge notes that one of the difficulties involved in this question is the fact that the word "church" is commonly used in a number of different senses. No one definition can adequately take into account all of these established usages. Sometimes the word "church" refers to the whole number of the elect from creation to consummation. Sometimes it is used to refer to all true believers living on earth at any given point in history. It is also used at times to refer to all of those who profess the Christian faith. Finally, as Hodge notes, the word "church" often means "an organized society professing the true religion, united for the purpose of worship and discipline, and subject to the same form of government and to some common tribunal."[16] It is very important to note that in this context Hodge does not mean perfect doctrine when he uses the phrase "true religion." By such definition, we would rule out the possibility of any visible church prior to the consummation. No communion on earth is absolutely perfect in knowledge and in faith. By "true religion" Hodge means the essential doctrines of the faith, without which no man may be saved.[17]

The visible church of which Hodge speaks then is "an organized society professing the true religion, united for the worship of God and the exercise of discipline, and subject to the same form of government and to common tribunal."[18] He observes that this definition is the one to which the principles of Scripture lead. A man becomes a Christian by faith in Christ. He becomes part of the visible Church by profession of faith in Christ. "The true, or invisible church consists of true believers; the visible church, of a society of such professors."[19] Or in other words, "all

[16] Ibid., 229.
[17] Ibid., 230.
[18] Ibid., 234.
[19] Ibid., 235.

true believers are in the true church, and all professing believers are in the visible church."[20]

We have already observed that if salvation is possible within a particular communion, then that communion must be part of the visible church in some sense. Hodge explains what this means in relation to the Roman Catholic question:

> All we contend for is that the church is the body of Christ, that those in whom the Holy Spirit dwells are members of that body; and consequently that whenever we have evidences of the presence of the Spirit, there we have evidence of the presence of the church. And if these evidences occur in a society professing certain doctrines by which men are thus born unto God, it is God's own testimony that such a society is still part of the visible church. . . . Wherever, therefore, there is a society professing truth, by which men are actually born unto God, that society is within the definition of the church given in our standards, and if as a society, it is united under one tribunal for church purposes, it is itself a church.[21]

The next question Hodge addresses is whether the church of Rome is within the definition of a visible church he has already established. He notes the obvious fact that Rome is an organized society, that its professed object is to unite for the worship of God and exercise of discipline, and that it is subject to the same form of government and a common tribunal. He also makes the important observation "that its rulers have left its true end out of view and perverted it into an engine of government and self-aggrandizement is true, and very wicked; but the same thing is true of almost all established churches."[22] The perversion of the true ends of a visible Church can be found within the leadership of Roman Catholicism, Orthodoxy, and Protestantism.

The question boils down to whether or not the Roman church

[20] Ibid.
[21] Ibid., 236–237.
[22] Ibid., 238.

professes the true religion. It is at this point that Protestants can sometimes fall into the same violation of the law of noncontradiction that Roman Catholicism and Eastern Orthodoxy fall into. All but a handful of individual Protestants grant that there are those who are genuinely saved within the Roman Catholic and Orthodox communions. But many Protestants will also say that neither of these two communions is a visible church in any sense and that neither profess or teach the true religion in any sense. These communions would be referred to as completely severed branches. The difficulty, as Hodge observes, is that if this is the true status of these visible communions; if the true religion is not professed in any way, shape or form; then salvation is not possible for anyone within them any more than it is for anyone within Judaism, Mormonism, or Unitarianism. If there are true Christians within these communions, then the true religion, however obscured it may be, must be present in some sense.

Hodge continues by explaining the exact sense in which the true religion is present within these communions. He writes,

> It is a historical fact, as far as such a fact can be historically known, that men have been saved who knew nothing of the gospel but that Jesus Christ came into the world to save sinners. The Scriptures do not warrant us in fixing the minimum of divine truth by which the Spirit may save the soul. We do know, however, that if any man believes that Jesus is the Son of God, he is born of God; that no true worshipper of Christ ever perishes. Paul sends his Christian salutations to all in every place, theirs and ours, who shall call upon the name of the Lord Jesus, their Lord and ours.[23]

Hodge argues that Rome does profess the true religion in a very specific sense. In addition to believing that the Scripture is the Word of God, Rome believes and receives the Apostles', the Nicene, and the Athanasian Creeds. Having cited the Nicene Creed which Rome professes, Hodge asks,

[23] Ibid., 241.

If this creed were submitted to any intelligent Christian without his knowing whence it came, could he hesitate to say that it was the creed of a Christian church? Could he deny that these are the very terms in which for ages the general faith of Christendom has been expressed? Could he, without renouncing the Bible, say that the sincere belief of those doctrines would not secure eternal life? Can any man take it upon himself in the sight of God, to assert that there is not truth enough in the above summary to save the soul? If not, then a society which professing that creed professes the true religion in the sense stated above.[24]

In response to those who assert that Rome is not part of the visible Church because she does not teach and profess the true religion, Hodge explains that "[t]he Jewish church at the time of Christ, by her officers, in the synagogue and in the sanhedrim [sic], and by all her great parties professed fundamental error, justification by the law, for example; and yet retained its being as a church, in the bosom of which the elect of God still lived."[25] The situation is similar to that which existed in the Galatian churches. Paul is able to address them as a church while at the same time admonishing them for turning away from the gospel (Gal. 1:2, 6; 3:1–3).

The matter boils down to this: Many Protestants object to Hodge's argumentation with the counter-argument that Rome does not teach the true religion and therefore cannot be considered a visible church. The problem is that Rome's teaching contradicts the Protestant interpretation of Scripture. This is obviously true. And Protestantism contradicts Rome's interpretation of the Scripture. But is Protestantism correct simply because Protestantism does not contradict Protestantism's interpretation of Scripture? The question dramatically illustrates the very problem that we have sought to address throughout these pages. It demonstrates how easily Protestants can fall into an individualistic and subjectivistic solo *scriptura* type of thinking.

---

[24] Ibid., 241–242.
[25] Ibid., 243.

The most obvious objection that can be raised against Hodge's argument in light of our discussion is the fact that the Reformers often referred to the Roman Catholic church as "antichrist." If the Reformers adhered to Tradition I and if Tradition I requires that any church (such as Rome) that adheres to the common creeds of the Church be considered a visible church in some sense, then how do we understand the Reformers' condemnations of Rome? In response it could be suggested that the Reformers at this point were not being entirely consistent with their own doctrines, but Hodge points out a more reasonable explanation. He points out that the Reformers denied that Rome was a true church in the sense of being a *pure* church, not in the sense of being a *real* church.[26]

The Reformers viewed Rome in two different senses—either in reference to the profession of Christianity she makes or in reference to her subjection to the papacy. In the first sense it was admitted that Rome may still be called a Christian church. In the other sense she was considered anti-Christian and apostate.[27] One clear example of this distinction is found in the writings of the great Protestant theologian Francis Turretin. He explains the distinction while dealing with the question of whether Rome can be called a true Church of Christ:

> The church of Rome can be regarded under a twofold view (*schesei*): either as it is Christian, with regard to the profession of Christianity and of gospel truth which it retains; or papal, with regard to subjection to the pope, and corruptions and capital errors (in faith as well as in morals) which she has mingled with and built upon those truths besides and contrary to the word of God. We can speak of it in different ways. In the former respect, we do not deny that there is some truth in it; but in the latter (under which it is regarded here) we deny that it can be called Christian and apostolic, but Antichristian and apostate. In this sense, we confess that it can still improperly and relatively be

---

[26] Ibid., 225–226.
[27] Ibid., 225.

called a Christian church in a threefold respect. First, with respect to the people of God or the elect still remaining in it, who are ordered to come out of her, even at the time of the destruction of Babylon (Rev. 18:4). (2) With respect to external form or certain ruins of a scattered church, in which its traces are seen to this day, both with respect to the word of God and the preaching of it (which, although corrupted, still remains in her); and with respect to the administration of the sacraments and especially of baptism, which is still preserved entire in her as to substance. (3) With respect to Christian and evangelical truths concerning the one and triune God, Christ the God-man (*theanthropo*) Mediator, his incarnation, death and resurrection and other heads of doctrine by which she is distinguished from assemblies of pagans and infidels. But we deny that she can simply and properly be called a true church, much less the one and only catholic church, as they contend.[28]

In another place, however, Turretin makes it clear that he considers the church of Rome to be a real visible church in some sense. In his defense of the validity of Roman baptism, he explains, "There are still remains of the church in the papacy (Rev. 18:4) and God has not yet wholly left that church."[29]

The issue of Roman Catholic baptism raises an important point. As noted above, many of the Reformers referred to the Roman Catholic Church as "antichrist." Yet virtually all of the magisterial Reformers also taught that Roman Catholic baptism was valid. This is a common position among the heirs of the Reformation as well. It is not unusual to find the staunchest critics of Rome following the Reformers and granting the validity of Roman baptism. This, however, raises a significant question. Can there be such a thing as a valid baptism that is not a Christian baptism? Obviously, the answer to this question is "no." In order for a baptism to be considered valid, it must be a Christian baptism.

---

[28] Francis Turretin, *Institutes of Elenctic Theology*, Trans. by George Musgrave Giger, Ed. by James T. Dennison, Jr., (Phillipsburg, NJ: P&R Publishing Co., 1992–97), III:121.

[29] Ibid., III:409.

A non-Christian baptism is by definition an invalid baptism. So, if Roman Catholic baptism is valid, then Roman Catholic baptism is Christian, and if Roman Catholic baptism is Christian, the Roman Catholic church must be a part of the true Church in some sense because a non-Christian church cannot administer Christian baptism. The Christian sacrament of baptism can only be administered within the context of the Christian Church.

What this means is that the problems raised concerning the relation of Rome to the true Church is not a problem caused solely by adherence to Tradition I. This is a difficulty that has existed since the Reformation in the sixteenth century. All of the magisterial Reformers and all of their heirs who share their belief in the validity of Roman baptism must also deal with the logical and theological implication of that belief—that despite her numerous serious errors, Rome must be considered in some sense to be part of the true visible Church.[30]

Rome has veered way off course doctrinally, but if Tradition I (*sola scriptura*) is true, then Rome's interpretation cannot be measured only against another branch's interpretation of Scripture. Unless we wish to fall into the same question-begging circular argumentation that Rome and Orthodoxy fall into, we cannot simply assert that our communion is the correct branch because our communion's interpretation of Scripture comes closest to our communion's interpretation of Scripture. Rome's aberrations must be measured against the ancient rule of faith to which she claims adherence. Her errant doctrines and practices must be demonstrated to be inconsistent with these foundational doctrines.

Unfortunately the difficult practical reality we face in the present state of the Church, with all of the division that has occurred, is that the Church has not spoken as a completely unified body since at least the eleventh century. Each branch of the Church has tried to find a way around this dilemma by either

---

[30] Regardless of one's conclusion regarding the status of the Roman Catholic communion, it is a separate issue from the case for *sola scriptura* presented throughout this book.

dogmatically declaring itself to be the only true branch of the Church, by functioning in practical terms as if that were the case, or by glossing over the real differences that exist among the branches. The problem is that by doing these things, the branches of the Church continually fall into logical absurdities.

PRACTICAL QUESTIONS

Regardless of where one lands on the issue of Rome's status as a branch of the true visible Church, a number of difficult practical questions remain. What, for example, does all of this mean to the individual believer? If any church which adheres to the apostolic rule of faith is part of the true visible Church, does it matter which of these churches one belongs to as an individual believer? If one believes that Rome, despite her doctrinal errors, remains a branch of the visible Church, does it matter whether he is a member of a Roman Catholic church as opposed to a presbyterian church or an anglican church? It actually matters a great deal.

We notice for example that in Revelation 2 and 3, letters are written to seven local churches which are all at that time addressed as being part of the true visible Church. But not all of these churches are equally as faithful and obedient to the Lord. Some churches, such as the church of Philadelphia (Rev. 3:7–13), are more faithful. Some churches, such as the church of Laodicea (Rev. 3:14–22), are on the verge of being completely broken off. In other words, even within true branches, there are healthy branches and diseased branches, strong branches and weak branches.

None of the branches of the present Church is perfect. Each has its own problems, but within Roman Catholicism and Eastern Orthodoxy there is the added problem of institutional autonomy. The claims of infallibility have rendered it impossible for these communions to correct themselves. The claims of ecclesiastical infallibility contradict, in the most fundamental way, the teaching of the Apostles and the early Church on the nature of Christ's authority. Within Protestantism, despite a plethora of its own problems, there remains the possibility of adhering to *sola scriptura*—

Tradition I. The majority of Protestant Evangelicals have abandoned this doctrine for their own more individualized version of autonomy, but there is no inherent requirement that they do so. This critically important doctrine of *sola scriptura* remains a viable option within Protestantism. It is not an option at present within either Rome or Orthodoxy.

What all of this means practically is that there is no good reason for Protestant conversions to Roman Catholicism or Eastern Orthodoxy. It is only within Protestantism at this time that the early Church's concept of authority can still be found at all. It is the minority position to be sure, but it still exists. This doctrine of *sola scriptura* [Tradition I] is absolutely crucial if the unity of the invisible Church is to be made visible. Rome and Orthodoxy, at this point in history, have rejected this concept of authority in favor of an ecclesiastical autonomy. Until God intervenes, it is virtually impossible for either of those communions to move in a positive direction. Their claims of infallibility force them to ignore their own deviations from the ancient faith. Protestantism has its own deviations from the ancient faith of the Church, but if it utilizes *sola scriptura*, it is at least possible for those deviations to be recognized and corrected. No such recognition and correction is possible within self-professed infallible communions until the claim of infallibility itself is recognized to be a usurpation of Christ's authority. Until that happens, Rome and Orthodoxy are locked in an everlasting stalemate with each other.

For those who are Protestants, one of the first steps that must be taken is a complete and total rejection of the individualized autonomy of solo *scriptura*. This doctrine has been a plague upon Protestantism, and the sooner it is recognized as such, the better. All of the problems will not immediately sort themselves out if Protestant denominations consciously return to *sola scriptura*, but a return to this foundational doctrine would lay the groundwork for future generations. Protestantism cannot continue to operate under the individualistic principles of solo *scriptura*, or Protestantism as a branch of the true visible Church will eventually cease to exist.

SOLA SCRIPTURA AND THE CREEDS

If *sola scriptura* is true, the Scripture is to be interpreted by the Church within the hermeneutical context of the *regula fidei* or rule of faith. This rule of faith has found written expression in the ecumenical creeds of the Church. The Nicene Creed and the definition of Chalcedon are the creedal confessions of all orthodox Christians and serve as the doctrinal boundaries of orthodox Christianity. Several questions remain, however. What is the relationship between these creeds and the Scripture? What is the purpose of creeds in the Church?

There is a tendency within the Church to run to extremes, and this tendency manifests itself clearly when the creeds of the Church are discussed. It would not be an exaggeration to say that modern Evangelicalism is anti-creedal. This is largely due to the effects of solo *scriptura,* but for whatever reason this anti-creedalism exists, it is a dangerous error. The simple truth of the matter is that creeds are inevitable. The question is not whether one will have a creed. The only question is *which* creed will one have—the Christian creed or a creed of one's own devising?

Part of the Evangelical aversion to creeds comes from misunderstanding exactly what a creed is. The English word "creed" comes from the Latin *credo* which simply means "I believe." This is why a creed is inevitable. If a Christian has any belief about what Scripture teaches, he has a creed whether he uses that word or not. Even the statement, "No creed but Christ" is itself a creed. It is simply another way of saying, "*I believe* there should be no creeds," or, "My creed is that there should be no creeds." The denial of creeds is simply a self-contradiction.

The most common objection to creeds is that they undermine the authority of Scripture. Ken Gentry cites a book in which the necessity of creeds is vehemently denied.

In one book leveling a critical assault on creedalism we find the following statement: "To arrive at truth we must dismiss religious prejudices from heart to mind. We must let God speak for

himself. . . . To let God be true means to let God have the say as
to what is the truth that sets men free. It means to accept his
word, the Bible, as the truth. Our appeal is to the Bible for
truth." The same writer spurns creeds as "man-made traditions,"
"the precepts of men," and "opinions."[31]

Evangelicals who adhere to solo *scriptura* have no trouble asserting these same type of arguments almost verbatim, but it is interesting to note the source from which these statements come.
They come from a publication of the Jehovah's Witnesses entitled
Let God be True.[32]

The truth of the matter is that a proper concept of creeds does
not result in the subordination of Scripture regardless of whether
the accusation comes from Evangelicals or cultists. There is a
significant difference between the Scriptures and the ecumenical
creeds. Scripture alone is God-breathed. Because of this, Scripture alone is inherently infallible. Scripture alone, being the very
Word of the living God, has the absolute and final authority of
God Himself. The creeds are not God-breathed. This fact alone
subordinates their authority to that of Scripture. The creeds were
written by fallible and noninspired councils of the Church. Scripture's authority is absolute—because it is the Word of God. The
authority of the creeds is derivative—because they are the
Church's summaries of the Word of God.

One of the difficulties that confuses discussion of creedal authority is the failure to distinguish between infallibility and inerrancy. As already pointed out, infallibility demands inerrancy,
but fallibility does not demand errancy. One who is infallible cannot make an error, but it is not true to say that one who is fallible
must make an error. Fallibility only means the *possibility* of error—not the necessity of error. The confusion arises because *sola
scriptura* assumes that these ecumenical creedal statements are
without error. In other words, it assumes that the doctrinal

---

[31] Kenneth L. Gentry, Jr., "In Defense of Creedalism," *Penpoint*, Vol. 9, no. 4 (Dec.
1998).
[32] Ibid.

statements in the Nicene Creed and the definition of Chalcedon are true. We would not confess them if we believed them to be false and erroneous.

Evangelical and cultic advocates of solo *scriptura* assume that an actual instance of inerrancy demands infallibility on the part of the one or ones who did not make an error—in this case several Church councils. This assumption, however, is simply not necessary. An inerrant creed does not require an infallible Church. Any fallible human being or group of human beings can produce a factually inerrant statement. Advocates of *sola scriptura* do not believe these creeds to be without error because of a belief in ecclesiastical infallibility. We believe them to be inerrant for the same reason we believe the table of contents of Scripture to be inerrant—because of the corporate testimony of the Holy Spirit to Christ's people.

In response to advocates of solo *scriptura* who deny the necessity of creeds in the Church, several additional points must be addressed. First, we must note that it is not enough for any individual or church to simply profess belief in the Bible. The Jehovah's Witness author cited above would profess to believe in the Bible. Samuel Miller explains that such a profession is not enough because "many who call themselves Christians, and profess to take the Bible for their guide, hold opinions, and speak a language as foreign, nay, as opposite, to the opinions and language of many others, who equally claim to be Christians, and equally profess to receive the Bible, as the east is to the west."[33] In other words, "there are multitudes who, professing to believe the Bible, and to take it for their guide, reject every fundamental doctrine which it contains."[34]

A second reason why these creeds are absolutely necessary is for the purpose of detecting and removing heresy when it arises

---

[33] Samuel Miller, *The Utility and Importance of Creeds and Confessions*, (Greenville, SC: A Press, 1991 [1839]), 4. Samuel Miller was one of the first professors of theology in the nineteenth century at the then-Reformed Princeton Theological Seminary.

[34] Ibid., 5.

in the Church. Solo *scriptura* cannot accomplish this necessary task because the simple proclamation of adherence to the Bible "would be doing nothing peculiar; nothing distinguishing; nothing which every heretic in Christendom is not ready to do, or rather is not daily doing, as loudly, and as frequently as the most orthodox church."[35] Douglas Wilson observes,

> Liars are experts in chopping logic and missing the truth *slightly* —"Did God say not to eat from *any* tree?" In order to pin a liar down, words must be defined in the most careful manner available. In this context, the only man who needs to be more precise than a liar is the man who would catch the liar. This is why people who hate the Bible say they want the language of the Bible, not the language of creeds, and why men who faithfully apply a faithful creed (containing words and language found nowhere in Scripture), are doing exactly what the Bible requires of them. "Thou hast tried them which say" (Rev. 2:2). The nature of the testing can and should include very carefully crafted verbal formulae designed to trip up the dishonest. "And every spirit that confesseth not that Jesus Christ is come in the flesh is not of God" (1 John 4:3).[36]

Heretics are liars, and the creeds are necessary to detect and remove them from the Church. Solo *scriptura* cannot even begin to accomplish this necessary task. One of the earliest heresies that arose in the Church was Arianism—a denial of the deity of Christ. As Miller points out, when Arius was brought before the Church, "he was not only as ready as the most orthodox divine present, to profess that he believed the Bible; but he also declared himself willing to adopt, as his own, all the language of the Scriptures, in detail, concerning the person and character of the Redeemer."[37] Arianism was only eradicated when the Church carefully dealt with it in terms of a creed.

---

[35] Ibid., 8.

[36] Douglas Jones and Douglas Wilson, *Angels in the Architecture*, (Moscow, ID: Canon Press, 1998), 193–194.

[37] Miller, op. cit., 13–14.

An important point that Miller observes about creeds is the fact that "men are seldom opposed to Creeds, until Creeds have become opposed to them."[38] The truth of this has already been noted in connection with the arguments of the Jehovah's Witnesses. The practice continues in our own day in the writings of heretical authors. We are reminded again of the assertions made by proponents of the hyper-preterist heresy such as Ed Stevens, who writes,

> Even if the creeds were to clearly and definitively stand against the preterist view (which they don't), it would not be an overwhelming problem since *they have no real authority anyway.* They are no more authoritative than our best opinions today, but they are valued because of their antiquity.[39]

And elsewhere,

> We must not take the creeds any more seriously than we do the writings and opinions of men like Luther, Zwingli, Calvin, the Westminster Assembly, Campbell, Rushdoony, or C.S. Lewis.[40]

These are the words, not of the apostolic Church, not of the Reformers, but of heretics and apostates attempting to conceal their false doctrine, yet many Evangelicals find nothing in these sentences with which they would object. That is how pervasive the error of solo *scriptura* is.

If Evangelical Christians would simply reflect upon what statements such as the ones above entail, the error would be very clear. If the creeds are not to be taken any more seriously than the writings of, say, C.S. Lewis, what that necessarily means is that the *doctrines* of the creeds are not to be taken any more seriously than the *doctrines* of C.S. Lewis. That places the doctrine of the Trinity on the same level as the doctrinal speculations of C.S.

---

[38] Ibid., 17.

[39] Ed Stevens, "Creeds and Preterist Orthodoxy," Unpublished Paper. Emphasis mine.

[40] Ibid.

Lewis on the afterlife. It places the doctrines of the creeds on the same level as the doctrines of the heretics. And when they are on the same level, one cannot be used as a standard to rule out the other. That is why heretics reject the authority of creeds. They do not want authoritative doctrinal boundaries pointing out their heresy, so they reject the authority and even the possibility of having such creedal boundaries. And their claims are entirely consistent with solo *scriptura*.

As foreign as it may sound to individualistic modern Evangelical ears, a church that adheres to *sola scriptura* is a creedal church. The evangelical denial of real creedal authority is not only self-contradictory and foolish, it is an open invitation to every kind of heresy imaginable. A creedless Church, like a creedless Christian, is a ship tossed to and fro, carried about by every wind of doctrine, compelled to consider every contradictory theological fad and novelty that comes along as long as the one proclaiming it assures his audience that it is simply what the Bible teaches.

SUMMARY

This chapter has attempted to deal with some of the most difficult questions about Scripture, the Church, and the creeds that arise in any discussion of Christian authority. One source of the difficulty in answering these questions is the fact that the Holy Spirit is the ultimate criterion of truth, and the way He works this out in history does not always lend itself to tidy logical syllogisms. There is an element of mystery here that we must respect.

It becomes clear as we struggle with these questions that there is a mutually reciprocal and inseparable relationship between Scripture, the *regula fidei*, and the Church. The Holy Spirit is the ultimate criterion of truth, but He bears witness to the truth through this reciprocal relationship between Christian Scripture, the Christian Church, and the Christian creed. Each of these three relates to the other two in a unique way. The Scripture is the Spirit-inspired Word of God that bears witness to the truth of the *regula fidei* and bears witness to the identity of the Church.

The Creed provides the hermeneutical framework for the Church's interpretation of Scripture and serves as a means by which the true Church may be recognized. The Church bears witness to the Shepherd's voice in her recognition of the canon and her confession of the true *kerygma* in the creed.

Only *sola scriptura,* or Tradition I, does justice to the mystery involved in this intricate and balanced relationship. Only *sola scriptura* properly defines the unique role for each of these three while also maintaining the necessity of the proper relationship between them. If any of these three aspects of Christian authority are separated entirely from the other two or related incorrectly, the whole of Christian authority is compromised. The usual result of such compromise is either institutional autonomy or individual autonomy. The doctrine of *sola scriptura* is not merely the best option out of several. *Sola scriptura* is the only doctrine that relates the Christian Scripture, the Christian Church, and the Christian creed in a way that does not rob God of the sovereignty that is properly His and His alone.

Conclusion

For several centuries the debate over the authority of Scripture has too often been framed in terms of a false dilemma: Scripture vs. creeds, Scripture vs. the Church, or more commonly Scripture vs. tradition. As we have discovered, this way of stating the issue is highly misleading. This was not the way the discussion was framed by either the early church fathers or by the Reformers. The Reformers did not reject tradition; they rejected one particular concept of tradition in favor of another concept of tradition. The Reformation debate was originally between adherents of two different concepts of tradition. One concept, which had its origins in the first centuries of the Church, defined Scripture as the sole source of revelation and the only final and infallible standard. The other concept of tradition, which was not hinted at until the fourth century and which was not clearly expounded until the late Middle Ages, defined Scripture and tradition as two separate and complementary sources of revelation.

The Reformation arose during a time when both strands of thought could be found within the Church. The early Reformers rejected the two-source view of scriptural authority and called the Church back to the one-source view she had taught in the first three centuries. In rejecting the later concept of tradition, the Reformers coined the term *sola scriptura*. Rome reacted against this position by fully embracing the later two-source concept of tradition, which was soon dogmatized by the Council of Trent. During this conflict, another group arose which rejected both of the older concepts of tradition in favor of a radically new position. These radicals of the Reformation continued to use the term *sola scriptura*, but they altered its meaning dramatically. These men divorced Scripture entirely from its ecclesiastical and theological context. They called for a rejection of tradition regardless of how it was understood.

With the rise of Enlightenment rationalism and other trends such as American populism, the radically individualistic Anabaptistic version of *sola scriptura* (or more properly solo *scriptura*) found fertile ground. During the nineteenth century especially, both liberals and heretics used it as their starting point for rebuilding their own false versions of Christianity. Today, this counterfeit version of *sola scriptura* is almost universally assumed to have been the teaching of the magisterial Reformers. It is assumed to be so by many Evangelicals who, rather than study the teaching of the Reformers themselves within their own historical and ecclesiastical context, have instead read their own modernist Enlightenment assumptions back into the minds of these men. It is also assumed to be so by many Roman Catholic and Orthodox apologists who, rather than admit that *sola scriptura* as understood by the first Reformers was a legitimate strand of medieval thought, have instead chosen to attack a rather flimsy substitute.

The Evangelical church has not awakened readily to a fact that many Roman Catholic apologists have been quick to notice. The simple fact of the matter is this: the modern Evangelical doctrine of Scripture—solo *scriptura*—is self-contradictory and fundamentally absurd. If applied consistently it is fatal to Christianity. A growing number of Evangelicals are realizing this, and because they have been told that solo *scriptura* is the Reformation and Protestant doctrine, they are flocking to Rome and to Constantinople in an attempt to maintain a coherent faith.

If Evangelical Protestantism is to survive, if it is to regain its calling, it must reject the essentially man-centered doctrine of solo *scriptura*. The Evangelical church cannot call Christendom to reform and to a return to apostolic Christianity by rejecting one of the fundamental tenets of apostolic Christianity. Why should we expect or even want those within Roman Catholicism or

Eastern Orthodoxy to reject institutional autonomy in favor of individual autonomy? Solo *scriptura* cannot result in anything other than doctrinal chaos.

Instead of advocating chaos, the Evangelical church must regain an understanding of the Reformation doctrine of *sola scriptura,* which is essentially nothing more than the early Church's doctrine of Scripture and tradition framed within a different historical context. The Church must affirm that Scripture is the sole source of revelation. The Church must affirm that Scripture is the sole, final, and infallible norm of faith and practice. And the Church must affirm that Scripture is to be interpreted in and by the communion of saints within the theological context of the rule of faith. Only by rejecting all forms of autonomy, institutional or individual, can any branch of the Church be in obedience to Jesus Christ the Lord.

Soli Deo Gloria

Bibliography

Arand, Charles P., "The Church's Dogma and Biblical Theology," in Horton, Michael S., *A Confessing Theology for Postmodern Times*. Wheaton, IL: Crossway Books, 2000.

Archimandrite, Chrysostomos and Archimandrite, Auxentios. *Scripture and Tradition*. Etna, CA: Center for Traditionalist Orthodox Studies, 1984.

Aulen, Gustaf. *Reformation and Catholicity*. Translated by Eric H. Wahlstrom. Edinburgh: Oliver and Boyd, 1962.

Berkouwer, G.C. *The Conflict with Rome*. Translated by David H. Freeman. Grand Rapids: Baker Book House, 1958.

_____. *Holy Scripture*. Translated by Jack B. Rogers. Grand Rapids: William B. Eerdmans Publishing Company, 1975.

Bouyer, Louis. *The Spirit and Forms of Protestantism*. Translated by A.V. Littledale. Collins: The Fontana Library, 1956.

Bray, Gerald. *Creeds, Councils and Christ*. Fearn: Mentor, 1997.

Bromiley, G.W. *The Unity and Disunity of the Church*. Grand Rapids: William B. Eerdmans Publishing Company, 1958.

Bruce, F.F. *The Canon of Scripture*. Downers Grove: InterVarsity Press, 1988.

_____. *Tradition: Old and New*. Grand Rapids: Zondervan Publishing House, 1970.

Byrne, James M. *Religion and the Enlightenment: From Descartes to Kant*. Louisville: Westminster John Knox Press, 1997.

Callahan, Daniel J., Heiko A. Oberman and Daniel J. O' Hanlon, eds. *Christianity Divided: Protestant and Roman Catholic Theological Issues*. New York: Sheed and Ward, 1961.

Calvin, John. *Institutes of the Christian Religion*. Library of Christian Classics, vols. 20–21. Translated by Ford Lewis Battles. Edited by John T. McNeill. Philadelphia: Westminster Press, 1960.

Carlton, Clark. *The Way: What Every Protestant Should Know About the Orthodox Church*. Salisbury: Regina Orthodox Press, 1997.

Carson, D.A. and John D. Woodbridge, eds. *Scripture and Truth*. Grand Rapids: Zondervan Publishing House, 1983.

Chemnitz, Martin. *Examination of the Council of Trent*. 4 vols. Translated by Fred Kramer. St. Louis: Concordia Publishing House, 1971 [1565–1573].

Christie-Murray, David. *A History of Heresy*. Oxford: Oxford University Press, 1976.

Clendenin, Daniel B., ed. *Eastern Orthodox Theology: A Contemporary Reader*. Grand Rapids: Baker Book House, 1995.

Congar, Yves. *The Meaning of Tradition*. Translated by A.N. Woodrow. New York: Hawthorn Books, Publishers, 1964.

_____. *Tradition and Traditions: An Historical and a Theological Essay*. New York: The MacMillan Company, 1967.

Cullmann, Oscar. *Message to Catholics and Protestants*. Translated by Joseph A. Burgess. Grand Rapids: William B. Eerdmans Publishing Company, 1959.

Davies, Rupert E. *The Problem of Authority in the Continental Reformers*. London: The Epworth Press, 1946.

Davis, Leo Donald. *The First Seven Ecumenical Councils (325–787): Their History and Theology*. Collegeville: The Liturgical Press, 1983.

DiBerardino, Angelo and Basil Studer, eds. *History of Theology*. Vol. I. *The Patristic Period*. Translated by Matthew J. O'Connell. Collegeville: The Liturgical Press, 1997.

Estep, William R. *The Anabaptist Story: An Introduction to Sixteenth Century Anabaptism*. Third edition. Grand Rapids: William B. Eerdmans Publishing Company, 1996.

_____. *Renaissance and Reformation*. Grand Rapids: William B. Eerdmans Publishing Company, 1986.

Eusebius. *The History of the Church*. Rev. ed. Translated by G. A.

Williamson. Edited by Andrew Louth. London: Penguin Books, 1989.

Evans, Gillian R., Alister E. McGrath and Allan D. Galloway. *The Science of Theology*. The History of Christian Theology, vol. I. Edited by Paul Avis. Grand Rapids: William B. Eerdmans Publishing Company, 1986.

Florovsky, Georges. *Bible, Church, Tradition: An Eastern Orthodox View*. The Collected Works, vol. I. Edited by Richard S. Haugh. Vaduz: Buchervertriebsanstalt, 1987.

Geiselman, Joseph R. "Scripture and Tradition in Catholic Theology." *Theology Digest*. Vol. 6 (1958).

Geisler, Norman, ed. *Inerrancy*. Grand Rapids: Zondervan Publishing House, 1980.

Gerrish, B.A. *The Old Protestantism and the New: Essays on the Reformation Heritage*. Edinburgh: T.&T. Clark Limited, 1982.

Hall, Christopher A. *Reading Scripture With the Church Fathers*. Downers Grove: InterVarsity Press, 1998.

Hannah, John D., ed. *Inerrancy and the Church*. Chicago: Moody Press, 1984.

Hatch, Nathan O. *The Democratization of American Christianity*. New Haven: Yale University Press, 1989.

Headley, John M. *Luther's View of Church History*. New Haven: Yale University Press, 1963.

Henry, Carl F.H., ed. *Revelation and the Bible*. Grand Rapids: Baker Book House, 1958.

Hierodeacon, Gregory. *The Church, Tradition, Scripture, Truth, and Christian Life*. Etna, CA: Center for Traditionalist Orthodox Studies, 1995.

Higgins, A.J.B., ed. *The Early Church: Studies in Early Christian History and Theology*. Philadelphia: The Westminster Press, 1956.

Hodge, Charles. *Systematic Theology*. 3 vols. Grand Rapids: William B. Eerdmans Publishing Company, 1989.

Jones, Douglas and Douglas Wilson. *Angels in the Architecture: A Protestant Vision for Middle Earth*. Moscow, ID: Canon Press, 1998.

Kelly, J.N.D. *Early Christian Doctrines*. Rev. ed. San Francisco: HarperCollins Publishers, 1978.

Kistler, Don, ed. *Sola Scriptura: The Protestant Position on the Bible.* Morgan, PA: Soli Deo Gloria Publications, 1995.

Klotsche, E.H. and J. Theodore Mueller. *The History of Christian Doctrine.* Burlington: The Lutheran Literary Board, 1945.

Kung, Hans. *Structures of the Church.* Translated by Salvator Attanasio. New York: Thomas Nelson & Sons, 1964.

LaDue, William J. *The Chair of Saint Peter: A History of the Papacy.* Maryknoll: Orbis Books, 1999.

Lane, A.N.S. "Scripture, Tradition & Church: An Historical Survey." *Vox Evangelica.* 9 (1975).

Lee, Philip J. *Against the Protestant Gnostics.* New York: Oxford University Press, 1987.

Leith, John H. *Creeds of the Churches: A Reader in Christian Doctrine from the Bible to the Present.* Third edition. Louisville: John Knox Press, 1982.

Lohse, Bernhard. *A Short History of Christian Doctrine.* Translated by F. Ernest Stoeffler. Philadelphia: Fortress Press, 1966.

McBrien, Richard P. *Catholicism.* Rev. ed. San Francisco: HarperCollins Publishers, 1994.

McGrath, Alister E. *The Genesis of Doctrine: A Study in the Foundations of Doctrinal Criticism.* Oxford: Basil Blackwell, 1990.

_____. *The Intellectual Origins of the European Reformation.* Oxford: Blackwell Publishers, 1987.

_____. *Reformation Thought: An Introduction.* 2d ed. Oxford: Blackwell Publishers, 1993.

Metzger, Bruce M. *The Canon of the New Testament: Its Origin, Development, and Significance.* Oxford: Clarendon Press, 1987.

Meyendorff, John. *Byzantine Theology: Historical Trends and Doctrinal Themes.* New York: Fordham University Press, 1979.

_____, ed. *The Primacy of Peter: Essays in Ecclesiology and the Early Church.* Crestwood, NY: St. Vladimir's Seminary Press, 1992.

Miller, Samuel. *The Utility and Importance of Creeds and Confessions.* Greenville, SC: A Press, 1991 [1839].

Muller, Richard A. *Post-Reformation Reformed Dogmatics.* Vol. II. *Holy Scripture: The Cognitive Foundation of Theology.* Grand Rapids: Baker Book House, 1993.

Oberman, Heiko A. *The Dawn of the Reformation.* Edinburgh: T.&T. Clark, LTD, 1986.

_____. *Forerunners of the Reformation: The Shape of Late Medieval Thought.* Translated by Paul L. Nyhus. London: Lutterworth Press, 1967.

_____. *The Harvest of Medieval Theology: Gabriel Biel and Late Medieval Nominalism.* Cambridge: Harvard University Press, 1963.

_____. *Luther: Man Between God and the Devil.* Translated by Eileen Walliser-Schwarzbart. New Haven: Yale University Press, 1989.

_____. *The Reformation: Roots and Ramifications.* Translated by Andrew Colin Gow. Grand Rapids: William B. Eerdmans Publishing Company, 1994.

Olin, John C., ed. *John Calvin and Jacopo Sadoleto: A Reformation Debate.* New York: Harper & Row, Publishers, 1966.

Pelikan, Jaroslav. *Development of Christian Doctrine: Some Historical Prolegomena.* New Haven: Yale University Press, 1969.

_____. *The Christian Tradition.* 5 vols. Chicago: The University of Chicago Press, 1971–1989.

_____. *Obedient Rebels: Catholic Substance and Protestant Principle in Luther's Reformation.* London: SCM Press, Ltd., 1964.

_____. *The Vindication of Tradition.* New Haven: Yale University Press, 1984.

Placher, William C. *A History of Christian Theology: An Introduction.* Philadelphia: The Westminster Press, 1983.

Pomazansky, Michael. *Orthodox Dogmatic Theology.* Translated and Edited by Hieromonk Seraphim Rose. Platina, CA: Saint Herman of Alaska Brotherhood, 1983.

Previte-Orton, C.W. *The Shorter Cambridge Medieval History.* 2 vols. Cambridge: Cambridge University Press, 1952.

Ray, Stephen K. *Upon This Rock: St. Peter and the Primacy of Rome in Scripture and the Early Church.* San Francisco: Ignatius Press, 1999.

Salmon, George. *The Infallibility of the Church.* Third edition. London: John Murray, 1899.

Sandlin, Andrew, ed. *Keeping Our Sacred Trust: Biblical Authority, Creedal Orthodoxy, and Heresy.* Chalcedon Symposium Series, No. 1. Vallecito, CA: Chalcedon Foundation, 1999.

Schroeder, H.J., ed. *The Canons and Decrees of the Council of Trent.* Rockford: Tan Books and Publishers, Inc., 1978.

Smalley, Beryl. *The Study of the Bible in the Middle Ages.* Oxford: Basil Blackwell, 1952.

Strimple, Robert B. "The Relationship Between Scripture and Tradition in Contemporary Roman Catholic Theology." *Westminster Theological Journal.* Vol. 40, no. 1 (Fall 1977).

Sungenis, Robert A., ed. *Not By Scripture Alone: A Catholic Critique of the Protestant Doctrine of Sola Scriptura.* Santa Barbara: Queenship Publishing Company, 1997.

Tavard, G.H. "Tradition in Early Post-Tridentine Theology." *Theological Studies.* 23 (1962).

Thomas Aquinas. *Summa Theologiae.* London: Blackfriars, 1964.

Thompson, Bard. *Humanists and Reformers: A History of the Renaissance and Reformation.* Grand Rapids: William B. Eerdmans Publishing Company, 1996.

Tierney, Brian. *Origins of Papal Infallibility: 1150–1350.* Studies in the History of Christian Thought, vol. 6. Edited by Heiko A. Oberman. Leiden: E.J. Brill, 1988.

Torrance, J.B. "Authority, Scripture & Tradition." *Evangelical Quarterly.* 59 (1987), 245–251.

Turner, H.E.W. *The Pattern of Christian Truth.* London: A.R. Mowbray & Co., Limited, 1954.

Turretin, Francis. *Institutes of Elenctic Theology.* 3 vols. Translated by George Musgrave Giger. Edited by James T. Dennison, Jr. Phillipsburg, NJ: P&R Publishing Co., 1992–95.

Vassady, Bela. *Christ's Church: Evangelical, Catholic, and Reformed.* Grand Rapids: William B. Eerdmans Publishing Company, 1965.

von Campenhausen, Hans. *Ecclesiastical Authority and Spiritual Power in the Church of the First Three Centuries.* Translated by J.A. Baker. London: Adam & Charles Black, 1969.

Wallace, Ronald S. *Calvin's Doctrine of Word and Sacrament.*

Edinburgh: Oliver and Boyd, Ltd., 1953.

Ware, Timothy. *The Orthodox Church*. New ed. London: Penguin Books, 1993.

Webster, William. *The Church of Rome at the Bar of History*. Carlisle, PA: The Banner of Truth Trust, 1995.

Wendel, Francois. *Calvin: Origins and Development of His Religious Thought*. Translated by Philip Mairet. Durham: Labyrinth Press, 1963.

Whelton, Michael. *Two Paths: Papal Monarchy - Collegial Tradition*. Salisbury, MA: Regina Orthodox Press, 1998.

Zwingli, Ulrich. *Commentary on True and False Religion*. Edited by Samuel Macauley Jackson and Clarence Nevin Heller. Durham, NC: The Labyrinth Press, 1981.

Index of Authors

A

Armstrong, John H., 264
Athanasius, 29, 30, 47
Augustine, 39, 40, 41, 195
Auxentios, Archimandrite,
     225, 231, 232, 233, 234

B

Bainton, Roland H., 83, 87, 89, 90,
     91, 95
Barraclough, Geoffrey, 51, 53, 56
Basil the Great, 33, 35
Baukham, Richard, 168, 169
Beale, G.K., 171
Beecher, Charles, 145
Belknap, Jeremy 144
Berkhof, Louis, 261
Berkouwer, G.C., 85
Bigane, John, 184
Blosser, Philip, 290, 291, 292, 293,
     294, 295, 296, 297, 299, 300,
     301, 302, 304, 305, 306, 307
Boniface VIII, 221
Bromiley, Geoffrey W., 22
Brown, Colin, 141, 142
Brown, Raymond E., 51
Bruce, F.F., 20, 23, 24, 45, 46, 62,
     173, 316
Byrne, James, 142

C

Calvin, John, 103, 104, 105, 106,
     107, 108, 109, 110, 111, 112,
     113, 114, 115, 116, 117, 118,
     268
Campbell, Alexander, 144
Carlton, Clark, 13, 285, 308, 309
Carson, D.A., 176, 186, 188, 189,
     190, 191
Chadwick, Owen, 83
Chafer, Lewis Sperry, 241
Chauncy, Charles, 144
Chemnitz, Martin, 40
Chrysostom, John, 37, 38, 39
Chrysostomos, Archimandrite,
     225, 226, 227, 231, 232, 233,
     234
Clement of Alexandria, 24
Clouse, Robert G., 64
Congar, Yves, 50, 130, 131, 132
Currie, David, 13, 285
Cyprian, 27, 28, 29, 108, 195
Cyril of Jerusalem, 31

D

Davis, Leo Donald, 30, 46, 47, 52,
     218

E

Estep, William R., 124

357

Index of Scripture